D0940356

CONTENTS

SECTION 1 Overview of Military Opportunities

SECTION 2 Military Branches

SECTION 3 Military College Opportunities

SECTION 4 Military Career Fields

SECTION 5 Military Information

APPENDICES

ACKNOWLEDGMENTS

A VERY SPECIAL THANKS TO:

- ✪ Brig. Gen. Patrick Garvey, New York State National Guard
- ✪ Col. Thomas Cleland, New York State National Guard
- ✪ Michael Mydlarz, IBM (U.S. Army Veteran)
- ✪ Ens. Greer, Department of Defense Navy Information Office
- ✪ Sgt. First Class Mark A. George, U.S. Army Recruiting
- ✪ USMEPCOM (United States Military Entrance Processing Command)
- ✪ MEPS, Buffalo, NY

GOVERNMENT SOURCES CONSULTED INCLUDE:

"Military Careers: A Guide to Military Occupations and Selected Military Career Paths"— U.S. Department of Defense, Washington, DC 1995–1997

ASVAB 18/19 Manual— U.S. Department of Defense

All Hands—Official magazine of the U.S. Navy

Airman—Official magazine of U.S. Air Force

Army Reserve Magazine

Citizens Airman—Official magazine of the U.S. Air Force Reserve

Coast Guard—Official U.S. Coast Guard Magazine

The Coast Guard Reservist

Marines—Official magazine of the U.S. Marine Corps

Soldiers—Department of the Army magazine

Profile—An outstanding DOD monthly magazine designed to inform young people and career counselors about opportunities in the military

Defense—Official bimonthly publication of the DOD

The 1997 Pocket Recruiting Guide

U.S. Department of Army: Military Occupational Classification and Structure

DOD Occupational Conversion Index

To order any of the magazines:

Call   U.S. Government Printing Office
                        Washington, DC 20401
                        (202) 512-1800

Mail order to   U.S. Government Printing Office
                        Superintendent of Documents
                        PO Box 371954
                        Pittsburgh, PA 15250–7954

GUIDE DISCLAIMER

Every effort has been made to provide accurate and complete information in this guide. However, there may be mistakes made in the content, due to changes in U.S. military policy, which may change without notice. Therefore, this book should be used as only a general guide to Military Opportunities & Careers, and not as the final and permanent information source.

FOREWORD

by Lt. Gen. Vernon A. Walters
U.S. Army (Retired)

I entered the Army in 1941 as a private, and progressed through the grades to a three-star general, one grade from the top. I had neither a college nor a high school education, but I had an extensive knowledge of languages, which served me extraordinarily well. In a military career, if you don't have much competition (as I didn't, as I speak eight languages) you can attract the attention of people who will greatly affect your future career. I was able not only to serve my country but also to meet some of the most extraordinary people of this century as a translator for several presidents of the United States.

Once, with General DeGaulle, I didn't realize that he spoke English, and I began, during a translation session, to make comments to General Eisenhower, such as, "I don't think that he wants to do it, even though he [DeGaulle] says yes," or "He says no, but if you push him a little harder he'll do it." Finally, General DeGaulle tapped me on the shoulder and said in English, "Walters, you did a good job." That's when I learned never to tamper with translations.

But it doesn't have to be just languages; it can be anything at which you excel that draws you to the attention of other people and makes you stand out from the crowd. The military offers numerous opportunities that allow for people to excel in a variety of occupations.

In a global sense, the military is a good career choice because it is a fulfilling career and it gives one a sense of achievement and a sense of service to the whole country. Military careers are important; they can provide you with the ability to protect the things you believe in and preserve and defend your way of life, offering security for your children's future. You do that in the military in a very direct and immediate way. You are called upon to sacrifice and you are called upon to take risks. It is a special type of people who are willing to be called upon to sacrifice and risk, who will keep the world and this country free.

The fact that I was able to go from the rank of private to three-star general gives a sense of how flexible a career the military is, that it can allow individuals to rise continuously to posts of higher responsibility. The more you know, the more you can do; the more you know about how the services are composed and organized, and the careers and opportunities offered, the more chances you have of getting ahead in a military career. That's why a book such as Barron's *Guide to Military Careers* will be extremely valuable to young people.

Lt. Gen. Vernon A. Walters, U.S. Army (Retired), served his country for more than half a century as a military officer and diplomat. During those years, he carried out numerous sensitive missions on behalf of six U.S. Presidents. In addition, he served for four years as Deputy Director of the CIA, Ambassador-at-Large, Permanent Representative to the United Nations, and Ambassador to Germany. General Walters has received the Presidential Medal of Freedom and numerous other awards and decorations for his military and diplomatic service. He is the author of *Silent Missions* (1978) and *The Wall Falls* (1994), both outstanding and highly recommended books.

PREFACE

THE NATURE OF MILITARY "ACCESSION" (HIRING)

We have all heard the military slogans: *aim high, be all that you can be, it's not just a job, it's an adventure*, and the classic *the few, the proud, the Marines*. Maybe you've heard the radio or TV ads promising enlistment bonuses, up to $40,000 toward college, and so on. Of course, they didn't mention that the enlistment bonuses are for certain line-of-work specialties that a particular branch has a critical need for, and that you may have to enlist for an extended period of time, more than the normal four-year enlistment, and start at a low pay grade.

Unless you've had a veteran in the family, your opinion about the military branches and careers may be formed by television, the movies, or CD-ROM games, but beware—joining the military is a critical and complex decision for any person. And the military makes it more difficult by accidental design. How? During the research for this book, I made a casual observation. I walked into a typical military recruiting building where all five of the armed services maintained separate offices. As I went from office to office, I was struck by the fact that each service office, while it would not, of course, knock the other services, strongly stated that only its branch could fulfill your future. And therein lies the problem. It is not up to anyone to decide what branch, program, or occupation is right for you. Only you can decide that.

And to make matters worse, the military has faced its own version of downsizing in the early 1990s, just like the civilian world. While the United States needs a strong military and always will, the hiring or in military speak, *accession*, of new personnel has shifted.

For almost 45 years, the military's personnel requirements and overall strategies had been shaped by the need to be prepared to deal with a short-notice, global war with the former Soviet Union. Given the dramatic developments in Eastern Europe, the former Soviet Union, and Africa, the military services are refocusing their strategy on a peacetime mission and on readiness for regional conflicts and contingencies. As the military plans for the next century, it will reduce the numbers of active-duty officers. (Source: *Department of Defense Military Careers, 1995–1998*)

What does this mean? It means that the military branches may require, at the very least, a high school education from the pool of enlisted candidates; however, critical shortages of personnel, which we have now, change that mandate. Recruiters may always look for candidates with education, but they may steer other candidates into specialties in which the military has a critical need. In other words, you may go into a recruiter's office with the intent to sign up as an officer in a college ROTC program for computer engineering, and wind up settling for an enlisted position in the infantry.

This is not to say that military recruiters are a bunch of unsavory characters, but always remember that they have been assigned a mission to acquire as many qualified candidates to fill critical-need positions (such as infantry). Take, for example, the very creed of the recruiters:

RECRUITER'S CODE OF ETHICS

I am responsible for representing the United States Army in an important position during this period of the Army's history. My neglect or delay in fulfilling responsibility could place in danger the American way of life and the sacred course of human freedom.

I will encourage to enlist in the United States Army those young men and women who are morally, aptitudinally, physically, and administratively qualified young men and women who will serve with honor and distinction, and with whom I would be proud to serve in peace as well as in war.

I will always maintain the highest standards of military and moral conduct in the performance of my duties while conducting recruiting operations throughout the United States, its territories, and overseas. I will leave no questions as to the correctness of my ethical standards or moral purpose, and I will always demonstrate an unshakable sense of integrity.

I dedicate myself to the support of my Army and my country. And, when I have fulfilled my responsibilities and discharged my duties, I will have strengthened the United States, its Army and this code that I will represent. I am in the Army and in my community. (Source: *U.S. Army Recruiting*)

While compiling the information for this book, I examined my own military career, and found that the path I chose was unusual. Or was it? During my senior year of high school, I joined the U.S. Coast Guard at the age of 17. After being processed at the recruiting command, and officially sworn in, I left to complete my high school year (the standard *delayed entry program*). In July of that year, I traveled from upstate New York to Cape May, New Jersey, for Coast Guard basic training, which lasted eight weeks.

After basic training, I went to Yorktown, Virginia, for the Boatswain's Mate/Port Security (BM/PS) Class A School. The BM/PS School trained me in both military occupational specialties. After graduation, I left active duty and began both my reserve duty and my civilian career as a police officer. As a reservist, I was *initially assigned* to a marine safety office in Albany, New York, where I was able to use my training in the port security field. Later, I *transferred* to the Coast Guard Intelligence Office as a reserve special agent, *lateraled* to the Investigator Rating (IV). After several years, my civilian job required me to transfer to a new reserve unit, where I performed the duties as a mobilization and augmentation petty officer (administration) until I retired with an honorable discharge.

The reason for my story is to point out several terms: *initially assigned, transferred,* and *lateraled.* The point is that military opportunities allow you to change your career path if you want. If I had to do it all over again, I might have joined the Air Force ROTC program or applied to the Naval Military Academy; however, I have no regrets about my Coast Guard career. If anything, I am extremely proud of the work I did for my service, my comrades, and my country.

This book is intended for anyone interested in a military career as well as for those currently in the military who are looking for a change. It was prepared to make candidates aware of the real possibilities that exist in the United States military.

Donald B. Hutton
August 1998
Semper Paratus

SECTION

1

OVERVIEW OF
MILITARY
OPPORTUNITIES

Chapter 1

INTRODUCTION

☐ **How to Use This Book**

☐ **Anticipated Positions: Planning for the Future**

☐ **Plan Your Course of Action**

☐ **General Military Opportunities Defined**

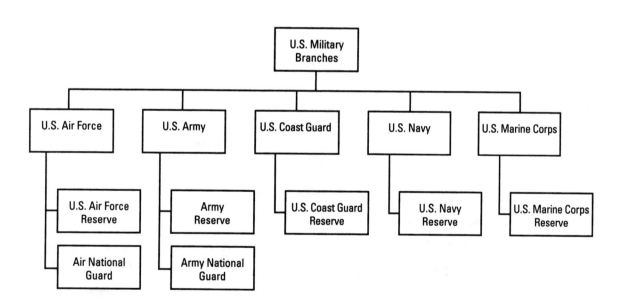

HOW TO USE THIS BOOK

This book is designed to be a *user-friendly* guide to military careers and opportunities. Whenever possible, a helpful hint or comment has been included; however, readers are strongly encouraged to conduct follow-up research into the military branch they are interested in.

The book is divided into five sections and the appendices.

SECTION 1 *Overview of Military Opportunities*

This section is dedicated to explaining basic choices, common requirements, and opportunities as well as pay grades and rank, enlistment paperwork, and entrance examinations.

SECTION 2 *Military Branches*

This section outlines the specific enlisted and officer careers and opportunities in the Air Force, Army, Coast Guard, Marine Corps, and Navy. Also, an inventory of weapons and equipment used and additional resources (films, books, and videos) on each branch is discussed in each chapter.

SECTION 3 *Military College Opportunities*

This section is devoted to military academy preparatory schools, military academies, and the Reserve Officer Training Corps (ROTC) programs.

SECTION 4 *Military Career Fields*

This is a special cross-reference section that identifies career specialties and defines the military and federal government counterparts.

SECTION 5 *Military Information*

Additional information is provided here on the Pentagon, the history of war and the U.S. military, and an overview of military career planning.

APPENDICES *Glossary of Military Terms*

The Author

Military Careers Action (Tear-Out) Sheet

ANTICIPATED POSITIONS: PLANNING FOR THE FUTURE

Twenty years ago, a group of military service members started their careers; now they are about to retire and a new group is about to enter the service. Will you be with them? Military personnel planners have a formula that determines the anticipated number of new personnel who will be needed for a particular service. Planners have to consider the number of military personnel retiring each year and the time it will take to test, process, hire, and train new ones to fill the ranks. Finally, and most important, they must decide if there is sufficient budget for the new personnel. Using all this information, military recruiters find their mandates to enlist candidates.

According to the Department of Defense, more than 400,000 new military personnel need to be recruited each year to replace those who complete their enlistment or retire in over 100 career occupations.

What Do You Want to Do?

Basically, your interest in seeking a military career or opportunity has assigned you to a complex investigation that you may find both thrilling and time-consuming. First, however, you have to make a choice—what do you want to do? While you may presently think you want to work in one particular branch or service, you should keep an open mind and consider the other options.

PLAN YOUR COURSE OF ACTION

You should not just walk into a military career. Most successful candidates planned a course of action that enabled them to obtain their desired position. Make a list of several positions you are interested in. Check the qualifications for those positions. Do you qualify? If not, obtain more education and experience. As you plan your career, ask yourself some important questions:

1. *Are you ready for a military life?*
   Military life is not for everyone: The pay is predominantly low to start, a majority of personnel are stationed on overseas bases, personnel are subject to transfer at a moment's notice, and, most important, they have signed a commitment, meaning they cannot simply quit if they do not like the service.

2. *Are you willing to travel and be reassigned?*
Military personnel may be transferred throughout the world several times during their careers, which means they may have to live on military bases until retirement. They may also have to conduct extensive travel for their duties. Not everyone can handle the military life. If you are single, it is your decision alone; however, if you have a family, it must be a family decision.

3. *How do you feel about submarines, ships, and planes?*
Before you sign up for a career that takes you into the air or under the sea make sure that you are prepared for it; do not make a career decision based on a movie or CD-ROM attraction.

4. *Are you ready for military responsibility?*
Being a member of the military entails more than a job; the duties and responsibilities for the most part are a significant burden that an individual must accept both on and off duty, 24 hours a day; therefore, the decision to pursue a particular position must be well thought out and planned in advance. Unlike civilian jobs, you cannot simply tell the boss you quit and then leave; when you sign on, you are obligated to serve for a certain time.

5. *Is this a service career with a future?*
Choose your career wisely from the start. Does it have a future? Will you be able to have a clear promotion path? And, for future consideration, does the career specialty have a civilian counterpart?

6. *What type of military career or opportunities do you want? At what level?*
A majority of those joining the U.S. military do so at the enlisted personnel level, which is fine, because today the military is geared toward education of its enlisted personnel. In many cases, a person joining the military as an enlisted member can serve and earn a college degree at the military's expense; however, as you will learn in this book, there are several paths that can lead not only to a college education, but to an officer's career, in which there is higher pay and prestige, and greater federal and civilian hiring opportunities.

GENERAL MILITARY OPPORTUNITIES DEFINED

Enlisted Personnel

Enlisted personnel begin at the lowest rank in the military and serve as the main workforce. The military prefers candidates with a high school education. With time, good service, and education, advancement can be expected.

Officers

Officers begin at a supervisory rank. They must have a four-year college degree from an accredited institution before being commissioned; however, the military has several programs that lead to becoming a commissioned officer:

- Military Academies

- Officer Candidate Schools

- Reserve Officer Training Corps (ROTC)

- Direct Appointments

Do You Want a Full-Time or Part-Time Military Career?

The next question you should ask should be the degree of commitment you are willing to make. The military is flexible and has several full-time and part-time options.

Regular Service

In the regular service, personnel serve on a full-time basis. After enlisting in the service, members are sent to basic training. After graduation, they are sent to specialty job training schools. Upon completion, they are assigned to a station or unit for duty. After 20 years of regular service, members qualify for a military retirement.

Reserve Service

The reserves are part-time military soldiers. Personnel serve an initial period on active duty after attending basic training and job training. After the training period, which usually lasts several months, reservists are free to return to civilian life, but for the remainder of the service obligation they attend training sessions and perform work in the job specialty one or two days a month with their local unit. Once a year, reservists participate in an active-duty training session for 14 days. When reservists have completed 20 years of service and have reached age 60, they are entitled to retirement, based on reserve pay.

National Guard

In addition to reserve forces, the Army and Air Force have National Guard units in every state. Duty is similar to that of a reservist. Over the years, the function and mission of the National Guard units have increased to include domestic emergencies as well as drug and illegal alien interdiction efforts. National Guard members can earn a retirement after 20 years of service and after reaching age 60.

THE MILITARY BRANCHES: YOUR CHOICE	
Branches	**Main Mission**
U.S. Air Force Air Force Reserve Air National Guard	Defends the United States through control of air and space; flies and maintains aircraft, missiles, and spacecraft. Air Force personnel are stationed worldwide. *See Chapter 5.*
U.S. Army Army Reserve Army National Guard	Protects and defends the United States and its interests by way of ground troops, tanks, helicopters, and missile systems; conducts land-based operations around the world. *See Chapter 6.*
U.S. Coast Guard Coast Guard Reserve	A branch of the armed services and a service within the U.S. Department of Transportation; the primary maritime law enforcement agency for the United States. *See Chapter 7.*
U.S. Marine Corps Marine Corps Reserve	An elite fighting force that is part of the Department of the Navy. Marines serve on ships, protect naval bases, guard U.S. embassies, and provide a quick, ever-ready strike force to protect U.S. interests worldwide. *See Chapter 8.*
U.S. Navy Navy Reserve	Maintains freedom on the seas; defends the United States and its allies, and enables them to travel and trade freely on the world's oceans. Navy personnel serve on ships, on submarines, in aviation positions, and at shore bases around the world. *See Chapter 9.*

ENLISTED CAREERS—GENERAL ENLISTMENT REQUIREMENTS	
Age	Must be between the ages of 17 and 35 years. If age 17, parents' signed consent is required.
Citizenship	Must be a U.S. citizen or have been legally admitted to the United States for permanent residence and possess immigration and naturalization documents.
Males: Physical Condition (Some military occupations have additional requirements.)	Height: 5'0" to 6'8" Weight: 100 lb to 255 lb
Females: Physical Condition (Some military occupations have additional requirements.)	Height: 4'10" to 6'8" Weight: 90 lb to 227 lb
Vision (in general) (Some military occupations have additional requirements.)	At least 20/400 or 20/200 vision corrected to 20/20 with eyeglasses or contact lenses. Depth perception and color blindness is also tested.
General Health	Must be able to pass a medical exam.
Education	High school is now a requirement in most enlisted occupations.
Aptitude	Must qualify for enlistment on the Armed Services Vocational Aptitude Battery (ASVAB) test.
Background Investigation	Background investigation must reveal that person is of strong moral character.
Marital Status and Dependents	May be either single or married, with or without dependents.

OFFICER CAREERS—GENERAL ENLISTMENT REQUIREMENTS	
Age	Age requirement is based on selected program OCS/OTS: Between 19 and 29 years ROTC: Between 17 and 21 years Academy: Between 17 and 22 years (If age 17, parents' signed consent is required.)
Citizenship	Must be a U.S. citizen.
Males: Physical Condition (Some military occupations have additional requirements.)	Height: 5'0" to 6'8" Weight: 100 lb to 255 lb
Females: Physical Condition (Some military occupations have additional requirements.)	Height: 4'10" to 6'8" Weight: 90 lb to 227 lb
Vision (in general) (Some military occupations have additional requirements.)	At least 20/400 or 20/200 vision corrected to 20/20 with eyeglasses or contact lenses. Depth perception and color blindness is also tested.
General Health	Must be able to pass a medical exam.
Education	Must have a four-year college degree from an accredited institution. Some officer occupations require advanced degrees or four-year degrees in a specialized field.
Aptitude	Must qualify for enlistment on an officer qualification test. Each service uses its own officer qualification test.
Background Investigation	Background investigation must reveal that person is of strong moral character.
Marital Status and Dependents	OCS/OTS/ROTC: May be either single or married. Academy: Must be single to enter and graduate from service academies. Single persons with one or more minor dependents are not eligible for officer commissioning.

STANDARD MILITARY ENLISTMENT PROGRAMS
—ENLISTED ENTRANCE PROGRAMS

Opportunity	Overview	Branches
Delayed Entry	Enlistee can delay entry into active duty for up to one year (normally used by high school students).	Air Force Army Coast Guard Marine Corps Navy
Buddy Deal	Buddies join together, may be stationed together, and may also receive a grade-in-pay advance.	Air Force Army Coast Guard Marine Corps Navy
Guaranteed Training Enlistment Program	Selected line of work or military occupation is guaranteed under contract for training and placement.	Air Force Army Coast Guard Marine Corps Navy
Advanced Rank Enlistment Program	Based on civilian experience or college education, enlistee is given an advance in rank above the starting Recruit (E-1).	Air Force Army Coast Guard Marine Corps Navy
Enlistment Bonus	If enlistee selects and is needed for a critical occupational specialty, the military branch can offer cash incentives for signing.	Air Force Army Coast Guard Marine Corps Navy
Reserve Enlistment	Reserve duty after initial training is served on a part-time basis. Reservists meet one weekend a month and complete two weeks active duty a year toward retirement.	Air Force Army Coast Guard Marine Corps Navy
National Guard	National Guard duty is much like reserve duty, a part-time basis. In recent decades, Guard units have been activated for domestic emergencies and to assist on border drug and illegal alien interdiction.	Air Force Army
Reenlistment Bonus	Much like the enlistment bonus, active duty personnel in critical fields are offered cash bonuses to stay in the service.	Air Force Army Coast Guard Marine Corps Navy

MAIN ENLISTED EDUCATION PROGRAMS

Opportunity	Overview	Branches
Montgomery GI Bill Tuition Assistance Programs	Active duty personnel may deduct a set amount from their pay per month toward their future education. The military will also contribute a set amount of funds. In addition, each service has a variation and may provide additional funds to the member (such as the Army College Fund). *Candidates:* Must have a high school diploma. Must have nonprior service or have only initial active duty for training (IADT). Must have completed at least two years active duty. All members participating in the program contribute $1,200 their first year ($100 per month). There are also Reserve and National Guard Montgomery GI Bill program(s).	Air Force Army Coast Guard Marine Corps Navy
Loan Repayment Program	Incentive designed to increase enlistments of recruits with a college education.	Army Navy Air Force
Commissioning Programs	Most of the services have their own enlisted-commissioning program in which the member attends college on either a full-time or part-time basis.	Air Force Army Coast Guard Marine Corps Navy

OFFICER ENLISTMENT PROGRAMS		
Opportunity	**Overview**	**Branches**
Military Academy Preparatory Schools	Designed to strengthen a candidate's education background in a crash-course military environment. *See Chapter 10.*	Air Force Army Navy/Marine Corps Coast Guard
Military Academies: U.S. Military Academy at West Point, New York (Army) U.S. Naval Academy at Annapolis, Maryland (Navy and Marine Corps) U.S. Air Force Academy at Colorado Springs, Colorado (Air Force) U.S. Coast Guard Academy at New London, Connecticut (Coast Guard)	Four of the services maintain outstanding and legendary military academies that provide not only some of the best college education programs, but also train and form young persons into military leaders and managers. Competition is extremely fierce for entrance to the military academies; nominations are needed for three of them. Once accepted, cadets or midshipmen receive full benefits along with a tuition-free education. *See Chapter 10.*	Air Force Army Coast Guard Navy/Marine Corps
Officer Candidate School or Officer Training School (OTS) (21 percent of new officers)	Program for college graduates with no prior military training who wish to become military officers. The intensive military training lasts up to 20 weeks, after which candidates are commissioned as officers.	Air Force Army Coast Guard Marine Corps Navy
Direct Commission (11 percent of new officers)	Similar to the OCS/OTS programs, direct commission candidates are trained professionals in the medical, legal, engineering, or religious fields. Due to their expertise, direct commission candidates are not required to face a full schedule of military training.	Air Force Army Coast Guard Marine Corps Navy

OFFICER ENLISTMENT PROGRAMS (continued)		
Opportunity	**Overview**	**Branches**
ROTC (44 percent of officers)	Depending on service and ROTC option selected, students train for two, three, or four years. Often, they receive scholarships for tuition, books, fees, uniforms, and a monthly allowance. In addition to their military and college coursework, ROTC candidates perform drills for several hours each week and participate in military training exercises for several weeks each summer. Graduating ROTC candidates become commissioned as military officers and either go on active duty or become members of Reserve or National Guard units. ROTC programs for the Army, Navy, Air Force, and Marine Corps are available in more than 1,400 colleges and universities nationwide. *See Chapter 11.*	Air Force Army Marine Corps Navy

OFFICER EDUCATION PROGRAMS		
Opportunity	**Overview**	**Branches**
Aviation Programs	The military branches provide flight training and aviation programs.	Air Force Army Coast Guard Marine Corps Navy
Graduate Degree Programs	Postgraduate degrees can be earned while serving in the military and at the military's expense.	Air Force Army Coast Guard Marine Corps Navy
Medical Programs	All military branches are in constant need of medical personnel in a variety of specialties.	Air Force Army Coast Guard Marine Corps Navy
Legal Programs	The services have legal programs to assist and encourage legal education to include tuition assistance.	Air Force Army Coast Guard Marine Corps Navy

SPECIAL YOUTH PROGRAMS (UNDER 17)		
Opportunity	**Overview**	**Branches**
Junior ROTC	Junior ROTC programs are directed at high school students and gear them toward military life. May receive advance grade on active enlistment based on Junior ROTC experience.	Army Navy
Challenge Program	A special, federally funded program for certain "youths at risk" that allow the military the opportunity to help them turn their lives around. Outstanding and noteworthy program. *See Chapter 6 (Army National Guard).*	National Guard (Army)

STANDARD MILITARY PERSONNEL BENEFITS	
Opportunity	**Overview**
20 Year Retirement	After 20 years of active military service members qualify for a military retirement. This allows for a second career and possibly a second retirement source. Individuals who retire with more than 20 years of military service receive higher pay. In addition to the military pay, retirees also receive medical care and commissary/exchange privileges. Reservists and National Guard members also earn 20-year retirements; however, the payment formula is separate due to the part-time basis of their duty.
Paid Vacations	Military leave time of up to 30 days per year.
Medical	Full medical, hospitalization, dental, and eye care services for active military personnel, and most health care costs for family members.
Continuing Education	A variety of educational programs for undergraduate and graduate degrees, including tuition assistance for programs at colleges and universities.
Life Insurance	Military personnel are offered a low-cost *Serviceman Group Life Insurance* policy upon enlistment.
Housing and Food	Military personnel and their immediate family are offered housing and food entitlements.
Department of Veterans Affairs Home Loan Guarantee Program	Qualified veterans can obtain a guaranteed home loan with no money down.

\multicolumn{3}{c}{**GENERAL MILITARY OCCUPATIONS CHART**}		
\multicolumn{3}{l}{(Note: this chart reflects a sample of the career or line-of-work specialties that are available to candidates. *See Chapters 12 and 13 for additional information.*)}		
Occupational Category	**Enlisted Title**	**Officer Title**

Administration Occupations	Administrative Support
	Computer Systems Specialist
	Finance and Accounting
	   Specialist
	Personnel Specialist
	Postal Specialist
	Preventive Maintenance
	   Specialist
	Recruiting Specialist
	Sales and Stock Specialist
	Supply and Warehousing
	   Specialist
	Training Specialist and
	   Instructor
		Communications Manager
		Emergency Management Officer
		Finance and Accounting Officer
		Health Services Administrator
		International Relations Manager
		Management Analyst
		Personnel Manager
		Postal Director
		Purchasing/Contracting Officer
		Recruiting Manager
		Store Manager
		Supply and Warehousing Officer
		Teacher and Instructor
		Training/Education Director

Aviation Occupations	Air Crew Member Air Traffic Controller Flight Operations Specialist Survival Equipment Specialist Aircraft Launch and Recovery Specialist Flight Engineer	Airplane Navigator Airplane Pilot Helicopter Pilot Air Traffic Manager
Combat Occupations	Artillery Crew Member Combat Engineer Infantryman Tank Crew Member	Artillery Officer Infantry Officer Missile System Officer Tank Officer
Construction Occupations	Building Electrician Construction Specialist Equipment Operator Plumber and Pipe Fitter	N/A

Electronics and Electrical Repair Occupations	Aircraft Electrician
	Communications Repairer
	Computer Equipment
	   Repairer
	Electrical Products Repairer
	Electronic Instrument Repairer
	Photographic Equipment
	   Repairer
	Power Plant Electrical Repairer
	Precision Instrument Repairer
	Radar/Sonar Equipment
	   Repairer
	Ship Electrician
	Weapons Maintenance
	   Repairer
		N/A

GENERAL MILITARY OCCUPATIONS CHART (continued)		
Occupational Category	**Enlisted Title**	**Officer Title**
Engineering, Science, and Technical Occupations	Chemical Lab Technician Communications Equipment Specialist Compressed Gas Specialist Computer Programmer Emergency Management Specialist Environmental Health and Safety Specialist Meteorological Non-Destructive Tester NBC and Ordnance Specialist Radar and Sonar Operator Radio Intelligence Specialist Space Operations Specialist Surveying, Mapping, and Drafting Technician	Aerospace Engineer Chemist Civil Engineer Computer Systems Officer Electrical and Electronics Officer Environmental Health and Safety Officer Industrial Engineer Life Scientist Marine Engineer Meteorologist Nuclear Engineer Oceanographer Physicist Space Operations Officer Surveying and Mapping Officer
Health Care Occupations	Cardiopulmonary and EEG Technician Dental Specialist Medical Care Technician Medical Lab Technician Optometric Technician Pharmacy Technician Physical and Occupational Therapist Radiologic Technician	Administrator Dietitian Pharmacist Physical and Occupational Therapist Physician Assistant Registered Nurse Speech Therapist
Health Diagnosing and Treatment Practitioners	N/A	Dentist Optometrist Physician and Surgeon Psychologist
Human Services Occupations	Caseworker Counselor Religious Specialist	Chaplain Social Worker
Intelligence Occupations	Intelligence Specialist	Intelligence Officer
Investigative, Law Enforcement, Corrections, Security Occupations	Criminal Investigator Military Police Corrections Officer Security Guard	Inspector General Police Supervisor
Legal Occupations	Court Reporter Legal Specialist	Lawyer Military Judge

GENERAL MILITARY OCCUPATIONS CHART (continued)		
Occupational Category	**Enlisted Title**	**Officer Title**
Machine Operators and Precision Work Occupations	Aircraft Mechanic Automotive and Heavy Equipment Machinist Dental and Optical Lab Machinist Heating and Cooling Mechanic Marine Engine Mechanic Precision Instrument Repairer Welder/Metal Worker	N/A
Media and Public Affairs Occupations	Audiovisual and Broadcast Technician Broadcast Journalist Graphic Designer-Illustrator Interpreter/Translator Newswriter Photographic Specialist Printing Specialist	Audiovisual and Broadcast Director Public Information Officer
Music/Band Occupations	Musician	Music Director
Nuclear Power and Power Plant Operations	Power Plant Electrician Power Plant Operator Powerhouse Mechanic	Nuclear Engineer
Ship and Submarine Occupations	Seaman Quartermaster Boat Operator Diver	Ship/Submarine Officer Ship Engineer
Special Operation Forces	Air Force Special Operation Command (SOC) Army Green Berets Marine Expeditionary Unit (MEU) Navy SEAL	Air Force SOC Army Green Berets Marine MEU Navy SEAL
Support Service Occupations	Firefighter Food Service Specialist	Food Service Manager
Transportation and Material Handling Occupations	Cargo Specialist Petroleum Supply Specialist Railroad Operations Specialist Transportation Specialist Vehicle Driver	Transportation Maintenance Manager Transportation Manager

Chapter 2

MILITARY RANK
AND PAY

Military Rank Structure ——————————

☐ Promotions in the Military

Military Pay and Allowances ——————————

☐ **Regular Pay**
☐ Reserve Pay
☐ Flight Pay
☐ Sea Pay
☐ Submarine Pay
☐ Dive Pay
☐ Medical Field Pay
☐ Basic Allowance for Quarters
☐ Reenlistment Bonus
☐ Prior Service Enlistment Bonus
☐ Household Goods Allowance

MILITARY RANK STRUCTURE

There is an old saying that *rank has its privileges*. *Rank* is everything in the military—the higher you go, the more pay, benefits, respect, and opportunities you will receive. A military person can start as a lowly Private (E-1 pay grade) and retire as General or Admiral (0-9).

Enlisted

Enlisted personnel begin at the lowest rank in the military and the lowest end of the pay scale; however, even at the low end, the military now prefers candidates with a high school education. While beginning at a low point, with time, good service, and education, advancement can be a steady path upward. Enlisted personnel serve as the main workforce or backbone of the military.

Warrant Officer

Between *Enlisted* and *Officer* is the level known as *Warrant Officer*. The rank of Warrant Officer is restricted to members of each branch of the military who have demonstrated a potential for greater responsibility than normally expected of senior enlisted personnel. This is not an entry-level position. Warrant Officers are assigned responsibilities and have authority commensurate with their rank including assignments as small-unit commanding officers.

Commissioned Officer

Officers begin at a supervisory rank. They must have a four-year college degree from an accredited institution before being commissioned. Officers serve as the mainstream managers for the military and are given a wide spectrum of responsibilities and authority.

SAMPLE OATH OF COMMISSION

I, _____, having been appointed an officer in the _____of the United States, do solemnly swear that I will support and defend the Constitution of the United States against all enemies, foreign and domestic, that I will bear true faith and allegiance to the same; that I take this obligation freely, without any mental reserve or purpose of evasion; and that I will well and faithfully discharge the duties of the office to the office upon which I am about to enter, SO HELP ME GOD.

PROMOTIONS IN THE MILITARY

The military offers a wide area of advancement. Promotions in the military are based on several factors that include:

- Job specialty (whether the field is overpopulated or there is a critical shortage with the service)

- Length of time in the position

- Time in present pay grade

- Job performance

- Leadership ability

- Awards or commendations

- Educational achievement through technical, on-the-job, or civilian instruction

ENLISTED MILITARY RANK CHART

PAY GRADE / SERVICE	ARMY	NAVY	AIR FORCE	MARINE CORPS	COAST GUARD
E-9	COMMAND SERGEANT MAJOR / SERGEANT MAJOR	MASTER CHIEF PETTY OFFICER	CHIEF MASTER SERGEANT	SERGEANT MAJOR / MASTER GUNNERY SERGEANT	MASTER CHIEF PETTY OFFICER
E-8	FIRST SERGEANT / MASTER SERGEANT	SENIOR CHIEF PETTY OFFICER	SENIOR MASTER SERGEANT	FIRST SERGEANT / MASTER SERGEANT	SENIOR CHIEF PETTY OFFICER
E-7	SERGEANT FIRST CLASS	CHIEF PETTY OFFICER	MASTER SERGEANT	GUNNERY SERGEANT	CHIEF PETTY OFFICER
E-6	STAFF SERGEANT	PETTY OFFICER FIRST CLASS	TECHNICAL SERGEANT	STAFF SERGEANT	PETTY OFFICER FIRST CLASS
E-5	SERGEANT	PETTY OFFICER SECOND CLASS	STAFF SERGEANT	SERGEANT	PETTY OFFICER SECOND CLASS
E-4	CORPORAL SPECIALIST	PETTY OFFICER THIRD CLASS	SENIOR AIRMAN	CORPORAL	PETTY OFFICER THIRD CLASS
E-3	PRIVATE FIRST CLASS	SEAMAN	AIRMAN FIRST CLASS	LANCE CORPORAL	FIREMAN SEAMAN
E-2	PRIVATE	SEAMAN APPRENTICE	AIRMAN	PRIVATE FIRST CLASS	FIREMAN APPRENTICE SEAMAN APPRENTICE
E-1	No Insignia / PRIVATE	SEAMAN RECRUIT	No Insignia / AIRMAN BASIC	No Insignia / PRIVATE	No Insignia / SEAMAN RECRUIT

(Military Ranks, Source: DOD Military Careers)

OFFICER MILITARY RANK CHART

SERVICE / PAY GRADE	ARMY	NAVY	AIR FORCE	MARINE CORPS	COAST GUARD
O-9	★★★★ GENERAL	★★★★ ADMIRAL	★★★★ GENERAL	★★★★ GENERAL	★★★★ ADMIRAL
O-9	★★★ LIEUTENANT GENERAL	★★★ VICE ADMIRAL	★★★ LIEUTENANT GENERAL	★★★ LIEUTENANT GENERAL	★★★ VICE ADMIRAL
O-8	★★ MAJOR GENERAL	★★ REAR ADMIRAL (UPPER HALF)	★★ MAJOR GENERAL	★★ MAJOR GENERAL	★★ REAR ADMIRAL (UPPER HALF)
O-7	★ BRIGADIER GENERAL	★ REAR ADMIRAL (LOWER HALF)	★ BRIGADIER GENERAL	★ BRIGADIER GENERAL	★ REAR ADMIRAL (LOWER HALF)
O-6	COLONEL	CAPTAIN	COLONEL	COLONEL	CAPTAIN
O-5	LIEUTENANT COLONEL	COMMANDER	LIEUTENANT COLONEL	LIEUTENANT COLONEL	COMMANDER
O-4	MAJOR	LIEUTENANT COMMANDER	MAJOR	MAJOR	LIEUTENANT COMMANDER
O-3	CAPTAIN	LIEUTENANT	CAPTAIN	CAPTAIN	LIEUTENANT
O-2	FIRST LIEUTENANT	LIEUTENANT JUNIOR GRADE	FIRST LIEUTENANT	FIRST LIEUTENANT	LIEUTENANT JUNIOR GRADE
O-1	SECOND LIEUTENANT	ENSIGN	SECOND LIEUTENANT	SECOND LIEUTENANT	ENSIGN

(Military Ranks, Source: DOD Military Careers)

MILITARY PAY AND ALLOWANCES

Regular Pay (Full-Time Monthly Pay)

In addition to regular pay, service members are entitled to BAQ (Basic Allowance for Quarters) and other allowances.

Rank	<2	2	3	4	6	8	10	12	14	16	18	20	22	24	26
							Years of Service								

Commissioned Officers

Rank	<2	2	3	4	6	8	10	12	14	16	18	20	22	24	26
O-10	7360.20	7619.10	7619.10	7619.10	7619.10	7911.60	7911.60	8349.90	8349.90	8947.20	8947.20	9546.30	9546.30	9546.30	10140.90
O-9	6522.90	6693.90	6836.70	6836.70	6836.70	7010.40	7010.40	7302.00	7302.00	7911.60	7911.60	8349.90	8349.90	8349.90	8947.20
O-8	5908.20	6085.50	6229.80	6229.80	6229.80	6693.90	6693.90	7010.40	7010.40	7302.00	7619.10	7911.60	8106.60	8106.60	8106.60
O-7	4909.20	5243.10	5243.10	5243.10	5478.30	5478.30	5795.70	5795.70	6085.50	6693.90	7154.40	7154.40	7154.40	7154.40	7154.40
O-6	3638.40	3997.50	4259.70	4259.70	4259.70	4259.70	4259.70	4259.70	4404.60	5100.90	5361.30	5478.30	5795.70	5991.60	6285.60
O-5	2910.30	3417.00	3653.40	3653.40	3653.40	3653.40	3763.50	3966.60	4232.40	4549.20	4809.60	4955.70	5128.80	5128.80	5128.80
O-4	2452.80	2987.10	3186.30	3186.30	3245.40	3388.50	3619.80	3823.20	3997.50	4173.30	4287.90	4287.90	4287.90	4287.90	4287.90
O-3	2279.40	2548.50	2724.90	3014.70	3159.00	3272.10	3449.40	3619.80	3708.60	3708.60	3708.60	3708.60	3708.60	3708.60	3708.60
O-2	1987.80	2170.80	2608.20	2695.80	2751.60	2751.60	2751.60	2751.60	2751.60	2751.60	2751.60	2751.60	2751.60	2751.60	2751.60
O-1	1725.90	1796.10	2170.80	2170.80	2170.80	2170.80	2170.80	2170.80	2170.80	2170.80	2170.80	2170.80	2170.80	2170.80	2170.80

(Commissioned officers with more than four years active duty service as an enlisted member or warrant officer.)

Rank	<2	2	3	4	6	8	10	12	14	16	18	20	22	24	26
O-3E	0.00	0.00	0.00	3014.70	3159.00	3272.10	3449.40	3619.80	3763.50	3763.50	3763.50	3763.50	3763.50	3763.50	3763.50
O-2E	0.00	0.00	0.00	2695.80	2751.60	2838.90	2987.10	3101.40	3186.30	3186.30	3186.30	3186.30	3186.30	3186.30	3186.30
O-1E	0.00	0.00	0.00	2170.80	2319.30	2404.50	2491.80	2578.20	2695.80	2695.80	2695.80	2695.80	2695.80	2695.80	2695.80

Warrant Officers

Rank	<2	2	3	4	6	8	10	12	14	16	18	20	22	24	26
W-5	0.00	0.00	0.00	0.00	0.00	0.00	0.00	0.00	0.00	0.00	0.00	3963.60	4113.60	4232.70	4410.90
W-4	2322.30	2491.80	2491.80	2548.50	2664.60	2781.90	2898.60	3101.40	3245.40	3359.40	3449.40	3560.70	3679.80	3794.40	3966.60
W-3	2110.80	2289.60	2289.60	2319.30	2346.30	2517.90	2664.60	2751.60	2838.90	2923.80	3014.70	3132.30	3245.40	3245.40	3359.40
W-2	1848.60	2000.10	2000.10	2058.30	2170.80	2289.60	2376.60	2463.60	2548.50	2638.20	2724.90	2810.40	2923.80	2923.80	2923.80
W-1	1540.20	1765.80	1765.80	1913.40	2000.10	2085.90	2170.80	2260.20	2346.30	2433.60	2517.90	2608.20	2608.20	2608.20	2608.20

Enlisted Members

Rank	<2	2	3	4	6	8	10	12	14	16	18	20	22	24	26
E-9	0.00	0.00	0.00	0.00	0.00	0.00	2701.80	2762.40	2824.80	2889.90	2954.70	3011.70	3169.80	3293.40	3478.50
E-8	0.00	0.00	0.00	0.00	0.00	2265.60	2330.70	2391.90	2454.00	2519.10	2576.40	2639.70	2794.80	2919.30	3106.50
E-7	1581.90	1707.90	1770.60	1833.00	1895.40	1955.70	2018.40	2081.40	2175.30	2237.10	2298.90	2329.20	2485.50	2609.10	2794.80
E-6	1360.80	1483.50	1545.00	1610.70	1671.30	1731.30	1794.90	1887.30	1946.70	2009.40	2040.00	2040.00	2040.00	2040.00	2040.00
E-5	1194.30	1299.90	1362.90	1422.30	1515.90	1577.70	1639.80	1700.40	1731.30	1731.30	1731.30	1731.30	1731.30	1731.30	1731.30
E-4	1113.60	1176.30	1245.60	1341.60	1394.70	1394.70	1394.70	1394.70	1394.70	1394.70	1394.70	1394.70	1394.70	1394.70	1394.70
E-3	1049.70	1107.00	1151.10	1196.70	1196.70	1196.70	1196.70	1196.70	1196.70	1196.70	1196.70	1196.70	1196.70	1196.70	1196.70
E-2	1010.10	1010.10	1010.10	1010.10	1010.10	1010.10	1010.10	1010.10	1010.10	1010.10	1010.10	1010.10	1010.10	1010.10	1010.10
E-1	900.90	900.90	900.90	900.90	900.90	900.90	900.90	900.90	900.90	900.90	900.90	900.90	900.90	900.90	900.90

(Source: Office of the Undersecretary of Defense, Personnel and Readiness, Compensation April 17, 1997)

RESERVE PAY (FOR ONE DRILL) Reservists receive pay per drill for their monthly weekend service. While on two weeks active duty, reservists receive full-time regular pay and benefits.

Rank	<2	2	3	4	6	8	10	12	14	16	18	20	22	24	26
						Years of Service									
Commissioned Officers															
O-10	245.34	253.97	253.97	253.97	253.97	263.72	263.72	278.33	278.33	298.24	298.24	318.21	318.21	318.21	338.03
O-9	217.43	223.13	227.89	227.89	227.89	233.68	233.68	243.40	243.40	263.72	263.72	278.33	278.33	278.33	298.24
O-8	196.94	202.85	207.66	207.66	207.66	223.13	223.13	233.68	233.68	243.40	253.97	263.72	270.22	270.22	270.22
O-7	163.64	174.77	174.77	174.77	182.61	182.61	193.19	193.19	202.85	223.13	238.48	238.48	238.48	238.48	238.48
O-6	121.28	133.25	141.99	141.99	141.99	141.99	141.99	141.99	146.82	170.03	178.71	182.61	193.19	199.72	209.52
O-5	97.01	113.90	121.78	121.78	121.78	121.78	125.45	132.22	141.08	151.64	160.32	165.19	170.96	170.96	170.96
O-4	81.76	99.57	106.21	106.21	108.18	112.95	120.66	127.44	133.25	139.11	142.93	142.93	142.93	142.93	142.93
O-3	75.98	84.95	90.83	100.49	105.30	109.07	114.98	120.66	123.62	123.62	123.62	123.62	123.62	123.62	123.62
O-2	66.26	72.36	86.94	89.86	91.72	91.72	91.72	91.72	91.72	91.72	91.72	91.72	91.72	91.72	91.72
O-1	57.53	59.80	72.36	72.36	72.36	72.36	72.36	72.36	72.36	72.36	72.36	72.36	72.36	72.36	72.36
(Commissioned officers with more than four years active duty service as an enlisted member or warrant officer.)															
O-3E	0.00	0.00	0.00	100.49	105.30	109.07	114.98	120.66	125.45	125.45	125.45	125.45	125.45	125.45	125.45
O-2E	0.00	0.00	0.00	89.86	91.72	94.63	99.57	103.38	106.21	106.21	106.21	106.21	106.21	106.21	106.21
O-1E	0.00	0.00	0.00	72.36	77.31	80.15	83.06	85.94	89.86	89.86	89.86	89.86	89.86	89.86	89.86
Warrant Officers															
W-5	0.00	0.00	0.00	0.00	0.00	0.00	0.00	0.00	0.00	0.00	0.00	132.12	137.12	141.09	147.03
W-4	77.41	83.06	83.06	84.95	88.82	92.73	96.62	103.38	108.18	111.98	114.98	118.69	122.66	126.48	132.22
W-3	70.36	76.32	76.32	77.31	78.21	83.93	88.82	91.72	94.63	97.46	100.49	104.41	108.18	108.18	111.98
W-2	61.62	66.67	66.67	68.61	72.36	76.32	79.22	82.12	84.95	87.94	90.83	93.68	97.46	97.46	97.46
W-1	51.34	58.86	58.86	63.78	66.67	69.53	72.36	75.34	78.21	81.12	83.93	86.94	86.94	86.94	86.94
Enlisted Members															
E-9	0.00	0.00	0.00	0.00	0.00	0.00	90.06	92.08	94.16	96.33	98.49	100.39	105.66	109.78	115.95
E-8	0.00	0.00	0.00	0.00	0.00	75.52	77.69	79.73	81.80	83.97	85.88	87.99	93.16	97.31	103.55
E-7	52.73	56.93	59.02	61.10	63.18	65.19	67.28	69.38	72.51	74.57	76.63	77.64	82.85	86.97	93.16
E-6	45.36	49.45	51.50	53.69	55.71	57.71	59.83	62.91	64.89	66.98	68.00	68.00	68.00	68.00	68.00
E-5	39.81	43.33	45.43	47.41	50.53	52.59	54.66	56.68	57.71	57.71	57.71	57.71	57.71	57.71	57.71
E-4	37.12	39.21	41.52	44.72	46.49	46.49	46.49	46.49	46.49	46.49	46.49	46.49	46.49	46.49	46.49
E-3	34.99	36.90	38.37	39.89	39.89	39.89	39.89	39.89	39.89	39.89	39.89	39.89	39.89	39.89	39.89
E-2	33.67	33.67	33.67	33.67	33.67	33.67	33.67	33.67	33.67	33.67	33.67	33.67	33.67	33.67	33.67
E-1	30.03	30.03	30.03	30.03	30.03	30.03	30.03	30.03	30.03	30.03	30.03	30.03	30.03	30.03	30.03

FLIGHT PAY   Flight pay is issued as a career incentive for two reasons: First, it recognizes that flying in military aircraft has inherent dangers, and second, it keeps qualified personnel on flight status.

COMMISSIONED OFFICERS

More than 6	$650	More than 25	$585
More than 4	206	More than 22	495
More than 3	188	More than 20	385
More than 2	156	More than 18	250
Fewer than 2	125		

(Phase 1—for years of aviation service, in grades O-1 through O-6 and Warrant Officers)

(Phase 2—for years of active commissioned service)

AVIATOR CONTINUATION PAY

Up to $12,000 per year through fourteenth year of commissioned service.

RESERVES

One-thirtieth of monthly aviation pay for each drill period of at least two flying hours.

ENLISTED MEMBERS—
Hazardous Duty (Crew Member) Pay

Rank	Pay
E-9	$200
E-8	200
E-7	200
E-6	175
E-5	150
E-4	125
E-3	110
E-2	110
E-1	110

SEA PAY   Sailors in pay grade E-5 and below are entitled to an extra $100 a month in career sea pay after serving 36 consecutive months at sea. The benefit ends at the beginning of the fifth year of sea service. Officers are entitled to the same $100 benefit at any point in their career in which they serve more than three consecutive years at sea.

YEARS OF SEA DUTY

Rank	<2	2	4	6	8	10	12	14	16	18	20	22	24	26
Commissioned Officers														
O-6	225	230	230	240	255	265	280	290	300	310	325	340	355	380
O-5	225	225	225	225	230	245	250	260	265	265	285	300	315	340
O-4	185	190	200	205	215	220	220	225	225	240	270	280	290	300
O-3	150	160	185	190	195	205	215	225	225	240	260	270	280	290
O-2	150	160	185	190	195	205	215	225	225	240	250	260	270	280
O-1	150	160	185	190	195	205	215	225	225	240	250	260	270	280
Warrant Officers														
W-4	150	150	150	150	170	290	310	310	310	310	350	375	400	450
W-3	150	150	150	150	170	270	280	285	290	310	350	375	400	425
W-2	150	150	150	150	170	260	265	265	270	310	340	340	375	400
W-1	130	135	140	150	170	175	200	250	270	300	325	325	340	360
Enlisted Members														
E-9	100	100	120	175	190	350	350	375	390	400	400	410	420	450
E-8	100	100	120	175	190	350	350	375	390	400	400	410	420	450
E-7	100	100	120	175	190	350	350	375	390	400	400	410	420	450
E-6	100	100	120	150	170	315	325	350	350	365	365	365	380	395
E-5	50	60	120	150	170	315	325	350	350	350	350	350	350	350
E-4	50	60	120	150	160	160	160	160	160	160	160	160	160	160

SUBMARINE PAY Submariners are also recognized with additional pay for living under the sea. In addition to regular pay, they receive the following:

Rank	<2	2	4	6	8	10	12	14	16	18	20	22	24	26
YEARS OF SERVICE														
Commissioned Officers														
O-6	595	595	595	595	595	595	595	595	595	595	595	595	595	595
O-5	595	595	595	595	595	595	595	595	595	595	595	595	595	595
O-4	365	365	365	405	595	595	595	595	595	595	595	595	595	595
O-3	355	355	355	390	595	595	595	595	595	595	595	595	595	595
O-2	235	235	235	235	235	235	355	355	355	355	355	355	355	355
O-1	175	175	175	175	175	175	355	355	355	355	355	355	355	355
Warrant Officers														
ALL	310	355	355	355	355	355	355	355	355	355	355	355	355	355
Enlisted Members														
E-9	225	225	225	270	295	310	315	330	345	355	355	355	355	355
E-8	225	225	225	250	270	295	310	315	330	330	345	345	345	345
E-7	225	225	225	250	255	265	275	295	310	310	310	310	310	310
E-6	155	170	175	215	230	245	255	265	265	265	265	265	265	265
E-5	140	155	155	175	190	195	195	195	195	195	195	195	195	195
E-4	80	95	100	170	175	175	175	175	175	175	175	175	175	175
E-3	80	90	100	170	175	175	0	90	90	90	90	90	90	90
E-2	75	90	90	90	90	90	90	90	90	90	90	90	90	90
E-1	75	75	75	75	75	75	75	75	0	75	75	0	75	75

DIVE PAY Divers work in hazardous conditions under ships, submarines, or in special operations. The minimum diving pay is $110 monthly.

MEDICAL FIELD PAY Due to the sharp difference between military pay and the amount of money those in medical professions would make as civilians, medical field pay is necessary to retain qualified personnel. Certain medical specialties also command yearly bonuses and additional special pay.
Doctors $450 monthly
Dentists $350 monthly

BASIC ALLOWANCE FOR QUARTERS (BAQ) This chart shows 1997 BAQ rates.

Rank	SINGLE FULL RATE	PARTIAL RATE	MARRIED FULL RATE
O-10	824.70	50.70	1015.20
O-9	824.70	50.70	1015.20
O-8	824.70	50.70	1015.20
O-7	824.70	50.70	1015.20
O-6	756.60	39.60	914.10
O-5	728.70	33.00	881.10
O-4	675.30	26.70	776.70
O-3	541.20	22.20	642.60
O-2	429.30	17.70	548.70
O-1	361.50	13.20	490.50
O-3E	584.40	22.20	690.60
O-2E	496.80	17.70	623.10
O-1E	427.20	13.20	575.70
W-5	686.10	25.20	749.70
W-4	609.30	25.20	687.30
W-3	512.10	20.70	629.70
W-2	454.80	15.90	579.30
W-1	380.70	13.80	501.00

	SINGLE FULL RATE	PARTIAL RATE	MARRIED FULL RATE
Rank			
E-9	500.40	18.60	659.70
E-8	459.30	15.30	608.10
E-7	392.40	12.00	564.60
E-6	355.20	9.90	521.70
E-5	327.60	8.70	469.20
E-4	285.00	8.10	408.00
E-3	279.60	7.80	379.80
E-2	227.10	7.20	361.50
E-1	202.50	6.90	361.50

REENLISTMENT BONUS   The military offers qualified personnel in special needs areas reenlistment bonuses to keep them in the service. The amount varies according to the need and availability of funding.

PRIOR SERVICE ENLISTMENT BONUS   Like the reenlistment bonus, certain veterans who have special training or skills are paid bonuses to reenlist.

HOUSEHOLD GOODS ALLOWANCE Limit, in pounds, for shipping or storing personal goods for permanent change of station moves.

HOUSEHOLD GOODS ALLOWANCE		
Rank	**Without Dependents**	**With Dependents**
O-10–O-6	18,000	18,000
O-5–W-5	16,000	17,500
O-4–W-4	14,000	17,000
O-3–W-3	13,000	14,500
O-2–W-2	12,500	13,500
O-1–W-1	10,000	12,500
E-9	12,000	14,500
E-8	11,000	13,500
E-7	10,500	12,500
E-6	8,000	11,000
E-5	7,000	9,000
E-4 >2	7,000	8,000
E-4 <2	3,500	7,000
E-3	2,000*	5,000
E-2	1,500*	5,000
E-1	1,500	5,000

(*E-3s, E-2s, and E-1s married to E-3s, E-2s, or E-1s are entitled to a combined weight allowance of 5,000 pounds when both are without dependents.)

(Source: Office of the Undersecretary of Defense, Personnel and Readiness, Compensation)

Chapter 3

JOINING THE MILITARY

☐ Overview
☐ **Enlisting in the Military**
☐ The Basic Paperwork Process
☐ Standard Enlistment Forms
☐ **Military Background Investigations and Security Clearances**
☐ **Medical and Physical Examinations**
☐ **Basic Training (Enlisted)**
☐ Overview
☐ What to Expect
☐ Military Time
☐ First Duty: Security Watch
☐ Military Boot Camp Terms

OVERVIEW After reading this book and conducting your own research, select a list of Military Occupational Specialties (MOS) or programs you desire. When you are ready, meet with a recruiter. Be sure to prepare a list of questions. You may also wish to bring the detachable sheet located at the end of this book.

Step 1: Meet with a service recruiter for more than one branch.

Step 2: Qualify for enlistment.

This will mean a trip to the Military Enlistment Processing Station (MEPS) nearest you (at government expense). Basically, it is a one-stop processing station that will:

• administer the ASVAB or CAT-ASVAB exam to test your aptitude in certain career fields (this will be explained in depth in the next chapter)

• conduct comprehensive medical and physical exams

- evaluate the results and provide career counseling with the military branch of your choice

Step 3: Obtain a guaranteed agreement for the career field (line-of-work) specialty training program after basic training or educational opportunity.

Step 4: Agree on the service obligation in years.

Step 5: Enlist in the service.

Hint

Be careful: Sign nothing on your first meeting. Recruiters are geared for high-pressure dealings and will try to have you sign up on the first meeting. Meet with recruiters or representatives from all of the services in which you are interested. Obtain all the publications that will clearly explain the programs that you are interested in.

ENLISTING IN THE MILITARY

Enlisting in the military is a complex process. After you have finally reached an agreement with the recruiter about your particular career or military training, you must then fill out numerous official forms. The standard military saying is *hurry up and wait.* There is some truth to this saying in day-to-day military operations and dealings; however, you are signing several years of your future into the military. When in doubt, or if you are not sure, tell the recruiters you need a little time to think it out, then reach out to someone you trust and respect, perhaps a current or former military veteran who may help you in reaching your decision.

THE BASIC PAPERWORK PROCESS (OR MAZE) When you join the military, you create a source of information about yourself for the U.S. government. The government by its nature and military mission needs to know everything about you. You are several things to the military, chief among them an investment. The government is about to give you specialized training and possibly a college education. It wants to know exactly who and what it is investing in; for instance, are you trustworthy, loyal, healthy, and moral?

STANDARD ENLISTMENT FORMS
- Record of Military Processing (DD 1966/1/2/3/4)
- Department of Defense Personnel Security Questionnaire (DD 398)
- Applicant Medical Prescreening Form (DD 2246)

Additional forms may include Drug and Alcohol Testing, Enlistment Eligibility Questionnaire, Police Records Check (DD 369), and A.E. Fingerprint Check (DD 2280).

RECORD OF MILITARY PROCESSING - ARMED FORCES OF THE UNITED STATES
(Before completing this form, read Privacy Act Statement, Warning, and Instructions on back of form.)

Form Approved
OMB No. 0704-0173
Expires Feb 28, 1996

Public reporting burden for this collection of information is estimated to average 20 minutes per response, including the time for reviewing instructions, searching existing data sources, gathering and maintaining the data needed, and completing and reviewing the collection of information. Send comments regarding this burden estimate or any other aspect of this collection of information, including suggestions for reducing this burden, to Washington Headquarters Services, Directorate for Information Operations and Reports, 1215 Jefferson Davis Highway, Suite 1204, Arlington, VA 22202-4302, and to the Office of Management and Budget, Paperwork Reduction Project (0704-0173), Washington, DC 20503

PLEASE DO NOT RETURN YOUR COMPLETED FORM TO EITHER OF THESE ADDRESSES.

A. SERVICE PROCESSING FOR	B. PRIOR SERVICE				C. SELECTIVE SERVICE CLASSIFICATION	D. SELECTIVE SERVICE REGISTRATION NO.
	YES	NO	(1) DIEUS (YYMMDD)			
	NUMBER OF DAYS		(2) DIERC (YYMMDD)			

SECTION I - PERSONAL DATA

1. SOCIAL SECURITY NUMBER

2. NAME *(Last, First, Middle Name (and Maiden, if any), Jr., Sr., etc.)*

3. CURRENT ADDRESS *(Street, City, County, State, Country, ZIP Code)*

4. HOME OF RECORD ADDRESS *(Street, City, County, State, Country, ZIP Code)*

5. CITIZENSHIP *(X one)*
- a. U.S. AT BIRTH *(If this box is marked, also X (1) or (2)*
  - (1) NATIVE BORN
  - (2) BORN ABROAD OF U.S. PARENT(S)
- b. U.S. NATURALIZED
- c. U.S. NON-CITIZEN NATIONAL
- d. IMMIGRANT ALIEN *(Specify)*
- e. NON-IMMIGRANT FOREIGN NATIONAL *(Specify)*

6. SEX
- a. MALE
- b. FEMALE

8. MARITAL STATUS *(Specify)*

9. NUMBER OF DEPENDENTS

7. a. RACIAL CATEGORY
- (1) AMERICAN INDIAN/ALASKAN NATIVE
- (2) BLACK/NEGRO/AFRICAN AMERICAN
- (3) ORIENTAL/ASIAN/PACIFIC ISLANDER
- (4) WHITE/CAUCASIAN
- (5) OTHER *(Specify)*

7. b. ETHNIC CATEGORY
- (1) SPANISH / HISPANIC   YES   NO
- (2) OTHER *(Specify)*

10. DATE OF BIRTH *(YYMMDD)*

11. RELIGIOUS PREFERENCE *(Optional)*

12. EDUCATION *(Yrs / Highest Ed Gr Compl)*

13. PROFICIENT IN FOREIGN LANGUAGE *(If Yes, specify. If No, enter NONE.)*   1st   2nd
/

14. VALID DRIVER'S LICENSE *(X one)*   YES   NO   *(If Yes, list State, number, and expiration date)*

15. PLACE OF BIRTH *(City, State and Country)*

SECTION II - EXAMINATION AND ENTRANCE DATA PROCESSING CODES
FOR OFFICE USE ONLY - DO NOT WRITE IN THIS SECTION - GO ON TO PAGE 2, QUESTION 23

16. APTITUDE TEST RESULTS

a. TEST ID	b. TEST SCORES											
	AFQT PERCENTILE	GS	AR	WK	PC	NO	CS	AS	MK	MC	E I	VE

17. DEP ENLISTMENT DATA

a. DATE OF DEP ENLIST-MENT (YYMMDD)	b. PROJ ACTIVE DUTY DATE (YYMMDD)	c. ES	d. RECRUITER IDENTIFICATION	e. PROGRAM ENLISTED FOR	f. T-E MOS/AFS	g. WAIVER	h. PAY GRADE

18. ACCESSION DATA

a. ENLISTMENT DATE (YYMMDD)	b. ACTIVE DUTY SERVICE DATE (YYMMDD)	c. PAY ENTRY DATE (YYMMDD)	d. TOE	e. WAIVER	f. PAY GRADE	g. DATE OF GRADE (YYMMDD)	h. ES	i. YRS HIGHEST ED GR COMPL

j. RECRUITER IDENTIFICATION	k. PROGRAM ENLISTED FOR	l. T-E MOS/AFS	m. PMOS/AFS	n. YOUTH	o. OA	p. TRANSFER TO (UIC)

19. SERVICE REQUIRED CODES

1	2	3	4	5	6	7	8	9	10	11	12	13	14	15	16	17	18	19	20	21	22	23	24	25
26	27	28	29	30	31	32	33	34	35	36	37	38	39	40	41	42	43	44	45	46	47	48	49	50
51 52 53 54 55	56	57	58	59	60	61	62	63	64	65	66	67	68	69	70	71	72	73	74	75	76	77	78	79	80

51	52	53	54	55	56	57	58	59	60	61	62	63	64	65	66	67	68	69	70	71	72	73	74	75	76	77	78	79	80
81	82	83	84	85	86	87	88	89	90	91	92	93	94	95	96	97	98	99	100	101	102	103	104	105	106	107	108	109	110
111	112	113	114	115	116	117	118	119	120	121	122	123	124	125	126	127	128	129	130	131	132	133	134	135	136	137	138	139	140

DD Form 1966/1, APR 94

| 20. NAME *(Last, First, Middle Initial)* | | | | 21. SOCIAL SECURITY NUMBER | |

SECTION III - OTHER PERSONAL DATA

22. EDUCATION

a. List all high schools and colleges attended. *(List dates in YYMM format.)*

(1) FROM	(2) TO	(3) NAME OF SCHOOL	(4) LOCATION	(5) GRADUATE	
				YES	NO

	YES	NO
b. Have you ever been enrolled in ROTC, Junior ROTC, Sea Cadet Program or Civil Air Patrol?		

23. MARITAL / DEPENDENCY STATUS AND FAMILY DATA *(If "Yes," explain in Section VI, "Remarks.")*

a. Is anyone dependent upon you for support?		
b. Is there any court order or judgment in effect that directs you to provide alimony or support for children?		
c. Do you have an <u>immediate relative</u> (father, mother, brother, or sister) who: (1) is now a prisoner of war or is missing in action (MIA); or (2) died or became 100% permanently disabled while serving in the Armed Services?		
d. Are you the only living child in your immediate family?		

24. PREVIOUS MILITARY SERVICE OR EMPLOYMENT WITH THE US GOVERNMENT *(If "Yes," explain in Section VI, "Remarks.")*

a. Are you now or have you ever been in any regular or reserve branch of the Armed Forces or in the Army National Guard or Air National Guard?		
b. Have you ever been rejected for enlistment, reenlistment, or induction by any branch of the Armed Forces of the United States?		
c. Are you now or have you ever been a deserter from any branch of the Armed Forces of the United States?		
d. Have you ever been employed by the United States Government?		
e. Are you now drawing, or do you have an application pending, or approval for: retired pay, disability allowance, severance pay, or a pension from any agency of the government of the United States?		

25. ABILITY TO PERFORM MILITARY DUTIES *(If "Yes," explain in Section VI, "Remarks.")*

a. Are you now or have you ever been a conscientious objector? *(That is, do you have, or have you ever had, a firm, fixed, and sincere objection to participation in war in any form or to the bearing of arms because of religious belief or training?)*		
b. Have you ever been discharged by any branch of the Armed Forces of the United States for reasons pertaining to being a conscientious objector?		
c. Is there anything which would preclude you from performing military duties or participating in military activities whenever necessary *(i.e., do you have any personal restrictions or religious practices which would restrict your availability?)*		

26. DRUG USE AND ABUSE *(If "Yes," explain in Section VI, "Remarks.")*

Have you ever tried or used or possessed any narcotic (to include heroin or cocaine), depressant (to include quaaludes), stimulant, hallucinogen (to include LSD or PCP), or cannabis (to include marijuana or hashish), or any mind-altering substance (to include glue or paint), or anabolic steroid, except as prescribed by a licensed physician?	

SECTION IV - CERTIFICATION

27. CERTIFICATION OF APPLICANT *(Your signature in this block must be witnessed by your recruiter.)*

a. I certify that the information given by me in this document is true, complete, and correct to the best of my knowledge and belief. I understand that I am being accepted for enlistment based on the information provided by me in this document: that if any of the information is knowingly false or incorrect, I could be tried in a civilian or military court and could receive a less than honorable discharge which could affect my future employment opportunities.

b. TYPED OR PRINTED NAME *(Last, First, Middle Initial)*	c. SIGNATURE	d. DATE SIGNED *(YYMMDD)*

28. DATA VERIFICATION BY RECRUITER *(Enter description of the actual documents used to verify the following items.)*

a. NAME *(X one)*	b. AGE *(X one)*	c. CITIZENSHIP *(X one)*
(1) BIRTH CERTIFICATE	(1) BIRTH CERTIFICATE	(1) BIRTH CERTIFICATE
(2) OTHER *(Explain)*	(2) OTHER *(Explain)*	(2) OTHER *(Explain)*
d. SOCIAL SECURITY NUMBER (SSN) *(X one)*	e. EDUCATION *(X one)*	f. OTHER DOCUMENTS USED
(1) SSN CARD	(1) DIPLOMA	
(2) OTHER *(Explain)*	(2) OTHER *(Explain)*	

DD Form 1966/2, APR 94

29. NAME (*Last, First, Middle Initial*) | **30. SOCIAL SECURITY NUMBER**

31. CERTIFICATION OF WITNESS

a. I certify that I have witnessed the applicant's signature above and that I have verified the data in the documents required as prescribed by my directives. I further certify that I have not made any promises or guarantees other than those listed and signed by me. I understand my liability to trial by courts-martial under the Uniform Code of Military Justice should I effect or cause to be effected the enlistment of anyone known by me to be ineligible for enlistment.

b. TYPED OR PRINTED NAME (*Last, First, Middle Initial*)	**c. PAY GRADE**	**d. RECRUITER I. D.**	**e. SIGNATURE**	**f. DATE SIGNED** (*YYMMDD*)

32. SPECIFIC OPTION / PROGRAM ENLISTED FOR, MILITARY SKILL, OR ASSIGNMENT TO A GEOGRAPHICAL AREA GUARANTEES

a. **SPECIFIC OPTION / PROGRAM ENLISTED FOR** (*Completed by Guidance Counselor, MEPS Liaison NCO, etc., as specified by sponsoring service - use clear text English.*)

b. I fully understand that I will not be guaranteed any specific military skill or assignment to a geographic area except as shown in Item 32.a. above and annexes attached to my Enlistment/ Reenlistment Document (DD Form 4).	**c. APPLICANT'S INITIALS**

33. CERTIFICATION OF RECRUITER OR ACCEPTOR

a. I certify that I have reviewed all information contained in this document and, to the best of my judgment and belief, the applicant fulfills all legal policy requirements for enlistment. I accept him/her for enlistment on behalf of the United States (*Enter Branch of Service*) _____ and certify that I have not made any promises or guarantees other than those listed in Item 32 above. I further certify that service regulations governing such enlistments have been strictly complied with and any waivers required to effect applicant's enlistment have been secured and are attached to this document.

b. TYPED OR PRINTED NAME (*Last, First, Middle Initial*)	**c. PAY GRADE**	**d. RECRUITER I.D. OR ORGANIZATION**	**e. SIGNATURE**	**f. DATE SIGNED** (*YYMMDD*)

SECTION V - RECERTIFICATION

34. RECERTIFICATION BY APPLICANT AND CORRECTION OF DATA AT THE TIME OF ACTIVE DUTY ENTRY

a. I have reviewed all information contained in this document this date. That information is still correct and true to the best of my knowledge and belief. If changes were required, the original entry has been marked "See Item 34" and the correct information is provided below.

b. ITEM NUMBER	**c. CHANGE REQUIRED**

d. APPLICANT		**e. WITNESS**		
(1) SIGNATURE	**(2) DATE SIGNED** (*YYMMDD*)	**(1) TYPED OR PRINTED NAME**	**(2) RANK / GRADE**	**(3) SIGNATURE**

SECTION VI - REMARKS (*Specify item(s) being continued by item number. Continue on separate pages if necessary.*)

	DD FORM 1966/4 ATTACHED (*X one*)	YES
		NO

DD Form 1966/3, APR 94

35. NAME (Last, First, Middle Initial)	36. SOCIAL SECURITY NUMBER

USE THIS DD FORM 1966 PAGE ONLY IF EITHER SECTION APPLIES TO THE APPLICANT'S RECORD OF MILITARY PROCESSING.

SECTION VII - PARENTAL / GUARDIAN CONSENT FOR ENLISTMENT

37. PARENT / GUARDIAN STATEMENT(S) (Line out portions not applicable)

a. I /we certify that (Enter name of applicant) _____

_____

has no other legal guardian other than me / us and I / we consent to his / her enlistment in the United States (Enter Branch of Service) _____ I/we certify that <u>no promises of any kind</u> have been made to me/us concerning assignment to duty, training, or promotion during his/her enlistment <u>as an inducement</u> to me/us to sign this consent. I/we hereby authorize the Armed Forces representatives concerned to perform medical examinations, other examinations required, and to conduct records checks to determine his/her eligibility. I/we relinquish all claim to his/her service and to any wage or compensation for such service.

b. <u>FOR ENLISTMENT IN A RESERVE COMPONENT.</u>
I/we understand that, as a member of a reserve component, he/she must serve minimum periods of active duty for training unless excused by competent authority. In the event he/she fails to fulfill the obligations of his/her reserve enlistment, he/she may be recalled to active duty as prescribed by law. I/we further understand that while he/she is in the ready reserve, he/she may be ordered to extended active duty in time of war or national emergency declared by the Congress or the President or when otherwise authorized by law.

c. PARENT

(1) TYPED OR PRINTED NAME (Last, First, Middle Initial)	(2) SIGNATURE	(3) DATE SIGNED (YYMMDD)

d. WITNESS

(1) TYPED OR PRINTED NAME (Last, First, Middle Initial)	(2) SIGNATURE	(3) DATE SIGNED (YYMMDD)

e. PARENT

(1) TYPED OR PRINTED NAME (Last, First, Middle Initial)	(2) SIGNATURE	(3) DATE SIGNED (YYMMDD)

f. WITNESS

(1) TYPED OR PRINTED NAME (Last, First, Middle Initial)	(2) SIGNATURE	(3) DATE SIGNED (YYMMDD)

38. VERIFICATION OF SINGLE SIGNATURE CONSENT

SECTION VIII - STATEMENT OF NAME FOR OFFICIAL MILITARY RECORDS

39. NAME CHANGE. If the preferred enlistment name (name given in Item 2) is not the same as on your birth certificate, and it has not been changed by legal procedure prescribed by state law, and it is the same as on your social security number card, complete the following:

a. NAME AS SHOWN ON BIRTH CERTIFICATE	b. NAME AS SHOWN ON SOCIAL SECURITY NUMBER CARD

c. I hereby state that I have not changed my name through any court or other legal procedure; that I prefer to use the name of

_____ by which I am known in the community as a matter of

convenience and with no criminal intent. I further state that I am the same person as the person whose name is shown in Item 2.

d. APPLICANT		e. WITNESS	
(1) SIGNATURE	(2) DATE SIGNED (YYMMDD)	(1) TYPED OR PRINTED NAME	(2) PAY GRADE
		(3) SIGNATURE	

DD Form 1966/4, APR 94

MILITARY BACKGROUND INVESTIGATIONS AND SECURITY CLEARANCES

☐ **Department of Defense Personnel Security Questionnaire (DD 398)**
☐ **Police Record Check (DD 369)**
☐ **Armed Forces Fingerprint Check (DD 2280)**

Background Investigation

Due to its very nature, the military is required to perform extensive background checks on its personnel to make sure they are trustworthy and loyal to the United States. When they enlist in the military, candidates will be required to fill out numerous forms with personal information and be fingerprinted. Depending on the sensitivity of the career that has been selected, military investigators will need to look into the candidate's background, including making inquiries at schools attended, in former neighborhoods, and at places of employment.

Security Clearance Terms

Security *clearances* are administrative determinations that an individual is eligible, from a security standpoint, for access to classified military information. Security *classifications* are levels of national security information and material and a determination of the degree of damage that unauthorized disclosure would cause to national defense or foreign relations of the United States and the degree of protection required. There are three categories:

Top Secret
This is the highest level of national security information or material and requires the highest degree of protection. Unauthorized disclosure of top secret material could reasonably be expected to cause *exceptionally grave damage* to the national security.

Secret
This level requires a substantial degree of protection. The unauthorized disclosure of national security information or material could reasonably be expected to cause serious damage to the national security.

Confidential
This level requires protection, the unauthorized disclosure of which could reasonably be expected to cause damage to the national security.

The forms on the following pages are more than likely the same ones that the military will ask you to complete.

DEPARTMENT OF DEFENSE
PERSONNEL SECURITY QUESTIONNAIRE *(BI/SBI)*

	FOR DIS USE ONLY

1.a. LAST NAME—FIRST NAME—MIDDLE NAME | **b. MAIDEN NAME** *(If any)*

2. ALIASES | **3. SOCIAL SECURITY NUMBER**

4. DATE OF BIRTH *(Year-Month-Day)* | **5. PLACE OF BIRTH** — **a. CITY** | **b. COUNTY** | **c. STATE** | **d. COUNTRY**

6. **a. CIVILIAN** **b. MILITARY** | **c. GRADE** | **d. IF MILITARY:** | ARMY / NAVY | AIR FORCE / MARINE CORPS

7. IDENTIFYING DATA

a. SEX	b. RACE	c. HEIGHT	d. WEIGHT	e. COLOR OF HAIR	f. COLOR OF EYES

8a. U.S. CITIZEN | **c. NATIVE** YES / NO | **d. IF NATURALIZED, CERTIFICATE NO.(S)** | **e. IF DERIVED, PARENT(S) CERTIFICATE NO.(S)** | **f. DATE** | **g. PLACE** | **h. COURT**

b. ALIEN | **i. REGISTRATION NO.** | **j. CURRENT CITIZENSHIP** | **k. DATE OF ENTRY** | **l. PORT OF ENTRY** | **m. FORM 1-151 NO.**

9. FORMER MILITARY SERVICE

a. FROM	b. TO	c. BRANCH	d. RANK	e. SERVICE NO(S)	f. TYPE OF DISCHARGE

10. FAMILY/ASSOCIATES *(List father, mother, spouse, and children.) (See DETAILED INSTRUCTIONS for others to be listed.)*

a. RELATIONSHIP AND NAME	b. DATE OF BIRTH	c. PLACE OF BIRTH	d. ADDRESS	e. CITIZENSHIP
FATHER				
MOTHER *(Maiden Name)*				
SPOUSE *(Maiden Name)*				

11. RESIDENCES *(List in chronological order beginning with the current address. Give the inclusive dates for each period of residence.) (See DETAILED INSTRUCTIONS.)*

a. DATES FROM / TO	b. NUMBER AND STREET	c. CITY	d. STATE	e. COUNTRY	f. ZIP CODE
Present					

12. DUTY OR EMPLOYMENT ORGANIZATION *(List in chronological order beginning with the present, each period of employment, self-employment, part-time employment, and/or unemployment. List inclusive dates for each period. If discharged for cause from any employment, so state. See DETAILED INSTRUCTIONS.)*

a. DATES FROM / TO	b. NAME OF EMPLOYER	c. ADDRESS	d. NAME OF IMMEDIATE SUPERVISOR
Present			

13. FEDERAL SERVICE, FOREIGN TRAVEL/CONNECTION *("Yes" answers must be explained in Item 18 in accordance with DETAILED INSTRUCTIONS.)*

Yes	No	
		a. HAVE YOU EVER BEEN IN THE FEDERAL CIVIL SERVICE?
		b. HAVE YOU TRAVELED OR RESIDED ABROAD FOR OTHER THAN THE U.S. GOVERNMENT?
		c. DO YOU HAVE ANY FOREIGN PROPERTY OR BUSINESS CONNECTIONS, OR HAVE YOU EVER BEEN EMPLOYED BY OR ACTED AS A CONSULTANT FOR A FOREIGN GOVERNMENT, FIRM, OR AGENCY?

FOR DIS USE ONLY

RETURN RESULTS TO: PERSONNEL INVESTIGATIONS CENTER DEFENSE INVESTIGATIVE SERVICE P.O. BOX 454 BALTIMORE, MARYLAND 21203

DD FORM 398
81 MAR
S/N 0102-LF-000-3982

* U.S. GOVERNMENT PRINTING OFFICE:

14.a. MARITAL STATUS			b. NAME(S) OF FORMER SPOUSE(S)		c. DATE(S) OF PRIOR MARRIAGE(S)		d. PLACE
MARRIED		UNMARRIED					
LEGALLY SEPARATED		DIVORCED	e. DATE OF DIVORCE	f. COURT		g. LOCATION	

15. EDUCATION *(List in chronological order, beginning with the last school attended.) (See DETAILED INSTRUCTIONS.)*

a. DATES		b. NAME OF SCHOOL	c. ADDRESS	d. MAJOR	e. DEGREE
FROM	TO				

16. CREDIT REFERENCES *(Complete this item only if you lived overseas within the past 5 years. List 3 individuals and/or firms who have extended credit to you during that time period.) (See DETAILED INSTRUCTIONS.)*

a. NAME	b. ACCOUNT NUMBER	c. NUMBER AND STREET	d. CITY	e. STATE	f. ZIP CODE

17. CHARACTER REFERENCES *(List 5 good friends, co-workers, colleagues, classmates, etc.) (See DETAILED INSTRUCTIONS.)*

a. NAME	b. FROM	c. TO	d. NUMBER AND STREET	e. CITY	f. STATE	g. ZIP CODE

18. REMARKS *(Attach additional sheets, if necessary.)*

19. ORGANIZATIONS

a. *(List all organizations, except those referred to in b. below, in which you hold or have held membership.)*

i. NAME	ii. ADDRESS	iii. TYPE	iv. FROM	v. TO

b. *("Yes" answers must be explained in accordance with the DETAILED INSTRUCTIONS.)*

Yes	No	
		i. Are you now or have you ever been a member of the Communist Party or any Communist organization?
		ii. Are you now or have you ever been affiliated with any organization, association, movement, group, or combination of persons which advocates the overthrow of our constitutional form of government or which has adopted the policy of advocating or approving the commission of acts of force or violence to deny other persons their rights under the Constitution of the United States or which seeks to alter the form of government of the United States by unconstitutional means?

20. MEDICAL/FINANCIAL *("Yes" answers must be explained in accordance with the DETAILED INSTRUCTIONS.)*

Yes	No	
		a. Have you ever used any narcotic, depressant, stimulant, hallucinogen (to include LSD or PCP), or cannabis (to include marijuana or hashish), except as prescribed by a licensed physician?
		b. Have you ever been involved in the illegal purchase, possession, or sale of any narcotic, depressant, stimulant, hallucinogen, or cannabis?
		c. Has your use of alcoholic beverages (such as liquor, beer, wine) ever resulted in the loss of a job, arrest by police, or treatment for alcoholism?
		d. Have you ever been a patient (whether or not formally committed) in any institution primarily devoted to the treatment of mental, emotional, psychological, or personality disorders?
		e. Have you ever petitioned to be declared bankrupt?

21. ARRESTS *("Yes" answers must be explained in accordance with the DETAILED INSTRUCTIONS.)*

Yes	No	
		a. Have you ever been arrested, charged, cited, or held by Federal, State, or other law enforcement or juvenile authorities, regardless of whether the citation was dropped or dismissed or you were found not guilty? Include all court martial or non-judicial punishment while in military service. *(You may exclude minor traffic violations for which a fine or forfeiture of $100 or less was imposed.)*
		b. As a result of being arrested, charged, cited, or held by law enforcement or juvenile authorities, have you ever been convicted, fined by or forfeited bond to a Federal, State, or other judicial authority or adjudicated a youthful offender or juvenile delinquent (regardless of whether the record in your case has been "sealed" or otherwise stricken from the court record)?
		c. Have you ever been detained, held in, or served time in any jail or prison, or reform or industrial school or any juvenile facility or institution under the jurisdiction of any city, state, federal, or foreign country?
		d. Have you ever been awarded, or are you now under suspended sentence, parole or probation, or awaiting any action on charges against you?

i. DATE	ii. NATURE OF OFFENSE OR VIOLATION	iii. NAME AND LOCATION OF POLICE AGENCY	iv. NAME AND LOCATION OF COURT	v. PENALTY IMPOSED OR OTHER DIS-POSITION IN EACH CASE

I CERTIFY THAT THE ENTRIES MADE BY ME ARE TRUE, COMPLETE, AND ACCURATE TO THE BEST OF MY KNOWLEDGE AND BELIEF AND ARE MADE IN GOOD FAITH. I UNDERSTAND THAT A KNOWING AND WILLFUL FALSE STATEMENT ON THIS FORM CAN BE PUNISHED BY FINE OR IMPRISONMENT OR BOTH. *(See U.S. Code, Title 18, Section 1001.)*

DATE	SIGNATURE OF PERSON COMPLETING FORM

MEDICAL AND PHYSICAL EXAMINATIONS

☐   **Applicant Medical Prescreening Form (DD 2246)**

The military conducts in-depth medical and physical examinations on all new recruits. For the most part, the military looks for recruits who are in good physical condition. Exact physical requirements depend on the type of military career and opportunity the recruit has selected; for example, the requirements for a navy pilot are different from those for a seaman. It goes without saying that use of illegal drugs and alcohol may prevent candidates from being selected. The samples on the next pages are typical of the forms that recruits are required to fill out before the medical examination.

APPLICANT MEDICAL PRESCREENING FORM

Authority: Sections 505, 510, and 3012, Title 10, U.S. Code. **Principal purpose:** To speed your medical examination processing by identifying possible medical problem areas and to aid the medical staff in determining your eligibility and physical capabilities. To prepare military service applicants for medical processing by identifying documents or medical history required. **Disclosure:** Voluntary; failure to provide the information requested will stop further processing of your enlistment application

PART I. PROCESSING REQUIREMENTS (RECRUITER COMPLETES – VERIFY PERSONAL DATA ENTERED)

1. a. ARMED SERVICE PROCESSED FOR:
   ☐ ARMY ☐ NAVY ☐ MARINE CORPS ☐ AIR FORCE ☐ COAST GUARD

   b. SERVICE COMPONENT
   ☐ REGULAR ☐ RESERVE ☐ NATIONAL GUARD

2. NAME OF APPLICANT *(Last, First, Middle)*
3. DATE OF BIRTH *(YYMMDD)*
4. SOCIAL SECURITY NUMBER
5. HEIGHT *(actual) (inches)*
6. WEIGHT *(actual) (lbs)*
7. MAX WT ALLOWED *(lbs)*
8. DATE SCREENED *(YYMMDD)*

PART II. MEDICAL HISTORY (APPLICANT) Check each item–explain "yes" and "unsure" answers in item 16.

9. PHYSICAL IMPAIRMENTS

Have you ever had or have you now
a. Back trouble
b. Ear trouble or loss of hearing
c. Eye trouble, injury or illness
d. Any deformities of, or missing fingers or toes
e. Any painful or "trick" joints or loss of movement in any joint
f. Impaired use of arms, legs, hands and feet
g. Have loss of vision in either eye

10. CORRECTIVE DEVICES

Do you
a. Wear braces on your teeth
b. Wear contact lenses or glasses
c. Wear a hearing aid

11. DISEASES

Have you ever had or have you now
a. Hepatitis
b. Rheumatic Fever

12. FEDERAL GOVERNMENT ACTIONS

Have you ever
a. Been rejected for military service
b. Been discharged from military service for mental, physical or other reasons.
c. Do you receive or have you applied for disability from any Federal Agency.

13. TREATMENT OF ILLNESS/INJURY

Have you ever
a. Taken any medicines
b. Been hospitalized
c. Had bones surgically repaired using pins screws or plates
d. Had or have you now any illness or injury including broken bones which required treatment by a physician / surgeon, hospitalization or a surgical operation

14. MEDICAL CONDITIONS

a. Do you have any difficulty standing for a long time?
Have you ever
b. Been treated for a mental condition.
c. Been a Sleepwalker since age 12.
Have you ever had or have you now
d. Addiction to drugs or alcohol
e. Allergies
f. Asthma or respiratory problems
g. Bedwetting, since age 12.
h. Epilepsy or seizures of any kind.
i. Other medical problems or defects of any kind.

15. (FEMALES ONLY) DATE OF LAST MENSTRUAL PERIOD *(YYMMDD)*:

16. EXPLANATION OF "YES" AND "UNSURE" ANSWERS: DESCRIBE PROBLEM. GIVE AGE AT TIME OF PROBLEM, NAME OF DOCTOR AND/OR HOSPITAL WHERE TREATED, AND YOUR CURRENT STATUS REGARDING THAT PROBLEM.

DD Form 2246, NOV 80

949/042

PART III. CERTIFICATION BY APPLICANT AND RECRUITER

WARNING: The information you have given constitutes an official statement. Federal law provides severe penalties (up to 5 years confinement or a $10,000 fine or both), to anyone making a false statement. If you are selected for enlistment based on a false statement, you can be tried by military courts-martial or meet an administrative board for discharge and could receive a less than honorable discharge that would affect your future. WARNING.

a. Applicant. I certify the information on this form is true and complete to the best of my knowledge and belief, and no person has advised me to conceal or falsify any information about my physical and mental history.	b. Recruiting Representative. I certify all information is complete and true to the best of my knowledge. I have conducted the medical prescreening requirements as directed by service regulations.

APPLICANT'S SIGNATURE

NAME OF RECRUITING REP. *(Last, First, M.I.)*

PAY GRADE OF RECRUITING REP.

DATE SIGNED *(YYMMDD)*

SIGNATURE OF RECRUITING REP.

DATE SIGNED *(YYMMDD)*

PART IV. MEDICAL PROCESSING INSTRUCTIONS TO APPLICANT (Rctg Rep Check Blocks – Applicant Initials)

The Armed Forces Examining and Entrance Station (AFEES) or other military medical facility will conduct a thorough medical examination. You should provide any medical records or documents regarding illness, hospitalization, injuries, treatment, or surgery which may be required/requested by the examining physician. The items below apply specifically to you and represent requirements of the medical staff. Please initial each checked item in the blank provided to indicate that you understand.

PREPARATION FOR MEDICAL EXAMINATION

INSTRUCTIONS

☐ 1. Take medical documents as discussed. ____

☐ 2. Take eye glasses. ____

☐ 3. Wear contact lenses. Also take your eye glasses with you or a statement from the optometrist/opthalmologist of visual acuity and eye glass refractive error. Statement must be less than one year old. ____

☐ 4. Bring a statement from your orthodontist saying that the braces you are wearing will be removed at your expense and active treatment ended before your active duty date. ____

☐ 5. Males wear undershorts; females wear bra and panties for medical examination. ___

ACKNOWLEDGMENTS

☐ 1. I understand that I will undergo a pelvic/rectal examination. (females only) ___

☐ 2. My medical examination may take more than 1 day if tests are required. ___

☐ 3. I've been briefed on the processing procedures and I understand them. ___

☐ 4. I must lose ____ lbs. before further processing can take place. ___

☐ 5. I appear to be ineligible for further processing for the following reasons:

_____
_____
_____
_____

NOTE: In questionable cases, use DIAL-A-MEDIC procedures to call or forward this form and other documents to the AFEES Chief Medical Officer through the service rep. prior to scheduling a medical examination.

PART V. MEDICAL OFFICER'S COMMENTS

Based on information provided, further processing is:

☐ Authorized   ☐ Not Justified

☐ Deferred pending review of additional documentation
(attach supplemental page for remarks)

SIGNATURE AFEES MEDICAL OFFICER

DATE SIGNED *(YYMMDD)*

DD Form 2246 Reverse, NOV 80

*U.S. Government Printing Office: 1993 — 360-350/99019

BASIC TRAINING (ENLISTED)

OVERVIEW Basic training is the most talked about and remembered event in most veterans' memories. First, be aware that you are going to be yelled at—a lot. You are also going to be dirty, tired, and confused, but when you graduate, you will also be in the best shape of your life.

DURATION/LOCATION CHART		
Branch	**Location**	**Standard Duration**
Air Force	Lackland AFB, TX	6 Weeks
Army	Fort Jackson, SC Fort Knox, KS Fort Sill, OK Fort Leonard Wood, MO	8 Weeks
Coast Guard	Cape May, NJ	8 Weeks
Marine	Parris Island, SC San Diego, CA	11 Weeks
Navy	Great Lakes, IL	8 Weeks

WHAT TO EXPECT

- As soon as you arrive, your hair will be cut—close. You lose your civilian clothing and become a number in a boot camp class.

- There is a lot of physical exercise. From morning to night you will be running, marching, and doing sit-ups, push-ups, and pull-ups. Get into shape before you go!

- You will do a lot of saluting; you will be saluting just about everyone you come into contact with except the other recruits.

- Introduction to the Military 101: During your stay at basic training you will learn a great deal about the military and the branch of service you have selected.

Subject matter may include:

- Advancement
- Branch Mission, Organization, Regulations
- Chain of Command
- Code of Conduct
- Drug and Alcohol Abuse Prevention
- Education Benefits
- Financial Responsibility
- Firefighting
- First Aid
- Fraternization
- General Orders
- Hand Salutes and Military Greetings
- History and Traditions of the Branch
- Honors and Ceremonies
- Inspections
- Leave and Earnings Statement
- Military Drill
- Military Leave and Conduct
- Military Ranks and Rates
- Military Terminology
- Occupational Safety and Health
- Personal Hygiene
- Physical Conditioning
- Security Information
- Sexual Harassment
- Ship and/or Aircraft Familiarization
- Survival
- Swim Qualification (Coast Guard, Navy, Marines)
- Uniform Code
- Watch Standing
- Weapons Familiarization
- Wearing and Care of Uniforms

MILITARY TIME   The military operates on a 24-hour clock; the hours are numbered from 1 to 24 in a day. They are worded as follows: 6 A.M. would now be 0600 (zero six hundred hours) and 6 P.M. would be 1800 (eighteen hundred hours).

Time	Hours
12 AM	2400
1 AM	0100
2 AM	0200
3 AM	0300
4 AM	0400
5 AM	0500
6 AM	0600
7 AM	0700
8 AM	0800
9 AM	0900
10 AM	1000
11 AM	1100
12 AM	1200
1 PM	1300
2 PM	1400
3 PM	1500
4 PM	1600
5 PM	1700
6 PM	1800
7 PM	1900
8 PM	2000
9 PM	2100
10 PM	2200
11 PM	2300

FIRST DUTY: SECURITY WATCH   One of the first military duties for recruits in most of the branches is that of security watch. Security watch takes place around the clock and involves the protection of the post against trespassers, fire, damage, theft, or other set activities. You will also be given a fixed *standing order,* which you will be required to memorize. You may or may not be armed with a weapon during sentry duty. The purpose of sentry duty is to give a crash course in responsibility.

Typical Standing Orders of a Sentry

1. Take charge of your post and all government property in view.
2. Walk your post in a military manner, always keeping on the alert and observing everything that takes place within sight or hearing.
3. Report all violations of orders you are instructed to enforce.
4. Repeat all calls from posts more distant from the guardhouse than your own.
5. Quit your post only when properly relieved.
6. Receive, obey, and pass on to the sentry who relieves you all orders from the commanding officer and officer of the watch *only*.
7. Talk to no one except in the line of duty.
8. Give the alarm in case of fire or disorder.
9. Call the officer of the watch in any case not covered by instructions.
10. Salute all officers and all colors and standards not cased.
11. Be especially watchful at night and other times for challenging; challenge all persons on or near your post, and allow no one to pass without military authority.

(Based on U.S. Navy General Sentry Orders)

MILITARY BOOT CAMP TERMS Learn these terms before boot camp to make your adjustment a little easier.

Term	Meaning
Barracks	Building where military personnel live
BDU	Battle Dress Uniform
Below	Downstairs
Brightwork	Brass or shiny metal
Bulkhead	Wall
Bunk or rack	Bed
Colors	Raising or lowering of the American flag
Deck	Floor
Galley	Kitchen
Head	Bathroom
Ladder	Stairs
Leave	Vacation
Liberty	Time off a base or ship for a set period of time
Overhead	Ceiling
Passageway	Hall
Rating	Job specialty
Reveille	Start of a new day
Scuttlebutt	Rumor or a drinking fountain

Term	Meaning
Secure	Lock, put away, or stop work
Sick bay	Hospital or clinic
Swab	Mop
Taps	Time to sleep; end of the day
Topside	Upstairs

Tips

1. Listen to what you are being told; do what you are told. Boot camp instructors are not looking for individual thinkers. The whole purpose of boot camp is to make individuals act as a team or unit.

2. Before you go to boot camp, read up on the history and customs of the service you are joining, including who makes up the current chain of command for your particular branch.

Chapter 4

ENTRANCE EXAMS

Military Placement Tests

- [ ] **Basic Enlisted/Officer Enlisted Entrance Exams**
- [ ] Overview
- [ ] ASVAB/CAT
- [ ] ASVAB/CAT-ASVAB Sample Test Questions
- [ ] **Officer Enlistment Exams**
- [ ] Overview
- [ ] College Entrance Testing Exams
    - ACT
    - SAT I
    - GRE
- [ ] Specialized Officer Enlistment Exams
    - Air Force Officer Qualifying Test
    - Officer Aptitude Test
    - Officer Aptitude Rating

MILITARY PLACEMENT TESTS

Basic Enlisted/Officer Enlisted Entrance Exams———

OVERVIEW   Presently, both the ASVAB and CAT-ASVAB are given in about 14,000 schools. About 900,000 students take them.

- ### *Armed Services Vocational Aptitude Battery (ASVAB)*

    ASVAB began in 1968 as a joint military effort to standardize military entrance testing. The ASVAB is largely a pencil and paper type of exam with several categories or subtests. The ASVAB is still given in high school and at several MEPS nationwide.

- ### *Computerized Adaptive Testing—Armed Services Vocational Aptitude Battery (CAT-ASVAB)*

    CAT-ASVAB began in 1997 and is largely an automated testing system. Several of the MEPS are currently giving the CAT-ASVAB.

1. *What is the difference between the ASVAB and the CAT-ASVAB?*
   The straightforward pencil and paper test is just that—a set list of questions that the candidate answers and then waits for military processing personnel to correct and compute. The CAT-ASVAB not only corrects the answers immediately, it is also adaptive to the candidate's answers.

2. *CAT-ASVAB: How does it work?*
   Students are seated in front of a computer station and terminal. The test is displayed on the screen. As the students answer the test questions, the program immediately scores and records the answers, including the subtests. When the candidates have completed the CAT-ASVAB, the AFQT (Armed Forces Qualification Test, the math and verbal sections of the ASVAB) and composite scores for all the services are already computed.

   Advantage (Alleged):
   The CAT-ASVAB bases the next question you answer on the ability level pattern you exhibited from the previous question's answer. In other words, if you answer the question correctly, you are given a harder question. If you answer the question incorrectly, you are then given an easier question. This process is continued for each subtest until you have completed the entire CAT-ASVAB.

Disadvantage:
Unlike the ASVAB, the CAT-ASVAB does not allow candidates to go back and change answers.

3. *Scoring*
The straightforward pencil and paper test ASVAB raw score equals the total number of questions answered correctly.

The CAT-ASVAB raw scores are not equal to the total number of correct answers. The CAT-ASVAB subtest scores are computed using formulas that take into account the difficulty level of the question and the number of correct answers. Because the test is adaptive, a process called "equating" is used to compute the standard scores, AFQT, and the service composites.

Although the CAT-ASVAB is designed so that individuals with no computer experience can take the exam, it is highly recommended that a candidate practice using a computer before taking the CAT-ASVAB. A well-prepared candidate will always do better than one who is not.

Tip

It is critical that you do well on either of these tests. The better your score, the more military career choices you will have. These exams are used to determine what military occupational specialties or opportunities you qualify for. They can literally limit your future in the military. This author strongly recommends that you study and practice before taking them.

Recommended Study Guides

- *ASVAB—How to Prepare for the Armed Services Vocational Aptitude Battery (1997)*

- *Pass Key to the ASVAB (1997)*
  Published by:
  Barron's Educational Series, Inc.
  250 Wireless Blvd.
  Hauppauge, NY 11788
  (516) 434-3311

**ASVAB/
CAT-ASVAB** To take the Armed Services Vocational Aptitude Battery (ASVAB) or the Computerized Adaptive Testing–Armed Services Vocational Aptitude Battery (CAT-ASVAB), ask your high school guidance counselors or call your nearest recruiter (listed in the blue pages in the phone book) or 1-800-323-0513 for the nearest Military Entrance Processing Station (MEPS). There are about 65 MEPSs located throughout the United States. The location of the nearest MEPS can also be obtained from your local recruiter.

ASVAB/CAT-ASVAB SUBTESTS

Test	Description	Test time
Science (GS)	A 16-item test measuring knowledge of physical science	8 minutes
Arithmetic Reasoning (AR)	A 16-item test measuring the ability to solve arithmetic problems	39 minutes
Word Knowledge (WK)	A 16-item test measuring the ability to select the correct meaning of words presented in context and to identify the best synonym for a given word	8 minutes
Paragraph Comprehension (PC)	A 22-item test measuring the ability to obtain information from written passages	11 minutes
Numerical Operations (NO)	A 50-item speed test measuring the ability to perform arithmetical computations	3 minutes
Coding Speed (CS)	An 84-item speed test measuring the ability to use a key in assigning code numbers to words	7 minutes
Auto Information (AI)	An 11-item test measuring knowledge of automobiles	11 minutes
Shop Information (SI)	An 11-item test measuring knowledge of tools and shop terminology and practices	11 minutes
Mathematics Knowledge (MK)	A 16-item test measuring knowledge of high school mathematical principles	18 minutes
Mechanical Comprehension (MC)	A 16-item test measuring knowledge of mechanical and physical principles and the ability to visualize how illustrated objects work	20 minutes
Electronics Information (EI)	A 16-item test of knowledge of electricity and electronics	8 minutes
TOTAL TEST TIME		180 minutes

Military Career Scores

The composite of your scores in the Word Knowledge, Paragraph Comprehension, Arithmetic Reasoning, Mathematics Knowledge, Mechanical Comprehension, and Electronics Information subtest scores are used to estimate the likelihood of qualifying for specific military occupations or opportunity.

Composites

The following general composites are formed from subsets of the ten ASVAB tests:

- **Verbal Ability.** Word Knowledge + Paragraph Comprehension = measuring potential for verbal activities.

- **Math Ability.** Arithmetic Reasoning + Mathematics Knowledge = measuring potential for mathematical activities.

- **Academic Ability.** Verbal Ability + Math Ability composites = measuring potential for further formal education.

Armed Forces Qualifying Test (AFQT) Score

The AFQT establishes a basic cut-off level for entrance to one of the military branches. The main area that is looked at is the candidate's ability to understand and write English.
Verbal (VE = WK + PC)

MOS Qualifying Test Scores

The options for the specific MOS (line of work) may be limited if you do not do well. Certain MOSs have established scores:

Example

Key Army MOS Areas	Aptitude Areas and Scores
Combat (CO)	AR + CS + AI/SI + MC
Clerical (CL)	VE + AR + MK
Field Artillery (FA)	AR + CS + MK + MC
General Maintenance (GM)	GS + AI/SI + MK + EI
Motor Maintenance (MM)	NO + AI/SI + MC + EI
Operators of Food (OF)	VE + NO + AI/SI + MC
Electronics (EL)	GS + AR + MK + MC
Surveillance and Communications	GS + AR + AI/SI + MC
Skilled Technician (ST)	GS + VE + MK + MC
General Technical (GT)	VE + AR

Army Examples

MOS Title	Key Entrance Aptitude Area Levels
Infantryman	CO 90
Military Police	ST 95
Patriots Systems Repairer	EL 110

ASVAB/CAT-ASVAB Results Sheet

A result sheet is issued by the military that translates specific percentile scores and score bands on all subtests, as well as the three composites. A sample ASVAB Results Sheet is shown on the following pages.

ASVAB STUDENT RESULTS SHEET

ARMED SERVICES VOCATIONAL APTITUDE BATTERY

PUBLIC JANE Q
GRADE 11
SSN 987-65-4321
TEST DATE 10/10/92
BETA HIGH SCHOOL
ANYTOWN   SEX F   IL

ASVAB Scores

Percentile Scores — Same Grade/Same Sex Percentile Score Bands

	Same Grade/Same Sex
Academic Ability (AA = VA + MA)	50
Verbal Ability (VA = WK + PC)	51
Math Ability (MA = AR + MK)	54
Word Knowledge (WK)	47
Paragraph Comprehension (PC)	67
Arithmetic Reasoning (AR)	55
Mathematics Knowledge (MK)	52
General Science (GS)	56
Auto & Shop Information (AS)	81
Mechanical Comprehension (MC)	65
Electronics Information (EI)	60
Numerical Operations (NO)	78
Coding Speed (CS)	62

ASVAB Codes 3, 4
Military Careers Score 194

(SEE BACK OF SHEET FOR EXPLANATION.)

Explanation of Your ASVAB Scores

ASVAB SCORES

When you took the Armed Services Vocational Aptitude Battery (ASVAB), there were 10 tests. These tests are listed under the column "ASVAB Scores." Two examples are Word Knowledge and Coding Speed. Also, three additional scores are provided: Academic Ability (AA), Verbal Ability (VA) and Math Ability (MA). All of these ASVAB scores are described on the back of this sheet.

PERCENTILE SCORES

Your ASVAB scores are reported as percentiles. Percentile scores show how well you did in relation to others. ASVAB scores compare you to a national sample of students. Two types of percentile scores are reported: same grade/same sex and same grade/opposite sex. If you are in grades 10, 11 or 12, your same grade/ same sex score compares you with students of your own grade and sex.In contrast, your same grade/opposite

sex score compares you with students of your own grade and the opposite sex. Postsecondary students are compared with two-year college students. Suppose an 11th grade female obtained a same grade/same sex score of 60 on Verbal Ability. This means she scored the same or better than 60 out of every 100 females at her grade level in the national sample.

As mentioned above, scores are provided that compare you with students of your own and opposite sex. Because life experiences of girls and boys can vary, they can score somewhat differently on tests. Being male or female, however, does not limit your career or educational choices. Using gender-based scores may broaden the range of career and educational areas you are considering. For help in exploring careers, ask your counselor for *Exploring Careers: The ASVAB Workbook.* Also, if you need help understanding your scores, see your counselor.

SEE YOUR COUNSELOR FOR FURTHER HELP IN INTERPRETING YOUR ASVAB SCORES

TURN THIS SHEET OVER TO LEARN MORE ABOUT YOUR ASVAB SCORES

ASVAB — ARMED SERVICES VOCATIONAL APTITUDE BATTERY

COUNSELOR NOTES

Student:
Summary:
Date:

COUNSELOR SUMMARY

PUBLIC JANE Q
GEN PUBLIC
SSN 987-65-4321
SEX F
GRADE 11
COUNSELOR CODE X   10/10/92
ASVAB 18a
BETA HIGH SCHOOL
ANYTOWN   IL

Percentile Scores — Same Grade/Same Sex Percentile Score Bands

ASVAB Scores	Same Grade/Same Sex	Same Grade/Opposite Sex
Academic Ability (AA = VA + MA)	50	52 / 53
Verbal Ability (VA = WK + PC)	51	51 / 51
Math Ability (MA = AR + MK)	54	55 / 56
Word Knowledge (WK)	47	45 / 44
Paragraph Comprehension (PC)	67	71 / 74
Arithmetic Reasoning (AR)	55	53 / 52
Mathematics Knowledge (MK)	52	55 / 59
General Science (GS)	56	49 / 43
Auto & Shop Information (AS)	81	62 / 43
Mechanical Comprehension (MC)	65	51 / 37
Electronics Information (EI)	60	49 / 38
Numerical Operations (NO)	78	84 / 89
Coding Speed (CS)	62	72 / 82

ASVAB Codes 3, 4
Military Careers Score 194

(SEE BACK OF SHEET FOR EXPLANATION.)

30079 (Rev 10-90) GL

SCORE BANDS

Because a test score is never an exact measure of your ability, it might change somewhat if you took the test again. Each ASVAB score is represented by dashed lines known as a score band. This band indicates that if you took the ASVAB again, your score would likely fall within this band. Where score bands overlap, differences between these scores may not be meaningful.

ASVAB CODES & MILITARY CAREERS SCORE

Two additional types of results are reported in the bottom left-hand corner on the front of this results sheet: ASVAB Codes and Military Careers Score. ASVAB Codes are used with the OCCU-FIND exercise in *Exploring Careers: The ASVAB Workbook*. If you have not received this book, ask your counselor for a copy. The Military Careers Score is used with graphs found in *Military Careers*. These graphs can help you estimate your chances of qualifying for enlisted occupations in the military. See your counselor to review a copy of *Military Careers*.

UNDERSTANDING YOUR SCORES

Keep in mind the limitations of all aptitude tests. They are neither absolute measures of abilities nor perfect predictors of success or failure. Just as a high score does not guarantee success, a low score does not necessarily mean failure in a future educational program or occupation. For example, if you have never worked with shop equipment or automobiles, you might be unfamiliar with certain terms and could score low on Auto & Shop Information. By gaining experience through relevant hobbies or coursework, you may be able to raise your score in this area, as well as in other technical areas.

To use your scores for career exploration, you should consider them in connection with other important information you know about yourself such as your interests, school grades, motivation and personal goals. An aptitude test score is only one very general indicator for use in exploring careers. We recommend you read *Exploring Careers: The ASVAB Workbook* to learn more about how to interpret your ASVAB scores and use them for career exploration. Also, it might be helpful to talk with a counselor, teacher, parent or persons employed in careers you are considering.

ASVAB SCORE DESCRIPTIONS

Academic Ability

- Measures how well you did on the Verbal Ability and Math Ability sections combined
- A general indicator of future academic success

Verbal Ability

- Measures how well you did on the Word Knowledge and Paragraph Comprehension tests combined
- A general indicator of ability to learn from written material

Math Ability

- Measures how well you did on the Arithmetic Reasoning and Mathematics Knowledge tests combined
- A general indicator of success in future math courses

Word Knowledge

- Measures ability to select the correct meaning of words presented in context and to identify the best synonym for a given word
- Important for verbal and written communication

Paragraph Comprehension

- Measures ability to read and obtain information from written passages
- Important for activities that involve reading

Arithmetic Reasoning

- Measures ability to solve arithmetic word problems
- Important for school subjects such as mathematics and physics

Mathematics Knowledge

- Measures knowledge of high school mathematics principles
- Important for school subjects such as algebra and geometry

General Science

- Measures knowledge of scientific terms and concepts
- Important for school subjects such as the life and physical sciences

Auto & Shop Information

- Measures knowledge of automobiles, tools and shop terminology and practices
- Important for people interested in vehicle and mechanical repair occupations

Mechanical Comprehension

- Measures knowledge of mechanical and physical principles, and your ability to visualize how mechanical objects work
- Important for people interested in construction, mechanical repair, architectural and engineering occupations

Electronics Information

- Measures knowledge of electricity and electronics
- Important for people interested in the repair or installation of electrical products or an occupation such as electronics technician

Numerical Operations

- Measures ability to quickly and accurately perform arithmetic computations such as adding and subtracting
- Important for occupations requiring the accurate organization, checking and filing of records

Coding Speed

- Measures ability to use a reference key and quickly assign code numbers to words
- Important for occupations requiring the accurate organization, checking and filing of records

Every student who takes the ASVAB will receive a copy of *Exploring Careers: The ASVAB Workbook*. This book contains activities that will:

- Teach you strategies for career exploration and decision making
- Teach you how to use your ASVAB scores for career exploration
- Help you identify occupations that may match your interests, abilities and preferences
- Help you evaluate different occupations as possible career choices
- Show you where and how to gather career information

Exploring Careers: The ASVAB Workbook also contains a cartoon series that will introduce you to several high school students who are exploring careers. Their discussions and experiences may help you select careers to explore.

USE OF INFORMATION

Personal identity information (name, social security number, street address, and telephone number) and test scores will not be released to any agency outside of the Department of Defense, the Armed Forces, the Coast Guard and your school. Test scores provided to schools are handled in accordance with the policies of the school or local school system. For up to two years, information on your scores will be used by the Department of Defense for recruiting and research. After two years, personal identity information and test scores will be maintained by the Department of Defense for research purposes only.

COUNSELOR NOTES

COUNSELOR SUMMARY

THE ASVAB 18/19 CAREER EXPLORATION PROGRAM

The *ASVAB 18/19 Career Exploration Program* has developed several publications to help students learn more about themselves and the world-of-work.

Exploring Careers: The ASVAB Workbook

Schools are provided with one copy of *Exploring Careers: The ASVAB Workbook* for every student who takes the ASVAB. The *ASVAB Workbook* for your school to distribute the *Workbook* to students is when they receive their ASVAB Student Results Sheet. The *Workbook* is designed to help students interpret their ASVAB results and learn about career exploration. Each *Workbook* contains a copy of an interest measure, the Self-Directed Search™. Students can use the results from the Self-Directed Search and the ASVAB, along with their personal preferences, to explore more than 200 civilian and military occupations. The *Workbook* also directs students to additional sources of occupational information, including the U.S. Department of Labor's *Occupational Outlook Handbook* (OOH). The OOH provides descriptive information for 250 occupations.

Military Careers

Military Careers is a comprehensive source of information on enlisted and officer military occupations. For each of the 197 military occupations described in *Military Careers*, valuable information such as a description of primary work activities, training provided and work environment is included. For each military occupation described, similar civilian occupations are also identified.

ASVAB 18/19 SCORES

There are two sections to the ASVAB Student Results Sheet. The top section is for students and this detachable section is for your use. On the front side of this section, same grade percentile scores for three reference groups are reported in the columns under "Percentile Scores." These percentile scores, based on a nationally representative sample, show the student's standing compared to the following groups:

- Same grade/same sex
- Same grade/combined sex
- Same grade/opposite sex

The student score reports same grade/opposite sex and same grade/same sex percentile scores.

As mentioned above, scores are provided that compare students with students of their own sex and opposite sex. Because life experiences of girls and boys can vary, they can score somewhat differently on tests. Being male or female, however, does not limit their career or educational choices. Reporting scores based on sex may broaden the range of career and educational areas students are considering.

For further assistance in understanding the ASVAB or interpreting scores, read the *ASVAB 18/19 Counselor Manual* and the *ASVAB 18/19 Technical Manual*.

In addition, *Military Careers* describes the typical duties and assignments a person could expect when advancing along the path of a 20-year military career. In total, 25 enlisted and 13 officer career paths are described. One of the more interesting features of *Military Careers* is a "career profile" that summarizes the career progression of an actual service member in the illustrated occupation. Each profile details the places of assignment and duties the service member performed over his or her career.

ASVAB 18/19 Counselor Manual

The *ASVAB 18/19 Counselor Manual* provides counselors with background information on the entire program. The manual describes the technical characteristics of ASVAB 18/19 and the Self-Directed Search. It also suggests techniques for reporting and interpreting ASVAB and Self-Directed Search results with large groups, small groups and individual students. These techniques are illustrated in case studies. Also, information is provided on the following publications:

- *Exploring Careers: The ASVAB Workbook*
- *Military Careers*
- *Occupational Outlook Handbook*

To obtain a copy of the *ASVAB 18/19 Counselor Manual* or other ASVAB publications, please call toll free, 1-800-323-0513.

™ Self-Directed Search is a trademark of Psychological Assessment Resources, Inc.

**ASVAB/
CAT-ASVAB
Sample Test
Questions**

(Source: Department of Defense *ASVAB 18/19 Student and Parent Guide*)

The ASVAB and CAT-ASVAB subtests will look a lot like other tests you have taken. All test responses are multiple choice; the only difference will be how you record your test answers. For the ASVAB, you will use a pencil and paper; the CAT-ASVAB will be entered into a computer format. The following are actual examples from the Department of Defense *ASVAB 18/19 Student and Parent Guide*.

General Science

The General Science subtest consists of test questions that encompass both physical and biological sciences.

DOD Example:
A magnet will attract:
A. water
B. a flower
C. a cloth rag
D. a nail

(D is the correct answer.)

Arithmetic Reasoning

The Arithmetic Reasoning subtest consists of problems, similar to those below.

DOD Example:
If 12 workers are needed to run 4 machines, how many workers are needed to run 20 machines?
A. 20
B. 48
C. 60
D. 80

(C is the correct answer.)

Word Knowledge

The Word Knowledge test is designed to measure your understanding of the meanings of words. The test consists of underlined words. From the four choices, select the word or phrase meaning most nearly the same as the underlined word.

DOD Example:
<u>Small</u> most nearly means:

A. sturdy
B. round
C. cheap
D. little

(D is the correct answer.)

Paragraph Comprehension

The Paragraph Comprehension subtest consists of test questions that measure the ability to obtain information from written passages. In this section, you will find one or more paragraphs of reading material followed by incomplete statements or questions. Read each paragraph and select one of the lettered choices that best completes the statement or answers the question.

DOD Example:
From a building designer's standpoint, three things that make a home livable are the client, the building site, and the amount of money the client has to spend. According to this statement, to make a home livable:

A. the prospective piece of land makes little difference.
B. it can be built on any piece of land.
C. the design must fit the owner's income and site.
D. the design must fit the designer's income.

(C is the correct answer.)

Numerical Operations

The Numerical Operations subtest consists of simple mathematical computations. This is a speed test, so work as fast as you can to determine your answers without making mistakes.

DOD Example:

$3 \times 4 =$

A. 1
B. 7
C. 12
D. 14

(C is the correct answer.)

Coding Speed

The Coding Speed subtest contains questions that test how quickly and accurately you can find a number in a table. At the top of each section is a number table or "key." The key is a group of words with a code number for each word. Each item in the test is a word taken from the key at the top of that page. From among the possible answers listed for each item, find the one that is the correct code number for that word. This is a speed test, so work as fast as you can to determine your answers without making mistakes.

DOD Example:

Key

green	2715	man	3451	salt	4586
hat	1413	room	2864	tree	5972

Questions			*Answers*		
	A	B	C	D	E
1. room	1413	2715	2864	3451	4586
2. green	2715	2864	3451	4586	5972
3. tree	1413	2715	3451	4586	5972
4. hat	1413	2715	3451	4586	5972
5. room	1413	2864	3451	4586	5972

(The correct answers are lC, 2A, 3E, 4A, 5B.)

Auto and Shop Information

The Auto and Shop Information subtest has test questions about automobiles, shop practices, and the use of tools.

DOD Example:

A chisel is used for:

A. prying
B. cutting
C. twisting
D. grinding

(B is the correct answer.)

Mathematics Knowledge

The Mathematics Knowledge subtest contains problems designed to measure general mathematical knowledge. Included are questions on algebra and geometry.

DOD Example:

If 50 percent of $\times$ = 66, then $\times$ =

A. 33
B. 66
C. 99
D. 132

(D is the correct answer.)

Electronics Information

The Electronics Information subtest consists of test questions dealing with electricity, radio principles, and electronics.

DOD Example:

What does the abbreviation AC stand for?

A. additional charge
B. alternating coil
C. alternating current
D. ampere current

(C is the correct answer.)

Mechanical Comprehension

The Mechanical Comprehension subtest contains test questions designed to measure your understanding of mechanical principles. Many test questions use drawings to illustrate specific principles.

Officer Enlistment Exams ─────────────

OVERVIEW The college entrance placement testing exams are used by all of the military academies and ROTC programs to determine candidates' aptitude. For the most part, the ACT and SAT are the most important. These exams are given at area high schools or local colleges. Make arrangements with school officials or contact the services directly. Unlike the ASVAB, where the military makes the arrangements and gives the test, it is up to you to make your own arrangements.

COLLEGE ENTRANCE TESTING EXAMS

☐ **American College Testing (ACT)**
☐ **SAT I**
☐ **Graduate Record Exam (GRE)**

ACT

The American Standard Testing Assessment Program is a private testing corporation. The key composites are English, reading, mathematics, and science reasoning.

Write to:
Registration Department
ACT Assessment Program
PO Box 414
Iowa City, IA 52243
(319) 337-1270

SAT I

The College Board's SAT I exam measures verbal and mathematical abilities.

Write to:
College Board SAT Program
Box 6200
Princeton, NJ 08541
(609) 771-7600

GRE

The Graduate Record Exam is administered by the Educational Testing Service and is an aptitude test of verbal, quantitative, and analytical abilities beyond that of a bachelor's degree level in a specific field.

Contact:
Graduate Record Examination
PO Box 6000
Princeton, NJ 08541-6000
(609) 771-7670
(510) 873-8100 (California)
(609) 771-7906 (fax)
gre-info@ets.org
http://www.gre.org

Tip

It is critical that you do well on these tests. The better your score, the more military career choices you will be able to select from. This author strongly recommends that you study and practice before taking this exam.

Recommended Study Guides

- *How to Prepare for SAT I (1998)*

- *How to Prepare for the Graduate Record Exam (1997)*

Published by:
Barron's Educational Series, Inc.
250 Wireless Blvd.
Hauppauge, NY 11788
(516) 434-3311

SPECIALIZED OFFICER ENLISTMENT EXAMS

☐ **Air Force Officer Qualifying Test**
☐ **Officer Aptitude Test**
☐ **Officer Aptitude Rating**

Some of the services require that an entrance exam be given to candidates joining the officers' ranks from the Officer Candidate School or Direct Commission programs. For the most part, these are similar to the college placement exams listed above. Depending on what program and military occupation is desired, candidates are reviewed on the ASVAB exams or other military rating exams:

1. *Air Force Officer Qualifying Test* measures aptitude in 16 subtest areas. The difference in this exam is that there are sections geared for testing piloting and navigation.

2. *Officer Aptitude Test (Army)* or *Officer Aptitude Rating (Navy and Coast Guard)* measures knowledge in math, English composition and usage, physics, and simple machines.

SECTION

2

MILITARY
BRANCHES

Chapter 5

U.S. AIR FORCE

U.S. Air Force

United States Air Force
Recruiting Command
Arlington, VA 22203

☎ 800-423-USAF
http://www.USAF.MIL

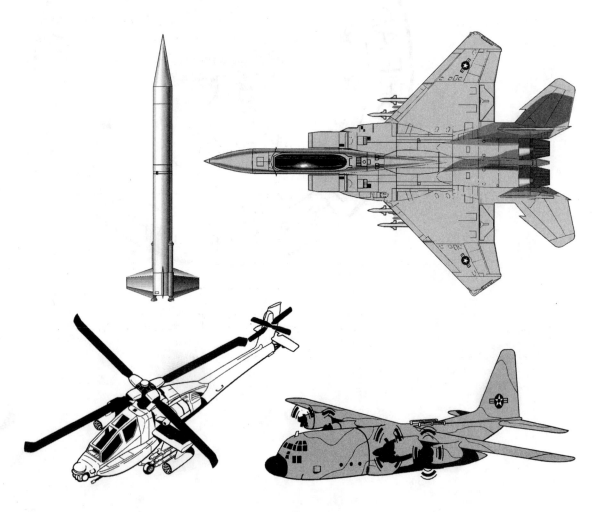

History:	**Established on September 18, 1947**
Special Units:	**Pararescue**
	Thunderbirds
	Special Operations Command
Recruiting Slogans:	**A Great Way to Serve**
	Aim High
	(Recruits more than 30,000 new personnel per year)

OVERVIEW The Air Force is the youngest of all the U.S. military services. It was created two years after World War II (ending a 40-year association with the U.S. Army to become a separate service). The Department of the Air Force was created when President Truman signed the National Security Act of 1947.

The Air Force offers a wide variety of career and educational opportunities. Both the Air Force Reserve and the Air National Guard offer the same career fields as the active Air Force.

MISSION The main mission of the Air Force is to defend the United States through the control and exploitation of air and space. The Air Force flies and maintains aircraft and maintains the bases that house them. Air Force personnel are stationed worldwide.

PROFILE OF AIR FORCE PERSONNEL

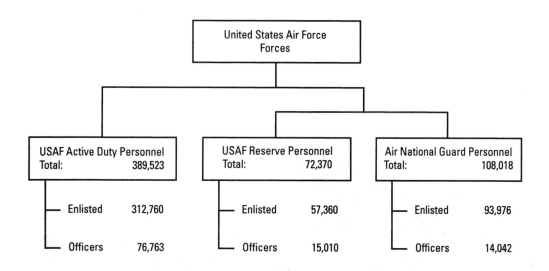

The Air Force:

- establishes air superiority, interdicts the enemy, and provides air support of combat ground forces.

- defends the nation against air and missile attack.

- is the major space research and development support for the Department of Defense.

- lends assistance to the National Aeronautics and Space Administration in conducting the nation's space program.

Special Operations Forces—Special Operations Command (AFSOC)

The AFSOC provides specialized air power for worldwide deployment and assignment to conduct unconventional warfare, special reconnaissance, counterterrorism, foreign internal defense, humanitarian assistance, psychological operations, personnel retrieval, and counternarcotics. AFSOC has approximately 9,700 personnel assigned.

MAJOR U.S. AIR FORCE COMMANDS AND BASES

Air Combat Command, Langley Air Force Base, VA
Air Force Intelligence Command, Kelly Air Force Base, TX
Air Force Material Command, Wright-Patterson Air Force Base, OH
Air Force Space Command, Peterson Air Force Base, CO
Air Force Special Operations Command, Hurlburt Field, FL
Air Mobility Command, Scott Air Force Base, IL
Air Training Command, Randolph Air Force Base, TX
Air University, Maxwell Air Force Base, AL
Pacific Air Forces, Hickam Air Force Base, HA
United States Air Forces in Europe, Ramstein Air Base, Germany

MAJOR U.S. AIR FORCE BASES

Alabama
Maxwell AFB, Montgomery

Alaska
Elmendore AFB, Anchorage

Arizona
Luke AFB, Phoenix

California
Edwards AFB, Rosamond
March AFB, Riverside
McClellan AFB, Sacramento
Travis AFB, Fairfield
Vandenberg AFB, Lompoc

Colorado
Patrick AFB, Cocoa Beach
Peterson AFB, Colorado Springs

Delaware
Dover AFB, Dover

Florida
Homestead AFB, Homestead

Georgia
Dobbins AFB, Marietta
Robins AFB, Warner Robins

Illinois
Scott AFB, Belleville

Indiana
Grissom AFB, Peru

Maryland
Andrews AFB, Camp Springs

Massachusetts
Westover AFB, Chicopee Falls

Minnesota
Minn-St. Paul IAP, Minneapolis

Mississippi
Kessler AFB, Biloxi

Missouri
Richards-Gebaur AFB, Belton

Louisiana
Barksdale AFB, Bossier City

Nevada
Nellis AFB, Las Vegas

New Jersey
McGuire AFB, Wrightstown

New York
Niagara Falls IAP, Niagara Falls

Utah
Hill AFB, Ogden

North Carolina
Seymour Johnson AFB, Goldboro

Virginia
Langley AFB, Hampton

Ohio
Wright-Patterson AFB, Fairborn

Washington
McChord AFB, Tacoma

Oklahoma
Tinker AFB, Oklahoma City

Wisconsin
General Mitchell IAP, Milwaukee

Oregon
Portland IAP, Portland

European Command
England
Germany

Pennsylvania
Greater Pittsburgh IAP, Pittsburgh

Italy
Turkey

South Carolina
Charleston AFB, Charleston

Pacific Command
Alaska
Guam

Texas
Kelly AFB, San Antonio
Lackland AFB, San Antonio

Hawaii
Japan
South Korea

Enlisted Opportunities

- ☐ **U.S. Air Force General Enlisted Career Fields**
- ☐ **Special Enlisted Opportunities and Programs**

Enlisted Entrance Overview

Age: 17 to 27 years old
Enlistments: 2, 3, 4, or 6 years

Recruit (Basic or Boot Camp) Training

Duration: 6 weeks
Location: Lackland Air Force Base, TX

Enlisted Promotion Path

After basic, most airmen attend a resident course (fully accredited) at one of the Air Force's four technical training centers or at one of the other service schools.

E-1   *Recruit*—(Basic or Boot) Training.
E-2   *Airman*—Basic must have 6 months time in grade and be recommended by the commander.
E-3   *Airman First Class*—Must have 10 months time in grade and commander recommendation.
E-4   *Senior Airman*—Must have 36 months time in service and 20 months time in grade or 28 months time in grade.
E-5–E-7   *Staff Sergeant, Technical Sergeant,* and *Master Sergeant*— Based on grade/time in service requirements and points. Performance reports, decorations, job knowledge, and Air Force knowledge tests also earn points toward promotion.
E-8–E-9   *Senior* and *Chief Master Sergeant*—Virtually the same as E-5 and above; also must meet a selection board.

Critical Needs—Enlisted Career Fields

Air Craft Maintenance
Electronics
Health Care
Pararescue

Special Operations Forces

Special Operations Command (AFSOC)

GENERAL ENLISTED CAREER FIELDS

Military Occupational Specialties

(See Chapter 12 for more information on Enlisted Career Fields.)

Administration
- ☐ Contracting Specialist
- ☐ Courier
- ☐ Education and Training Systems Specialist
- ☐ Financial Analysis Specialist
- ☐ Financial Management Specialist
- ☐ Historian
- ☐ Logistics Plans Specialist
- ☐ Manpower Management Specialist
- ☐ Military Training Manager
- ☐ Missile Facility Manager
- ☐ Operations Resource Management Specialist
- ☐ Personnel Specialist
- ☐ Personnel Systems Management Specialist
- ☐ Post Management Specialist
- ☐ Postal Specialist
- ☐ Recruiter
- ☐ Research and Development Technician
- ☐ Supply Management Specialist
- ☐ Supply Systems Analysis Specialist

Aviation
- ☐ Airborne Communications Specialist
- ☐ Airborne Computer Systems Technician
- ☐ Airborne Warning Command and Control Specialist
- ☐ Airborne Wing and Control Radar Specialist
- ☐ Aircraft Life Support Specialist
- ☐ Aircraft Loadmaster
- ☐ Aircraft Structural Maintenance Specialist
- ☐ Airfield Management Specialist
- ☐ Air Traffic Control Radar Specialist
- ☐ Air Traffic Control Specialist
- ☐ Avionics Guidance and Control System Specialist
- ☐ Avionics Sensor Maintenance Specialist
- ☐ Avionics Test Station and Component Specialist
- ☐ Communications Navigation Systems Specialist
- ☐ Flight Engineer
- ☐ Pararescue Specialist
- ☐ Survival Training Specialist

Combat
- ☐ Aerospace Control and Warning Systems Specialist
- ☐ Combat Control Specialist
- ☐ Command and Control Specialist
- ☐ Space Systems Operations Specialist
- ☐ Tactical Air Command and Control

Communications and Computer Systems
- ☐ Communications Computer Systems Controller
- ☐ Communications Computer Systems Programmer
- ☐ Communications Programmer
- ☐ Electronic Computer and Switching Specialist
- ☐ Electronic Spectrum Management Specialist
- ☐ Radio Communications Systems Specialist
- ☐ Secure Communications Systems Specialist
- ☐ Sensor Operator

Construction
- [ ] Pavement and Construction Equipment Specialist
- [ ] Utility Systems Specialist

Electronics and Electrical Repair
- [ ] Aircraft Communications and Navigation Systems Specialist
- [ ] Aircraft Electronic and Environmental Systems Specialist
- [ ] Aircraft Guidance and Control Specialist
- [ ] Avionics Systems Specialist
- [ ] Communications Cable and Antenna Systems Specialist
- [ ] Electrical Power Production Specialist
- [ ] Electronic Civil Engineer Specialist
- [ ] Electronic Warfare Systems Specialist
- [ ] Imagery Systems Maintenance Specialist
- [ ] Instrumentation and Telemetry Specialist

Engineering, Science, and Technical
- [ ] Aircraft Armament Specialist
- [ ] Combat Arms Training and Maintenance Technician
- [ ] Communications Systems Specialist
- [ ] Disaster Preparedness Specialist
- [ ] Explosive Ordnance Disposal Specialist
- [ ] Ground Radio Communications Specialist
- [ ] Information Management Specialist
- [ ] Liquid Fuel Systems Specialist
- [ ] Maintenance Data Systems Analyst Specialist
- [ ] Meteorology Navigation Systems Specialist
- [ ] Munitions Systems Specialist
- [ ] Nondestructive Inspection Specialist
- [ ] Nuclear Weapons Specialist
- [ ] Weather Technician
- [ ] Wideband Satellite Communications Specialist

Human Services
- [ ] Chapel Services Support Staff
- [ ] Social Actions Specialist

Intelligence
- [ ] Electronic Signals Intelligence Exploitation Specialist
- [ ] Imagery Interpreter
- [ ] Intelligence Operations Specialist
- [ ] Signals Intelligence Analysis Specialist
- [ ] Signals Intelligence Production Specialist

Law Enforcement
- [ ] Correctional Custody Supervisor
- [ ] Security Police
- [ ] Special Investigator

Legal
- [ ] Paralegal

Machinists, Mechanics, and Precision
- [ ] Aerospace Ground Equipment Specialist
- [ ] Aerospace Maintenance Specialist
- [ ] Aerospace Propulsion Specialist
- [ ] Aircraft Fabrication Specialist
- [ ] Aircraft Fuel Systems Specialist
- [ ] Aircraft Metals Technician
- [ ] Fabrication and Parachute Specialist
- [ ] General Purpose Vehicle Technician
- [ ] Heating, Ventilation, Air Conditioning, and Refrigeration Technician
- [ ] Helicopter Maintenance Specialist
- [ ] Precision Measurement Equipment Lab Specialist
- [ ] Special Purpose Vehicle and Equipment Specialist
- [ ] Special Vehicle Technician
- [ ] Tactical Aircraft Maintenance Specialist
- [ ] Vehicle Body Specialist
- [ ] Vehicle Maintenance Control and Analysis Specialist
- [ ] Vehicle Maintenance Specialist

Media
- [ ] Printing Management Specialist
- [ ] Public Affairs Specialist
- [ ] Still Photography Specialist
- [ ] Visual Information Production Specialist
- [ ] Visual Information Specialist

Medical and Health Care
- [ ] Aeromedical Specialist
- [ ] Aerospace Physiologist
- [ ] Bioenvironmental Engineer
- [ ] Biomedical Equipment Specialist
- [ ] Cardiopulmonary Laboratory Technician
- [ ] Cytotechnology Technician
- [ ] Dental Assistant Technician
- [ ] Dental Lab Technician
- [ ] Dental Management Technician
- [ ] Diet Therapy Specialist
- [ ] Health Services Management Specialist
- [ ] Histopathology Technician
- [ ] Medical Lab Technician
- [ ] Medical Services Technician
- [ ] Mental Health Specialist
- [ ] Occupational Therapist
- [ ] Optometry Technician
- [ ] Pharmacy Technician
- [ ] Physical Therapy Technician

- [ ] Public Health Specialist
- [ ] Radiologic Technician
- [ ] Surgical Technician

Military Intelligence Cryptologic Linguist
- [ ] Far East Crypto Specialist
- [ ] Germanic Crypto Specialist
- [ ] Mid-East Crypto Specialist
- [ ] Romance Crypto Specialist
- [ ] Slavic Crypto Specialist

Missile and Space Systems
- [ ] Missile and Space Facilities Specialist
- [ ] Missile and Space Systems Maintenance Specialist

Music
- [ ] Regional Band Specialist

Support Service
- [ ] Fire Protection Specialist

Transportation and Material Handling
- [ ] Air Transportation Specialist
- [ ] In-Flight Passenger Services Specialist
- [ ] Traffic Management Specialist
- [ ] Vehicle Operations Dispatch Specialist
- [ ] Vehicle Operations Specialist

Special Enlisted Opportunities and Programs

☐ **Special Enlistment Bonus**
☐ **Stripes for Education Training**
☐ **Community College of the Air Force**
☐ **Airman Education and Commissioning Program**
☐ **Bootstrap**

Special Enlistment Bonus

Candidates who qualify for specific Air Force specialties for a six-year term of enlistment may be entitled to an enlistment bonus. Bonuses range from $1,000 for explosives ordnance disposal specialists to $4,000 for cryptologic linguist specialists, and $6,000 for either a combat control apprentice or the pararescue apprentice specialties. Payment is contingent upon successful completion of technical training for the skill.

Stripes for Education Training

High school graduates with 45 semester hours or 67 quarter hours of college credit may qualify for enlistment as an E-3. Those with 20 semester hours or 30 quarter hours may qualify for enlistment at the rank of E-2. Enlistees who have been awarded a Boy Scout Eagle Scout Award or Girl Scout Gold Award enter active duty at E-2.

Community College of the Air Force

Enlisted members can earn an Associate in Applied Science degree directly corresponding to their Air Force job. The college is regionally accredited and offers more than 65 programs.

Airman Education and Commissioning Program

Enlisted members with 45 semester hours in scientific or technical disciplines can complete baccalaureate degrees and earn officer commissions.

Bootstrap

Selected enlisted members are reassigned to temporary duty at a civilian college for up to one year to complete degree requirements.

Officer Opportunities

☐ **Standard Officer Commissioning Programs**
☐ **Officer Career Fields**
☐ **Special Officer Opportunities and Programs**

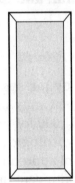

Standard Officer Commissioning Programs

☐ **U.S. Air Force Academy**
☐ **U.S. Air Force Academy Preparatory School**
☐ **Officer Training School**
☐ **Direct Commissions**
☐ **Reserve Officer Training Corps (AFROTC)**

U.S. Air Force Academy

The Air Force Academy offers 26 bachelor of science degrees plus a commission as an Air Force officer upon completion.
(See Chapter 10—Military Academies.)

U.S. Air Force Academy Preparatory School

The Air Force Academy Preparatory School candidates are automatically selected from among those individuals who applied to the Air Force Academy but did not receive appointments.
(See Chapter 10—Military Preparatory Schools.)

Officer Training School

Officer Training School (OTS), the Air Force, and the Air Force Reserve train selected college graduates to become commissioned officers. Potential pilots or navigators go directly to flight training after completing OTS. The applicant must be a graduate of an accredited college.

Direct Commissions

There are several direct commissioning programs. Programs e-xist for prior trained military officers, aviators, lawyers, medical and health professionals, engineers, and others who possess a four-year degree from a college or university

Reserve Officer Training Corps (AFROTC)

A program designed to allow college students to become Air Force officers while completing their bachelor's degree at over 147 colleges and universities (or at one of more than 680 institutions having a crosstown or consortium agreement with an Air Force ROTC host institution). The Air Force ROTC offers several options to earn an Air Force commission:

Four-Year Program
Two-Year Program
One-Year Program
AFROTC Three- and Four-Year Scholarships
AFROTC Pre-Health Professions Program
AFROTC Nurse Program

(*See Chapter 11—ROTC Opportunities.*)

Critical Needs—Officer Career Fields

Engineers
Medical
Nurses
Pilots

Special Operations Forces

Special Operations Command (AFSOC)

OFFICER CAREER FIELDS

Military Occupational Specialties

(See Chapter 13 for more information on Officer Career Fields.)

Administration
- ☐ Acquisition Manager
- ☐ Auditor
- ☐ Communications Computer Systems Officer
- ☐ Cost Analysis Officer
- ☐ Financial Management Officer
- ☐ Historian
- ☐ Information Management Officer
- ☐ Instructor
- ☐ Logistician
- ☐ Logistics Plans Officer
- ☐ Manpower Officer
- ☐ Personnel Officer
- ☐ Planning and Programming Officer
- ☐ Program Director
- ☐ Recruiting Service Officer
- ☐ Supply Officer
- ☐ Support Commander
- ☐ Transportation Officer

Aviation
- ☐ Aircraft Maintenance Munitions Officer
- ☐ Airlift Navigator
- ☐ Airlift Pilot
- ☐ Astronaut
- ☐ Bomber Navigator
- ☐ Bomber Pilot
- ☐ Fighter Navigator
- ☐ Fighter Pilot
- ☐ Generalist Navigator
- ☐ Generalist Pilot
- ☐ Helicopter Pilot
- ☐ Special Operations Navigator
- ☐ Special Operations Pilot
- ☐ Tanker Navigator
- ☐ Tanker Pilot
- ☐ Test Navigator
- ☐ Test Pilot
- ☐ Trainer Pilot

Combat
- ☐ Command and Control Officer
- ☐ Missile Officer
- ☐ Space and Missile Maintenance Officer

Engineering, Science, and Technical
- ☐ Aerospace Engineer
- ☐ Civil Engineer
- ☐ Developmental Engineer
- ☐ Space and Missile Officer
- ☐ Weather Officer

Human Services
- ☐ Chaplain
- ☐ Social Service Officer

Intelligence
- ☐ Air Attaché
- ☐ Intelligence Officer
- ☐ International Politics Military Affairs Officer

Law Enforcement
- ☐ Security Police Officer
- ☐ Special Investigator

Legal
- ☐ Judge Advocate
- ☐ Lawyer

Media and Public Affairs
- ☐ Public Affairs Officer
- ☐ Visual Information Officer

Medical and Health Care

- ☐ Aerospace Physiologist
- ☐ Allergist
- ☐ Anesthesiologist
- ☐ Audiology Speech Pathologist
- ☐ Bioenvironmental Engineer
- ☐ Biomedical Laboratory Technician
- ☐ Biomedical Scientist
- ☐ Clinical Nurse
- ☐ Clinical Social Worker
- ☐ Critical Care Medicine Specialist
- ☐ Dermatologist
- ☐ Diagnostic Radiologist
- ☐ Dietitian
- ☐ Family Physician
- ☐ Flight Nurse
- ☐ Health Physicist
- ☐ Health Services Administrator
- ☐ Medical Commander
- ☐ Medical Entomologist
- ☐ Mental Health Nurse
- ☐ Nurse Administrator
- ☐ Nurse Anesthetist
- ☐ Nurse Midwife
- ☐ Obstetrician/Gynecologist
- ☐ Occupational Therapist
- ☐ Operating Room Nurse
- ☐ Ophthalmologist
- ☐ Pathologist
- ☐ Pharmacist
- ☐ Physical Therapist
- ☐ Physician Assistant
- ☐ Podiatrist
- ☐ Public Health Officer
- ☐ Urologist
- ☐ Veterinary Clinician

Medical Diagnosing and Treatment

- ☐ Aerospace Medicine Physician
- ☐ Aerospace Medicine Specialist
- ☐ Clinical Psychologist
- ☐ Dentist
- ☐ Emergency Services Physician
- ☐ Endodontist
- ☐ Family Physician
- ☐ Family Practice Specialist
- ☐ General Practice Physician
- ☐ Internist
- ☐ Neurologist
- ☐ Nuclear Medicine Physician
- ☐ Occupational Medicine Specialist
- ☐ Optometrist
- ☐ Oral Pathologist
- ☐ Oral Surgeon
- ☐ Orthodontist
- ☐ Orthopedic Surgeon
- ☐ Pediatrician
- ☐ Periodontist
- ☐ Physical Medicine Physician
- ☐ Preventive Medicine Specialist
- ☐ Prosthodontist
- ☐ Psychiatrist
- ☐ Surgeon

Music

- ☐ Band Leader

SPECIAL OFFICER OPPORTUNITIES AND PROGRAMS

Air Force Institute of Technology

☎ 937-255-2321

AFIT offers education programs at the master's and doctoral levels through the School of Engineering, the School of Systems and Logistics, and the Civilian Institution Programs.

U.S. Air Force Reserve

☎ 800-257-1212

Special Opportunities and Programs
Air Reserve Technician Program

ARTs are full-time civil service employees for the Air Force and are at the same time members of the Air Force Reserve Command units where they work. The ARTs provide full-time support functions to maintain the reserve unit for readiness.

U.S. Air National Guard

☎ 800-638-7600 or local Air National Guard Unit

Special Opportunities and Programs
Air National Guard Academy of Military Science

The Air National Guard Academy of Military Science provides initial military training. Students attend the six-week course in pay grade E-5 (or their former enlisted grade, if higher) and are commissioned upon graduation. A degree is required in most career fields.

Inventory of U.S. Air Force Aircraft and Missiles ——————

- ☐ Air Tankers
- ☐ Airborne Tactical and Defense Missiles
- ☐ Attack and Observation
- ☐ Bombers
- ☐ Fighters
- ☐ Helicopters
- ☐ Reconnaissance and Special Duty
- ☐ Space Launch Vehicles
- ☐ Strategic Missiles
- ☐ Trainers
- ☐ Transports

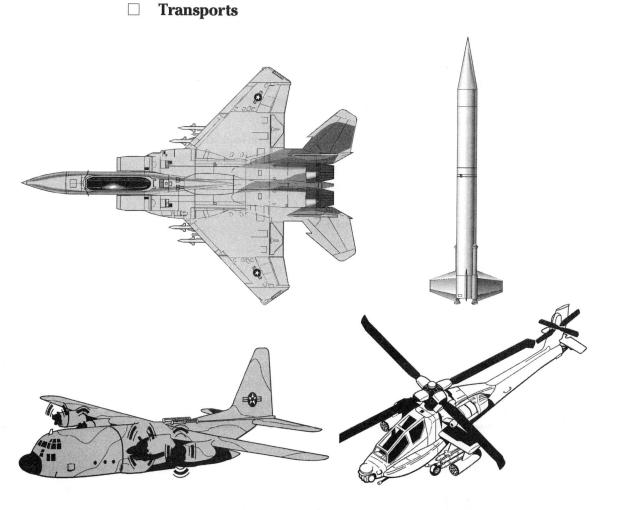

OVERVIEW   The Air Force has a wide assortment of aircraft, missiles, and space launch vehicles, including the famous Stealth Bomber, which made history in Desert Storm, and Air Force One, the presidential plane. In addition, the Air Force maintains intercontinental ballistic missiles.

Bombers

B1B	Lancer
B2A	Spirit
B52H	Stratofortress

Special Profile	**B1B Lancer**
Purpose:	multirole, long-range heavy bomber
Speed:	900 mph
Range:	intercontinental
Armament:	nuclear and conventional, including short-range attack missiles, gravity, and air-launched cruise missiles
Crew:	4

Fighters

F15C/D/E	Eagle
F16	Fighting Falcon
F117A	Nighthawk

Attack and Observation

A10/OA10	Thunderbolt 11
AC130H/U	Spectra

Transports

C9A/C	Nightingale
C12	Huron
C17A	Globemaster III
C20A/B	Gulf Stream
C21A	
C22B	
C27A	Spartan
C130	Hercules
C141B	Starlifter
VC137B/C	Stratoliner

Special Profile   **C5A/B Galaxy**
Purpose: long-range, heavy logistics transport
Speed: 541 mph
Range: 5,940 miles
Crew: 6

Special Profile   **Air Force One**
Purpose: presidential air transport
Speed: 630 mph
Range: 9,600 miles
Crew: 23

Reconnaissance and Special Duty

E3	Sentry (AWACS)
E4B	
E8C	Joint STARS
E9A	Telemetry Relay
EC130E	Airborne Command
EC130H	Compass Call
EF 111A	Raven
MC130E/H	Combat Talon I and 11
MC130P	Combat Shadow
RC135	Reconnaissance
SR71	
WC130H	Hercules

Special Profile   **U2R/S**
Purpose: high-altitude tactical reconnaissance; air sampling
Speed: 475 mph
Range: 7,000 miles
Crew: 1

Trainers

F4E	Phantom II
T1A	Jayhawk
T37B	Tweet
T38A and AT38B	Talon
T43A	Navigator Training

Tankers

KC10A	Aerial Tanker
KC135	Stratotanker

Helicopters

HH1H	Iroquois
MH53J	Pave Low IIIE
MH/HH60G	Pave Hawk

Strategic Missiles

LGM 118A	Peacekeeper

Special Profile	**LGM30F/G Minuteman**
Purpose:	intercontinental ballistic missile
Speed:	more than 15,000 mph
Range:	more than 6,000 miles
Payload:	3 MK12 or MK12A warheads

Airborne Tactical and Defense Missiles

AGM65	Maverick
AGM84	Harpoon
AGM86B/C	Air Launched Cruise Missile
AGM88A/B/C	HARM
AGM129A	ACM
AIM7	Sparrow
AIM120A	AMRAAM
GBU15	Glide Bomb
GBU24A/B	Guided Penetrator
GBU24/B	Guided Bomb
GBU27/B	Guided Bomb
GBU28	Guided Bomb

Space Launch Vehicles

Atlas II
Centaur
Delta 11
Pegasus
Titan II
Titan IV

ADDITIONAL   *Videos:*
RESOURCES   "Beyond the Wild Blue—A History of the U.S. Air Force"
"Fighter Pilots of the U.S. Air Force"
"Wings of Silver"

Books:
Airman's Guide by Wayne Valey (1994)
Air Force Officer Guide (31st Edition) by Jeffery Benton (1996)
Fighter Wing: A Guided Tour of an Air Force Combat Wing by Tom Clancy (1997)
From a Dark Sky: The Story of U.S. Air Force Special Operations by Orr Kelly (1997)

Official Magazine:
Airman, U.S. Air Force

Popular Movies:
Air Force (1943: John Garfield)—Classic WWII Drama
Air Cadet (1951: Rock Hudson)—Boot Camp Saga
Strategic Air Command (1955: James Stewart)—Cold War SAC Bombers Drama
Gathering of Eagles (1963: Rock Hudson)—SAC Command Drama
Catch-22 (1970: Alan Arkin)—Classic WWII Drama/Comedy
Firebirds (1990: Nicolas Cage)—Helicopter Drama
Memphis Belle (1990: Matthew Modine)—B-17 Saga

Advisory

You should not make a career decision based on a popular movie or television show. Remember: They are, for the most part, based loosely on facts or truths. Your final decision should be based on research into what will be good for you; however, popular movies and films can provide fine entertainment dealing with the military service.

Chapter 6

U.S. ARMY

U.S. Army

U.S. Army Recruiting Command
Building 1307, Third Avenue
Fort Knox, KY 40121-2726

☎ 800-USA-ARMY
http//www.goarmy.com

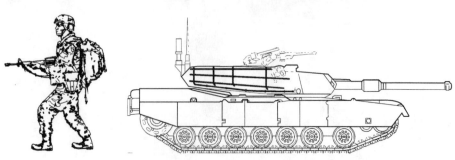

Famous Service Mottos:	**HOOAH** (Airborne motto; pronounced "Hu Ah") **Rangers Lead the Way**
Elite Units:	**Airborne Rangers** (training) **Green Berets**
Recruiting Slogan:	**Be All That You Can Be** (Recruits more than 80,000 new personnel per year)

PROFILE OF ARMY PERSONNEL

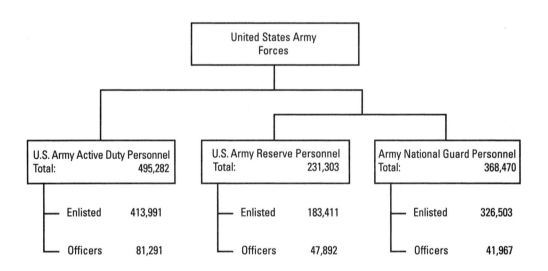

OVERVIEW The Army is the oldest of the military services, established technically on June 4, 1775 by the Continental Congress. The U.S. Army
protects the security of the United States and its vital resources. It
stands ready to defend American interests and the interests of our
allies through land-based operations anywhere in the world. The
largest of the military services, the Army offers a wide variety of
careers and opportunities. Both the Army Reserve and the Army
National Guard offer the same career fields as the active-duty Army.

MISSION The main missions of the Army include:
- Presence with forward units deployed
- Projection of land forces and contingency operations
- Peacetime and wartime reinforcement
- Evacuation and protection of U.S. citizens
- Support of the nation's war on drugs
- Assistance to friendly nations
- Support of national assistance and civil affairs

Special Operations Forces—Green Berets

The Green Berets are Special Forces soldiers who use guerrilla warfare
techniques, collect strategic intelligence, conduct raids and infiltration missions, and use unconventional warfare.

Special Trained Forces—Airborne Rangers

The Airborne Rangers are special Army soldiers who have been qualified
through rigorous training that includes parachuting from airplanes.

WHERE THEY SERVE

United States	393,536
Europe	64,853
East Asia and Pacific	29,409
Central and South America	8,388
Africa, Southeast Asia	3,363

MAJOR U.S. ARMY COMMANDS

U.S. Pacific Command
U.S. Atlantic Command
U.S. Europe Command
U.S. Forces Korea Command

MAJOR U.S. ARMY STATIONS/BASES*

Alabama
Fort Benning, Phoenix City
Fort Rucker, Ozark

Alaska
Fort Greely, Delta Junction
Fort Richardson, Anchorage
Fort Wainwright, Fairbanks

Arizona
Fort Huachuca, Sierra Vista
Yuma Proving Ground, Yuma

California
Fort Hunter Liggett, Monterey
Fort Irwin, San Bernardino
Presidio, Monterey
Sierra Army Depot, Herlong

Colorado
Fort Carson, Colorado Springs

District of Columbia
Fort Lesley McNair
Walter Reed Army Medical Center

Georgia
Fort Benning, Columbia
Fort Gillem, Atlanta
Fort Gordon, Augusta
Fort McPherson, Atlanta
Fort Stewart, Hinesville
Hunter Air Field, Savannah

Hawaii
Fort Shafter, Honolulu
Schofield Barracks, Wahiawa

Kansas
Fort Leavenworth, Leavenworth
Fort Riley, Junction City

Kentucky
Fort Campbell, Clarksville
Fort Campbell, Hopkinsville
Fort Knox, Louisville

Louisiana
Fort Polk, Leesville

Maryland
Aberdeen Proving Ground, Aberdeen
Fort Detrick, Frederick
Fort Meade, Laurel

Missouri
Fort Leonard Wood, Rolla

New Jersey
Fort Dix, Wrightstown
Fort Monmouth, Red Bank
Picatinny Arsenal, Picatinny

New Mexico
White Sands Missile Range, White Sands

New York
Fort Drum, Watertown
Fort Hamilton, Brooklyn
U.S. Military Academy, West Point

North Carolina
Fort Bragg, Fayetteville

Oklahoma
Fort Sill, Lawton

Pennsylvania
Carlisle Barracks, Carlisle

South Carolina
Fort Jackson, Columbia

Texas
Fort Bliss, El Paso
Fort Hood, Killen
Fort Houston, San Antonio

Virginia
Fort Belvoir, Fairfax County
Fort Eustis, Newport News
Fort Hill, Bowling Green

Fort Lee, Petersburg
Fort Monroe, Hampton
Fort Myer, Arlington
Fort Story, Virginia Beach
The Pentagon, Arlington

Washington
Fort Lewis, Tacoma

*As of publication, these bases still exist.

Enlisted Opportunities

☐ **Enlisted Career Fields**
☐ **Special Enlisted Opportunities and Programs**

Enlisted Entrance Overview

Age: 17 to 34 years
Enlistments: 2 to 6 years (Regular Active Duty)

Recruit (Basic or Boot Camp) Training

Duration: 8 weeks
Location: Fort Jackson, SC
             Fort Knox, KY
             Fort Leonard Wood, MO
             Fort Sill, OK

One-Station Unit Training

The Army maintains special stations that provide both common skills (Basic Combat Training) and skills required for *line-of-work* occupational fields (Advanced Individual Training) at the corresponding locations:

Infantry:	Fort Benning, GA
Armor:	Fort Knox, KY
Field Artillery:	Fort Sill, OK
Air Defense Artillery:	Fort Bliss, TX
Combat Engineer:	Fort Leonard Wood, MO
Military Police:	Fort McClellan, AL

Enlisted Promotion Path

E-1   *Recruit*—(Basic or Boot) Training

E-2   *Private*—Six months active duty and commander's recommendation.

E-3   *Private First Class*—12 months active duty service, 4 months as a private, and commander's recommendation.

E-4   *Specialist or Corporal*—12 months active duty service, 6 months time in grade, and commander's recommendation.

E-5–E-6   *Sergeant and Staff Sergeant*—Test against peers in job skill and other soldier skills; must also have high school diploma and meet Army promotion point system scores and promotion board criteria.

E-7–E-9   *Sergeant First Class and above*—Must meet Army centralized selection board criteria.

Critical Needs—Enlisted Career Fields

Cavalry Scout
Combat Engineer
Field Artillery Specialist
Hawk Missile Systems Specialist
Infantryman
Military Police
Patriot Launching Station Operator Maintainers

Special Operations Forces

Green Berets

Special Training

Airborne Rangers

ENLISTED CAREER FIELDS

Military Occupational Specialties

(See Chapter 12 for more information on Enlisted Career Fields.)

Administration
- ☐ Accounting Specialist
- ☐ Administrative Specialist
- ☐ Automated Logistical Specialist
- ☐ Chaplain Assistant
- ☐ Fabric Repair Specialist
- ☐ Finance Specialist
- ☐ Laundry and Bath Specialist
- ☐ Legal Specialist
- ☐ Mortuary Affairs Specialist
- ☐ Parachute Rigger
- ☐ Personnel Administration Specialist
- ☐ Recruiter Noncommissioned Officer
- ☐ Retention Noncommissioned Officer
- ☐ Unit Supply Specialist

Aircraft Maintenance
- ☐ Aircraft Armament Missile Systems Repairer
- ☐ Aircraft Electrician
- ☐ Aircraft Powerplant Repairer
- ☐ Aircraft Powertrain Repairer
- ☐ Aircraft Structural Repairer
- ☐ Airplane Repairer
- ☐ Avionic Mechanic
- ☐ Helicopter Repairer

Armor
- ☐ Armor Crewman
- ☐ Cavalry Scout

Aviation
- ☐ Aeroscout Observer
- ☐ Air Traffic Control Operator
- ☐ Aviation Operations Specialist

Combat
- ☐ Air Defense Command Control Computer Operator

- ☐ Air Defense System Specialist
- ☐ Automated Fire Support Systems Specialist
- ☐ Avenger Crewmember
- ☐ Bradley Linebacker Crewmember
- ☐ Bridge Crewmember
- ☐ Cannon Crewmember
- ☐ Cannon Fire Direction Specialist
- ☐ Chaparral Crewmember
- ☐ Combat Engineer
- ☐ Command/Control Operator/Maintainer
- ☐ Engineer Tracked Vehicle Crewman
- ☐ Enhanced Operator/Maintainer
- ☐ Field Artillery Firefinder Radar Operator
- ☐ Field Artillery Meteorological Crewmember
- ☐ Field Artillery Specialist
- ☐ Field Artillery Surveyor
- ☐ Fire Support Specialist
- ☐ HAWK Missile System Crewmember
- ☐ Infantryman
- ☐ Multiple Launch Rocket System Crewmember
- ☐ Patriot Fire Control Operator/Maintainer
- ☐ Patriot Launching Station Specialist

Construction
- ☐ Carpentry and Masonry Specialist
- ☐ Concrete and Asphalt Equipment Operator
- ☐ Crane Operator
- ☐ General Construction Equipment Operator
- ☐ Heavy Construction Equipment Operator
- ☐ Interior Electrician

☐ Plumber
☐ Quarrying Specialist

Electronic & Electrical Repair
☐ Air Traffic Control Equipment Repairer
☐ Automatic Test Equipment Repairer
☐ Avenger System Repairer
☐ Avionic Communications Equipment Repairer
☐ Avionic Flight Systems Repairer
☐ Avionic Radar Repairer
☐ Chaparral/Redeye Repairer
☐ Combat Electronic Missile System Repairer
☐ EW/Intercept Aviation System Repairer
☐ EW/Intercept Tactical System Repairer
☐ Hawk Fire Control/Continuous Wave Repairer
☐ Hawk Firing Section Repairer
☐ Land Combat Support System Test Specialist
☐ Multiple Launch Rocket System Repairer
☐ Operator/Maintainer
☐ Patriot System Repairer
☐ Radar Repairer
☐ Radio and Communications Security Repairer
☐ Special Electronic Devices Repairer
☐ Strategic Systems Repairer
☐ Surveillance Radar Repairer
☐ Telecommunications Terminal Device Repairer
☐ Test, Measurement, and Diagnostic Equipment Support Specialist
☐ Vulcan Repairer
☐ Wire Systems Equipment Repairer

Electronic Warfare/Cryptologic Operations
☐ Electronic Warfare/Signal Specialist
☐ Emitter Locator/Identifier
☐ Intelligence Voice Interceptor
☐ Morse Interceptor
☐ Signal Intelligence Analyst (Linguist)

Engineering, Science, and Technical
☐ Ammunitions Specialist
☐ Automatic Data Processing Specialist
☐ Cartographer
☐ Chemical Operations Specialist
☐ Explosive Ordnance Disposal Specialist
☐ Information Systems OperatorAnalyst
☐ Microwave Systems Operator-Maintainer
☐ Multichannel Transmission Systems Operator
☐ Printing and Bindery Specialist
☐ Radio Operator-Maintainer
☐ Satellite Communications Systems Specialist
☐ Signal Support Systems Specialist
☐ Telecommunications Operator Maintainer
☐ Terrain Analyst
☐ Topographic Analyst
☐ Topographic Surveyor
☐ Wire Signal Installer

Human Services
☐ Caseworker
☐ Religious Specialist

Intelligence
☐ Counterintelligence Assistant
☐ Ground Surveillance Systems Operator
☐ Imagery Analyst
☐ Imagery Ground Station Operator
☐ Intelligence Analyst
☐ Interrogator
☐ Psychological Operations Specialist
☐ Signal Security Specialist
☐ Translator/Interpreter
☐ Unmanned Aerial Vehicle Operator

Law Enforcement
- ☐ CID Investigator
- ☐ Corrections Specialist
- ☐ Military Police

Legal
- ☐ Paralegal

Machinists, Mechanics, and Precision Work
- ☐ Air Defense System Maintenance Repairer
- ☐ Armament Repairer
- ☐ Bradley Fighting Vehicle System Mechanic
- ☐ Chaparral System Mechanic
- ☐ Construction Equipment Repairer
- ☐ Fire Control Repairer
- ☐ Fuel and Electrical Systems Repairer
- ☐ Hawk Missile Systems Mechanic
- ☐ Heavy Wheel Vehicle Mechanic
- ☐ Light Wheel Vehicle Mechanic
- ☐ M1 Abrams Tank System Mechanic
- ☐ M1A1 Abrams Tank Turret Mechanic
- ☐ Machinist
- ☐ Metal Worker
- ☐ Self-Propelled Field Artillery Repairer
- ☐ Self-Propelled Field Artillery Turret Mechanic
- ☐ Small Arms/Artillery Repairer
- ☐ Track Vehicle Mechanic
- ☐ Track Vehicle Repairer
- ☐ Utilities Equipment Repairer

Media & Public Affairs
- ☐ Broadcast Journalist
- ☐ Combat Documentation and Production Specialist
- ☐ Journalist
- ☐ Multimedia Illustrator
- ☐ Visual Information/Audio Equipment Specialist

Medical & Health Care
- ☐ Animal Care Specialist
- ☐ Dental Specialist
- ☐ Hospital Food Service Specialist
- ☐ Medical Equipment Repairer
- ☐ Medical Laboratory Specialist
- ☐ Medical Specialist
- ☐ Medical Supply Specialist
- ☐ Mental Health Specialist
- ☐ Operating Room Specialist
- ☐ Optical Laboratory Specialist
- ☐ Patient Administration Specialist
- ☐ Pharmacy Specialist
- ☐ Practical Nurse
- ☐ Preventive Medicine Specialist
- ☐ Radiology Specialist
- ☐ Respiratory Specialist
- ☐ Veterinary Food Inspection Specialist

Music
- ☐ Baritone or Euphonium Player
- ☐ Bassoon Player
- ☐ Clarinet Player
- ☐ Electric Bass Guitar Player
- ☐ Flute or Piccolo Player
- ☐ French Horn Player
- ☐ Guitar Player
- ☐ Oboe Player
- ☐ Percussion Player
- ☐ Piano Player
- ☐ Saxophone Player
- ☐ Special Bandmember
- ☐ Trombone Player
- ☐ Trumpet Player
- ☐ Tuba Player

Petroleum and Water
- ☐ Petroleum Laboratory Specialist
- ☐ Petroleum Supply Specialist
- ☐ Water Treatment Specialist

Power Plant Operations
- ☐ Power Generation Equipment Repairer
- ☐ Prime Power Production Specialist
- ☐ Turbine Engine Drive/Generator Repairer

Service
☐ Firefighter
☐ Food Service Specialist

Special Forces
(not entry-level positions)
☐ Special Operations Communications
   Sergeant
☐ Special Operations Engineer
☐ Special Operations Medical Sergeant
☐ Special Operations Weapons Sergeant

Transportation
☐ Airbrake Repairer
☐ Cargo Specialist
☐ Locomotive Electrician
☐ Motor Transport Operator
☐ Railway Car Repairer
☐ Railway Equipment Repairer
☐ Railway Operations Crewmember
☐ Railway Section Repairer
☐ Traffic Management Coordinator
☐ Train Crewmember
☐ Watercraft Engineer
☐ Watercraft Operator

Special Enlisted Opportunities and Programs

Army Civilian Acquired Skills Program (ACASP)

Candidates who have certain civilian skills that are needed by the Army may be appointed to grade E-3 upon enlistment.

Army College Fund

In addition to the Montgomery GI Bill, the military has a separate education program in which applicants may be able to earn up to $20,000 for education with a $1,200 investment.

Concurrent Admissions Program (CONAP)

This is a joint program of the Army Recruiting Command and participating colleges. The concept of CONAP is to admit eligible Army enlistees to college concurrent with their enlistment, deferring enrollment for up to two years after they leave active duty. CONAP is also open to Army Reserve and Army National Guard personnel.

Warrant Officer (W-1 to W-4)

The rank of Warrant Officer in the Army is restricted to members who have demonstrated a potential for greater responsibility than normally expected of enlisted personnel. This is not an entry-level position. Warrant Officers are assigned responsibilities and have authority commensurate with their rank, including assignments as commanding officers and engineering officers in many types of units. The Army also hosts an Aviation Warrant Officer program.

Career Fields:

- Adjutant General
- Air Defense Aviation
- Aviation Maintenance
- Band
- Criminal Investigation Department
- Engineer
- Field Artillery
- Military Intelligence
- Ordnance (Ammunition)
- Ordnance (Maintenance)
- Quartermaster
- Signal
- Special Forces
- Transportation

Officer Opportunities

- ☐ **Standard Officer Commissioning Programs**
- ☐ **General Officer Career Fields**
- ☐ **Special Officer Opportunities and Programs**

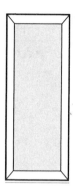

STANDARD OFFICER COMMISSIONING PROGRAMS

U.S. Military Academy

The United States Military Academy, located at West Point, NY, offers bachelor of science degrees with majors in both engineering and liberal arts. A graduate earns a commission as a second lieutenant in the U.S. Army.
(See Chapter 10—Military Academies.)

U.S. Military Academy Preparatory School

Candidates may apply to the U.S. Military Academy Preparatory School for one year to improve their academic skills and compete for an appointment to the following year's class.
(See Chapter 10—Military Academies.)

Army Reserve Officers' Training Corps (AROTC)

Army ROTC is the primary source for college-trained officers for the Army. Army ROTC is divided into two parts: the basic course and the advanced course. The basic course covers the first two years of college, the advanced course the third and fourth years. The Army ROTC offers several options to earn an Army commission:

Four-Year Program
Two-Year Program
One-Year Program
AROTC Three- and Four-Year Scholarships
AROTC Pre-Health Professions Program
AROTC Nurse Program

(See Chapter 11—ROTC)

Officer Candidate School

OCS is a 14-week course that trains enlisted personnel, warrant officers, and civilians with a college degree to be Army officers. Enlisted soldiers and warrant officers must have 60 hours of college for OCS. Civilian applicants must have a bachelor's degree.

Critical Needs—Officer Career Fields

Engineering
Infantry
Medical

Special Operations Forces

Green Beret Officers

Special Training

Airborne Rangers/Officers

GENERAL OFFICER CAREER FIELDS

Military Occupational Specialties

(See Chapter 13 for more information on Officer Career Fields.)

Administration
- [ ] Administrative System Management Officer
- [ ] Archivist
- [ ] Army Acquisition Corps Candidate Officer
- [ ] Army Research Associates Program Officer
- [ ] Branch Automation Officer
- [ ] Comptroller
- [ ] Contracting and Industrial Management Officer
- [ ] Cultural Affairs Officer
- [ ] Economist
- [ ] Equal Opportunity Advisor
- [ ] Finance Officer
- [ ] Force Development Officer
- [ ] Historian
- [ ] Instructor
- [ ] Joint Specialty Officer
- [ ] Operations Research Officer
- [ ] Personnel Management Officer
- [ ] Personnel Programs Management Officer
- [ ] Personnel Systems Management Officer
- [ ] Planner
- [ ] Postal Officer
- [ ] Quartermaster
- [ ] Recruiting Officer
- [ ] Strategist
- [ ] Strength Management Officer

☐ Supply and Material Management Officer
☐ Systems Automation Management Officer
☐ Training Development Officer
☐ USMA Professor

Armor
☐ Armor Officer
☐ Cavalry Officer

Aviation
☐ Air Operations Officer
☐ Air Traffic Services Officer
☐ Aviation All-Source Intelligence Officer
☐ Aviation Logistics Officer
☐ Aviation Safety Officer
☐ Experimental Test Pilot
☐ Instructor Pilot
☐ Maintenance Test Pilot
☐ Pilot

Combat
☐ Air Defense Artillery Officer
☐ Cannon Field Artillery Officer
☐ Combat Development Officer
☐ Combat Engineer
☐ Electronic Warfare Officer
☐ Field Artillery Officer
☐ Field Artillery Target Acquisition Officer
☐ Hawk Missile ADA Officer
☐ Light Missile Field Artillery Officer
☐ M1A2 Abrams Tank Officer
☐ M1/M1 A Abrams Tank Officer
☐ M2 Bradley Infantry Fighting Vehicle Officer
☐ M3 Cavalry Fighting Vehicle Officer
☐ M60 A1-A3 and M48 Series Tank Officer
☐ M551 Armor Reconnaissance Vehicle Officer
☐ Mortar Unit Officer

☐ NBC Reconnaissance Officer
☐ Patriot Missile ADA Officer
☐ Ranger Officer
☐ Short-Range Air Defense Artillery Officer

Engineering, Science, and Technical
☐ Agricultural Officer
☐ Chemical Munitions and Material Management Officer
☐ Chemical Officer
☐ Chemical Operations and Training Officer
☐ Civil Defense Officer
☐ Corps of Engineers Officer
☐ Electrical Engineer
☐ Electronics Engineer
☐ Explosive Ordnance Disposal
☐ Facilities/Contract Construction Management Engineer
☐ Munitions Material Management
☐ Nuclear Chemical Target Analyst
☐ Nuclear Weapons Research and Operations
☐ Radio Frequency Manager
☐ Robotics Officer
☐ Space Activities Officer
☐ Tank/Maintenance Management
☐ Topographic Engineer

Human Services
☐ Chaplain
☐ Clinical Pastoral Educator
☐ Social Worker

Intelligence
☐ All Source Intelligence Officer
☐ Artificial Intelligence Officer
☐ Attaché
☐ Counterintelligence Officer
☐ Human Intelligence Officer
☐ Imagery Intelligence Officer
☐ Psychological Operations and Civil Affairs Officer

☐ Signals Intelligence/Electronic
   Warfare Officer
☐ Strategic Debriefer and Interrogator
☐ Strategic Intelligence Officer
☐ Technical Intelligence Officer

Law Enforcement
☐ CID Investigations Officer
☐ Inspector General
☐ Military Police Officer

Legal
☐ Claims/Litigation Specialist
☐ Government Contract Law Specialist
☐ International Law Specialist
☐ Judge Advocate General
☐ Military Judge

Media & Public Affairs
☐ Broadcast Officer
☐ Public Affairs Officer
☐ Visual Information Officer

Medical and Health Care
☐ Aeromedical Evacuation Officer
☐ Behavioral Sciences Officer
☐ Clinical Nurse
☐ Clinical Psychology Officer
☐ Community Health Nurse
☐ Dietitian
☐ Health Care Administration Officer
☐ Health Services Administration
   Officer
☐ Health Services Comptroller
☐ Health Services Human Resources
   Officer
☐ Health Services Officer
☐ Health Services Systems Management
   Officer
☐ Laboratory Sciences Officer
☐ Medical-Surgical Nurse
☐ Nurse Administrator
☐ Nurse Anesthetist
☐ Obstetric and Gynecologic Nurse
☐ Occupational Therapy Officer

☐ Operating Room Nurse
☐ Optometrist
☐ Patient Administration Officer
☐ Pediatric Nurse
☐ Pharmacy Officer
☐ Physical Therapy Officer
☐ Physician's Assistant
☐ Podiatrist
☐ Preventive Medicine Sciences Officer
☐ Psychiatric/Mental Health Nurse

Medical Laboratory Science
☐ Biochemistry Officer
☐ Clinical Laboratory Officer
☐ Immunology Officer
☐ Microbiology Officer
☐ Parasitology Officer
☐ Research Psychology Officer

Medical (Preventive) Science
☐ Audiology Officer
☐ Entomology Officer
☐ Environmental Science Officer
☐ Nuclear Medical Science Officer
☐ Sanitary Engineer

Medical and Treatment Practitioner
☐ Allergist/Clinical Immunologist
☐ Anesthesiologist
☐ Cardiologist
☐ Child Neurologist
☐ Child Psychiatrist
☐ Clinical Pharmacologist
☐ Dentist
☐ Dermatologist
☐ Diagnostic Radiologist
☐ Emergency Physician
☐ Endocrinologist
☐ Endodontist
☐ Family Physician
☐ Field Surgeon
☐ Flight Surgeon
☐ Gastroenterologist
☐ General Surgeon
☐ Infectious Disease Officer

☐ Internist
☐ Medical Oncologist/Hematologist
☐ Nephrologist
☐ Neurologist
☐ Neurosurgeon
☐ Nuclear Medicine Officer
☐ Obstetrician/Gynecologist
☐ Occupational Medicine Officer
☐ Ophthalmologist
☐ Oral and Maxillofacial Surgeon
☐ Oral Pathologist
☐ Orthodontist
☐ Orthopedic Surgeon
☐ Otolaryngologist
☐ Pathologist
☐ Pediatric Cardiologist
☐ Pediatric Dentist
☐ Pediatrician
☐ Periodontist
☐ Peripheral Vascular Surgeon
☐ Plastic Surgeon
☐ Preventive Medicine Officer

☐ Prosthodontist
☐ Psychiatrist
☐ Public Health Dentist
☐ Pulmonary Disease Officer
☐ Rheumatologist
☐ Therapeutic Radiologist
☐ Thoracic Surgeon
☐ Urologist
☐ Veterinarian

Special Forces
☐ Green Beret Officer

Support
☐ Commissary Management Officer

Transportation
☐ Marine and Terminal Operations Officer
☐ Motor/Rail Transportation Officer
☐ Traffic Management Officer

Special Officer Opportunities and Programs

☐ **Judge Advocate General Corps**
☐ **Medical/Dental Corps Program**

Judge Advocate General Corps

Direct commissions are available to individuals who have graduated from an American Bar Association-accredited law school with a J.D. or L.L.B. degree. JAG Corps candidates are commissioned as first lieutenants, and promoted to captain after six to nine months of service.

Medical/Dental Corps Program

The Army offers financial assistance to students in medical and dental school and for certain medical corps specialties in return for specified periods of military service. Medical students who qualify receive tuition, books, fees, and a monthly allowance.

U.S. Army Reserve

☎ 800-USA-ARMY

SPECIAL OPPORTUNITIES AND PROGRAMS

Army Reserve Medical Programs

Registered nurses who are graduates of accredited diploma, associate degree, and baccalaureate degree programs may qualify for a commission in the reserves of the Army Nurse Corps.

Specialized Training Assistance Program (STRAP)

STRAP provides a stipend for physicians, dentists, and nurses who are training in certain specialties. In return for the stipend, the officer serves in the Selected Reserve or the Individual Ready Reserve. The stipend is available to the nurse specialties of critical care, pre-operative nursing, and nurse anesthesia, as well as R.N. to B.S.N. degree completion.

Health Professionals Loan Repayment (HPLR)

This program provides repayment of student loans at $3,000 per year up to $20,000 for physicians and nurses in selected specialties in return for service in the Selected Reserve.

Selected Reserve Recruitment Bonus Program

This program provides an annual bonus to critical skill physicians and nurses in return for service in the Selected Reserve.

U.S. Army National Guard

☎ 800-638-7600 or local National Guard Armory

Overview

The Army National Guard (ANG) has more than 2,600 units in about 3,600 communities across the nation and in its territories.

Special Opportunities and Programs

Program for Youths at Risk or the Challenge Program

Several states have a program for youths at risk. The goal of these programs is outstanding. These National Guard programs are federally funded (state-administered). Currently, many of the programs in the 14 states that administer them are at risk of losing their funding;

readers (particularly guidance counselors and educators) are strongly urged to contact their legislators and ask them to support these programs.

So noteworthy is this program that a sample state program is presented here. The purpose is two-fold. First, it may clearly depict a success program; second, it may serve as a template for other groups interested in developing a similar program.

The New York National Guard Youth Opportunity Program, called "ChalleNGe," is a federally funded, military-style youth corps program targeted at high school dropouts aged $16\frac{1}{2}$ to 18. Candidates must be drug-free and have no current involvement with law enforcement agencies (such as parole, probation, conditional/suspended sentence, and so on).

The purpose of this program is to instill values, teach skills, and provide the education necessary for young people to become responsible citizens. Candidates are housed at a National Guard camp for instructional training. The program encourages candidates who complete the program to obtain the High School Equivalency Diploma and pursue further education, obtain full-time employment in their communities, or join the military.

Candidates are given educational material; room and board are provided free of charge. They receive intensive two-week instruction geared for team building, evaluation, and feedback. Next, candidates receive 20 weeks of holistic focusing in several areas to include Educational Excellence, Community Service, Life Coping Skills, Physical Fitness, Health, Hygiene, and Citizenship. The post-residential activity centers around mentoring the candidates to help them stay focused through their transition into college, employment, or the military.

Age:	$16\frac{1}{2}$ to 18 (high school dropouts)
Comments:	Contact your state's National Guard headquarters or local National Guard recruiter to see if your state hosts a similar program.

[Sample Contract Oath]

I solemnly affirm that every statement that I have given as a part of this interview is true. I further understand that this is a contract and that I am morally obligated to abide by it. I understand that the New York National Guard ChalleNGe Program does not tolerate profanity, drug usage, disrespect, or any form of illicit or violent behavior.

I understand that if I do not abide by the terms of this contract or give false information either by speaking or in writing, I will be subject to severe penalties or dismissal from the program. I further submit, by signing this contract, that I will put forth 100 percent of my energy and strength to complete the program if selected to attend. I enter into this agreement on my own free will/choosing. I am of sound mind.

(YOUTH'S NAME)   (SIGNATURE)

(WITNESS NAME)   (SIGNATURE)

Inventory of U.S. Army Aircraft, Tanks, and Weapons——

- ☐ **Aircraft**
- ☐ **Tracked Vehicles**
- ☐ **Howitzers**
- ☐ **Missiles**

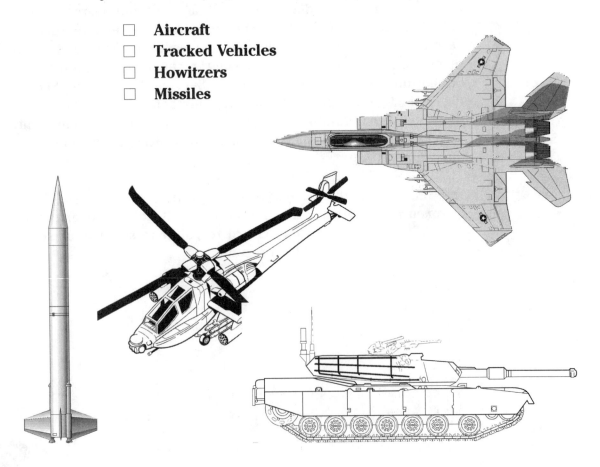

OVERVIEW The Army's fighting machines, such as the Bradley Tanks, are famous for winning battles quickly and decisively; however, during Desert Storm, the artillery, specifically the Patriot Missile systems, won the day. The Army also maintains an impressive helicopter fleet.

Aircraft

AH-1	Cobra Attack Helicopter
AH-60	Black Hawk Attack Helicopter
AH-64	Apache Attack Helicopter
CH-47	Chinook Medium Lift Transport Helicopter
OH-58	Kiowa Warrior (Scout) Helicopter
UH-1	Iroquois Utility Helicopter

Special Profile	**Black Hawk UH-60**
Mission:	light utility and assault capability
Max gross weight:	22,000 lb
Cruise speed:	139 kt
Endurance:	2.3 hr
Max range:	320 nm
Crew:	2 pilots, 1 crew
Armament:	two 7.62 mm machine guns
Payload:	2,640 lb (or 11 combat equipped troops)
External load:	8,000 lb

Tracked Vehicles

M1 Series Machine Battle Tank
M2/M3 Bradley Fighting Vehicle System
M9 Armored Combat Earthmover
M113 Series Armored Personnel Carrier

Special Profile	**M1 Abrams Tank**
Mission:	heavy armor superiority on the battlefield
Length:	32.04 ft
Width:	12 ft
Height:	7.79 ft
Top speed:	45 mph
Weight:	60 ton
Armament:	105 mm
Crew:	4

Howitzers

M109 Series 155mm Self-Propelled Howitzer
M198 Series 155mm Towed Howitzer

Missiles

Air-to-Ground Missile Systems
Avenger Surface-to-Air Missile Systems
Multiple-Launch Rocket System
Nuclear, Biological, and Chemical Reconnaissance System
Patriot Missile System (of Desert Storm fame)
Stinger Manportable Anti-Aircraft Missiles
TOW (Tube-Launched, Optically Tracked, Wire-Guided) Missile
System

ADDITIONAL RESOURCES

Videos:

"America's Elite: Elites of the U.S. Army, Navy, and Marines—82nd
Airborne Division, 101st Division, U.S. Marine Corps, and U.S. Navy
Seals"
"Army Rangers"

Books:

Armored Cav: A Guided Tour of an Armed Cavalry Regiment by Tom
Clancy (1997)
Army Officer's Guide by Lawrence Crocker (1996)
The Soldier's Guidebook by Col. Bluhm and Col. Motley (1997)

Magazines:

Army Times
Soldiers (official magazine of the U.S. Army)

Popular Movies:

You're in the Army Now (1941: Phil Silvers)—Army Comedy
The Story of GI Joe (1945: Burgess Meredith)—Classic WWII Drama
The Dirty Dozen (1967: Lee Marvin)—Classic WWII Saga
The Green Berets (1968: John Wayne)—Vietnam War Drama
M*A*S*H (1970: Donald Sutherland)—Korean War Comedy
Patton (1970: George C. Scott)—Classic WWII Saga
Apocalypse Now (1979: Marlon Brando)—Vietnam War Drama
Private Benjamin (1980: Goldie Hawn)—Boot Camp Comedy
The Big Red One (1980: Lee Marvin)—Infantry Classic Drama
Stripes (1981: Bill Murray)—Boot Camp Comedy
Streamers (1983: Matthew Modine)—Vietnam War Drama
Platoon (1986: Tom Berenger)—Vietnam War Drama
The Delta Force (1986: Lee Marvin)—Antiterrorist Drama
Full Metal Jacket (1987: Matthew Modine)—Boot Camp/Vietnam War Drama
Biloxi Blues (1988: Matthew Broderick)—Boot Camp Comedy
The Tank (1996: Jim Belushi)—WWII Comedy
Courage under Fire (1997: Meg Ryan)—Desert Storm Drama
G.I. Jane (1997: Demi Moore)—Navy SEAL Drama
Saving Private Ryan (1998: Tom Hanks)—WWII Drama

Advisory

You should not make a career decision based on a popular movie or television show. Remember: They are, for the most part, based loosely on facts or truths. Your final decision should be based on research into what will be good for you; however, popular movies and films can provide fine entertainment dealing with the military service.

Chapter 7

U.S. COAST GUARD

U.S. Coast Guard

U.S. Coast Guard Recruiting
4200 Wilson Boulevard
Arlington, VA 22203

☎ 800-GET USCG
http://www.dot.gov/dotinfo/uscg

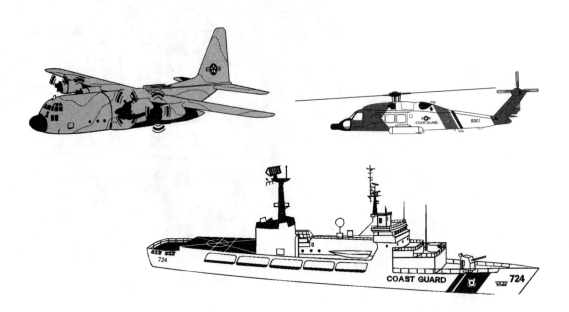

History:	**1790**—Established originally as the Revenue Cutter Service
	1915—Formed under the U.S. Treasury Department as U.S. Coast Guard
	1967—Became part of the U.S. Department of Transportation
Motto:	***Semper Paratus*** (Always Ready)
Recruiting Slogans:	**The Lifesavers**
	Jobs That Matter
	(Recruits 8,000 new personnel per year)

PROFILE OF USCG PERSONNEL

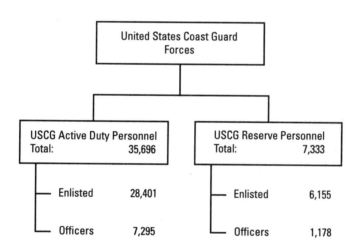

OVERVIEW   The Coast Guard has a proud history and good public image. Most people associate the Coast Guard not only with its search and rescue operations, but also with drug and illegal alien interdiction. Established by the Act of January 28, 1915, the Coast Guard became a component of the Department of Transportation on April 1, 1967. The predecessor of the Coast Guard—the Revenue Cutter Service—was established in 1790 as a federal maritime law enforcement agency. The United States Coast Guard is a service of the Armed Forces and is a branch of the U.S. Department of Transportation. In time of war or when the president so directs, it becomes a part of the Department of Defense and comes under the command of the U.S. Navy. The Coast Guard consists of ships, aircraft, boats, and shore stations that conduct a variety of missions. While it is one of the oldest services, it is also the smallest. It offers a wide variety of career and educational opportunities. The Coast Guard Reserve offers the same career fields as the active Coast Guard.

MISSION   The U.S. Coast Guard has a larger variety of missions than the other services. Here is a brief overview of each.

- *Aids to Navigation:* Establishes and maintains the U.S. aids to navigation system.

- *Bridge Administration:* Administers the statutes regulating the construction, maintenance, and operation of bridges and causeways across navigable waters.

- *Search and Rescue:* Maintains a system of rescue vessels, aircraft, and communications facilities to carry out the function of saving life and property.

- *Maritime Law Enforcement:* Serves as the primary maritime law enforcement agency for the United States.

- *Marine Inspection:* Formulates, administers, and enforces various safety standards for the design, construction, equipment, and maintenance of commercial vessels.

- *Marine Licensing:* Administers a system for evaluating and licensing of U.S. Merchant Marine personnel.

- *Marine Environmental Response:* Enforces the Federal Water Pollution Control Act and various other laws relating to the protection of the marine environment.

- *Port Safety and Security:* Oversees the safety and security of ports and anchorages, and the movement of vessels and prevention of pollution in U.S. waters.

- *Ice Operations:* Operates the nation's icebreaking vessels.

- ***Boating Safety:*** Develops and directs a national boating safety program aimed at making the operation of small craft in U.S. waters both pleasurable and safe.

- ***Military Readiness:*** Provides coastal and harbor defense, including port security.

MAJOR U.S. COAST GUARD COMMANDS

UNITED STATES COAST GUARD ORGANIZATION

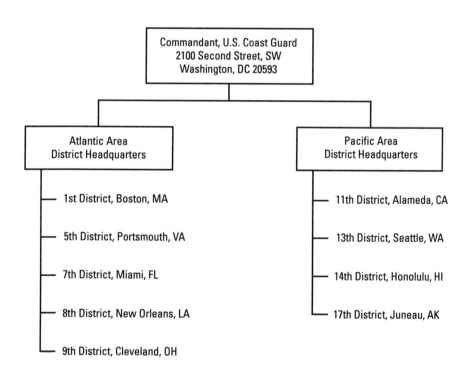

Ships and Stations of the Coast Guard
Coast Guard Large Vessels: 242
Coast Guard Shore Stations: 1,234

Typical Shore Stations/Units
1. Aids to Navigation Teams
2. Air Stations
3. Bases/Support Centers
4. Communications Stations
5. Electronic Shops
6. Group Offices
7. Light Stations
8. LORAN C Stations
9. Marine Inspection Offices
10. Marine Safety Offices
11. Reserve Port Security Units
12. Small Boat Stations
13. Vessel Traffic Services

Enlisted Opportunities

☐ **Enlisted Career Fields**
☐ **Special Enlisted Opportunities and Programs**

Enlisted Entrance Overview

Age: 17 to 28 years
Enlistments: 2 to 6 years (Regular Active Duty)

Recruit (Basic or Boot Camp) Training

Duration: 8 weeks
Location: Cape May, NJ
Instruction: seamanship, ordnance, damage control, Coast Guard history, and military and technical subjects

Enlisted Promotion Path

Promotions occur through a series of written and practical exams that test proficiency in a specialty. It is possible to advance from Seaman Recruit to Chief Petty Officer within 14 years.

E-1   *Recruit*—(Basic or Boot) Training

E-2   *Seaman or Fireman Apprentice*—Completion of basic training

E-3   *Seaman or Fireman*—Six months active duty service and commander's recommendation

E-4   *Petty Officer Third Class*—Six months active duty service, six months time in grade, and commander's recommendation

E-5–E-6   *Petty Officer Second Class to Petty Officer First Class*—Test against peers in job skill; must meet promotion criteria

E-7–E-9   *Chief Petty Officer and above*—Must meet selection board criteria

---

Critical Need—Enlisted Career Fields

Boatswain's Mates (BM)
Machinery Technicians (MK)
Radarmen (RD)
Subsistence Specialists (SS)

ENLISTED CAREER FIELDS

Rates/Military Occupational Specialties

(See Chapter 12 for more information on Enlisted Career Fields.)

Administrative
☐ Storekeeper (SK)
☐ Yeoman (YN)

Aviation
☐ Aviation Electrician's Mate (AE)
☐ Aviation Electronics Technician (AT)
☐ Aviation Machinist Mate (AD)
☐ Aviation Structural Mechanic (AM)
☐ Aviation Survivalman (ASM)

Communications and Computer
☐ Radioman (RM)
☐ Telecommunications Specialist (TC)
☐ Telephone Technician (TT)

Electrician and Electronics
☐ Electrician's Mate (EM)
☐ Electronics Technician (ET)

Engineering and Technical
☐ Damage Controlman (DC)
☐ Radarman (RD)

Mechanics
☐ Machinery Technician (MK)

Media and Public Affairs
☐ Public Affairs Specialist (PA)

Medical
☐ Health Services Technician (HS)

Music
☐ Musician (MU)

Ordinance
☐ Fire Control Technician (FT)
☐ Gunner's Mate (GM)

Science
☐ Marine Science Technician (MST)

Service (Cook)
☐ Subsistence Specialist (SS)

Ship and Boat Operations
☐ Boatswain's Mate (BM)
☐ Quartermaster (QM)

Reservist-Only Ratings
☐ Data Processing Technician (DP)
☐ Investigator (IV)
☐ Port Securityman (PS)

Special Enlisted Opportunities and Programs

☐ **Tuition Assistance Program**
☐ **Precommissioning Program for Enlisted Personnel**

Tuition Assistance Program

Coast Guard and Coast Guard Reserve personnel on active duty are eligible to participate in this program, which pays up to 75 percent of tuition fees.

Precommissioning Program for Enlisted Personnel

This program allows Coast Guard enlisted men and women to attend college fulltime for two years with a goal of qualifying for officer candidate school.

Warrant Officer (W-1 to W-3)

The rank of Warrant Officer in the Coast Guard is restricted to members who have demonstrated a potential for greater responsibility than normally expected of petty officers. This is not an entry-level position. Warrant Officers are assigned responsibilities and have authority commensurate with their rank, including assignments as commanding officers and engineering officers in many types of units. Warrant Officer example: CWO3—Chief Warrant Officer Boatswain's Mate.

Officer Opportunities

☐ **Standard Officer Commissioning Programs**
☐ **Officer Career Fields**
☐ **Special Officer Opportunities and Programs**

STANDARD ☐ **U.S. Coast Guard Academy**
OFFICER ☐ **U.S. Naval Academy Preparatory School**
COMMIS- ☐ **Officer Candidate School**
SIONING ☐ **Direct Commissions**
PROGRAMS

U.S. Coast Guard Academy

Largest source of U.S. Coast Guard Officers
The four-year academic program leads to a bachelor of science degree in a variety of majors. Upon graduation, the cadet is commissioned as an ensign in the Coast Guard.
(See Chapter 10—Military Academies.)

U.S. Naval Academy Preparatory School

The U.S. Naval Academy Preparatory School (NAPS) accepts qualified civilian applicants and applicants from the regular and reserve components of the Navy, Marine Corps, and Coast Guard.
(See Chapter 10—Military Preparatory Schools.)

Officer Candidate School

OCS is a rigorous 17-week course of instruction that prepares candidates to serve effectively as officers in the United States Coast Guard. Candidates must have already earned a bachelor's degree and meet specific age and medical requirements. Upon graduation, students are commissioned as ensigns in the United States Coast Guard.

Direct Commissions

There are several direct commissioning programs in the Coast Guard, along with programs for previously trained military officers, aviators, flight officers, lawyers, maritime academy graduates, engineers, and other critically needed specialists.

Critical Need—Officer Career Fields

Engineering
Environment Protection
Marine Science

OFFICER CAREER FIELDS

Military Occupational Specialties

(See Chapter 13 for more information on Officer Career Fields.)

Administration
- [ ] Communications Officer
- [ ] Computers Officer
- [ ] Finance and Accounting Officer
- [ ] Instructor
- [ ] Personnel Officer

Aviation
- [ ] Aircraft Pilot
- [ ] Aviation Engineer
- [ ] Helicopter Pilot
- [ ] Navigator

Combat
- [ ] Defense Operations Officer

Engineering, Science, and Technical
- [ ] Chemist
- [ ] Civil Engineer
- [ ] Environmental Protection Officer
- [ ] Industrial Manager
- [ ] Meteorologist
- [ ] Naval Engineer
- [ ] Nuclear Engineer
- [ ] Ocean Engineer

Human Services
- [ ] Religious Services Officer

Intelligence
- [ ] Attaché
- [ ] Intelligence Officer

Law Enforcement
- [ ] Boating Safety Officer
- [ ] Drug Interdiction Officer
- [ ] Maritime Law Enforcement Officer
- [ ] Port Security and Safety Officer

Legal
- [ ] Judge
- [ ] Lawyer

Marine Services
- [ ] Icebreaker Officer
- [ ] Marine Inspection Officer
- [ ] Marine Licensing Officer
- [ ] Marine Science Officer
- [ ] Navigation Systems Officer
- [ ] Vessel Inspection Officer
- [ ] Waterways Management Officer

Media and Public Affairs
- [ ] Public Information Officer

Medical
(U.S. Public Health Service Officers)
- [ ] Dental Officer
- [ ] Pharmacist
- [ ] Physician
- [ ] Registered Nurse
- [ ] Surgeon
- [ ] Therapist

Music
- [ ] Band Director

Ship Operations
- [ ] Search and Rescue Officer
- [ ] Ship Officer

Special Officer Opportunities and Programs

☐   **Aviation Program**
☐   **M.O.R.E.**
☐   **Physician's Assistant Program**
☐   **Postgraduate Education Program**
☐   **Tuition Assistance Program**
☐   **U.S. Public Health Service**

Aviation Program

Coast Guard aviation training is available to selected officers. Pilot trainees attend basic and advanced flight training at naval air stations. The Coast Guard also commissions a limited number of prior service aviators.

M.O.R.E.

The Minority Officer Recruiting Effort (M.O.R.E.) is open to minority students attending historically black colleges or other approved institutions with significant minority populations. After graduation, the M.O.R.E. student will attend Officer Candidate School and receive a reserve commission as an ensign.

Physician's Assistant Program

The Physician's Assistant Program is a two-year, full-time course of study. Upon successful completion, Coast Guard graduates receive their certificates as physician's assistants and direct commissions as ensigns. Completion of the program results in a bachelor's degree in health science.

Postgraduate Education Program

This program offers qualified officers an opportunity to obtain advanced education on a full-time basis at Coast Guard expense. They attend various colleges and universities in more than 30 major curriculum areas.

Tuition Assistance Program

The Coast Guard sponsors a tuition assistance program for off-duty education within the limits of available funds. This program allows Coast Guard officers to enroll in off-duty courses at accredited colleges and universities.

U.S. Public Health Service

The main source of U.S. Coast Guard Medical Officers. Coast Guard students enrolled in an accredited medical or osteopathy school may receive a monthly stipend plus tuition and fees. Upon receiving their degree, they serve with the U.S. Public Health Service (USPHS) on active duty with the Coast Guard or other USPHS agencies for one year for every year of subsidized training.

U.S. Coast Guard Reserve

☎ 1-800-GET USCG

Special Opportunities and Programs

U.S. Coast Guard Reserve Skills Program

This program allows first-time military enlistees with specialized professional skills to receive a Petty Officer rating (age 26–35 years). Prior service personnel up to age 42, who were E-4 and above, may be able to enlist/reenlist.

Inventory of U.S. Coast Guard Cutters, Aircraft, Boats, and Ships

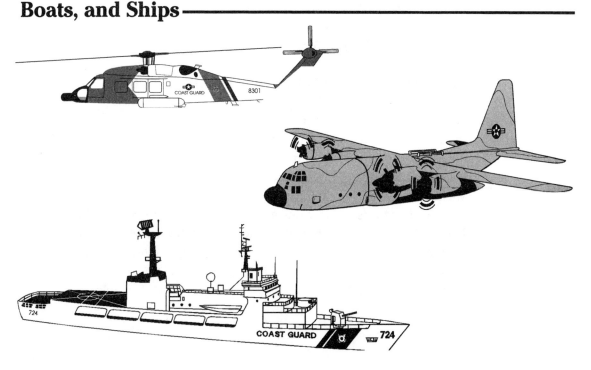

OVERVIEW   The Coast Guard operates a variety of cutters for ocean missions and small boats for coastal patrol and search and rescue. C-130 planes and helicopters assist in the missions of law enforcement, information gathering, and search and rescue. The Polar Icebreakers conduct scientific missions in the Arctic and Antarctic and perform icebreaking duties for shipping.

Cutters

(Any CG vessel 65 feet in length or greater)
399 feet—Polar Class Icebreaker
378 feet—High Endurance Cutter
295 feet—Training Barque Eagle (Academy)
290 feet—Inland Icebreaker
270 feet—Medium Endurance Cutter
225 feet—Seagoing Buoy Tender
210 feet—Medium Endurance Cutter
180 feet—Seagoing Buoy Tender
175 feet—Coastal Buoy Tender
160 feet—Inland Construction Tender
157 feet—Coastal Buoy Tender
140 feet—Icebreaking Tug
133 feet—Coastal Buoy Tender
115 feet—River Buoy Tender
110 feet—Patrol Boat
100 feet—Inland Buoy Tender
100 feet—Inland Construction Tender
 75 feet—River Buoy Tender
 65 feet—River Buoy Tender
 65 feet—Inland Buoy Tender

Special Profile	**378-Foot High Endurance Cutter**
Length:	378 ft
Beam:	43 ft
Displacement:	3,250 tons
Power Plant:	two diesel engines/two gas turbine engines
Maximum Range:	14,000 miles
Maximum Speed:	29 kt
Primary Missions:	law enforcement, defense, search and rescue
Typical Crew:	167 personnel (19 officers, 148 enlisted personnel)

Planes

C-130   Hercules
HU-25   Falcon

Helicopters

H-60   Jayhawk
HH-65   Dolphin

Boats

(Sizes range from 64 feet in length down to 12 feet)
64–45 feet—Aids to Navigation Boats
47 feet—Motor Lifeboat
44 feet—Motor Lifeboat
41 feet—Utility Boat
Port Security Unit (PSU) Boats
Transportable Port Security Boats (TPSB)
Rigid Inflatable Boat

Special Profile	**Transportable Port Security Boat (TPSB)**
Length:	22 feet 3 inches
Beam:	7 feet 6 inches
Engines:	twin 150 HP OMC outboards
Speed:	40+ kts
Crew:	3–4 (including coxswain)

ADDITIONAL *Television:*
RESOURCES "Coast Guard"—Fox TV
"Icebreakers"—A&E

Books:
Guardians of the Sea: History of the U.S. Coast Guard by Robert Erwin Johnson (1987)
The Coast Guardsman's Manual by George Krietemeyer (1991)

Official Magazine:
Coast Guard

Popular Movies:
(Note: Hollywood apparently has had no love affair with the Coast Guard, but here are a few oldies.)
Sea Devils (1937: Victor McLaglen) Classic Saga
Coast Guard (1939: Randolph Scott) Classic Saga
Fighting Coast Guard (1951: Forrest Tucker) Classic WWII Saga

---

Advisory

You should not make a career decision based on a popular movie or television show. Remember: They are, for the most part, based loosely on facts or truths. Your final decision should be based on research into what will be good for you; however, popular movies and films can provide fine entertainment dealing with the military service.

Chapter 8

U.S. MARINE CORPS

U.S. Marine Corps

U.S. Marine Corps Recruiting Command
2 Navy Annex
Washington, DC 20380

☎ 800-MARINES
http://www.usmc.mil/mar

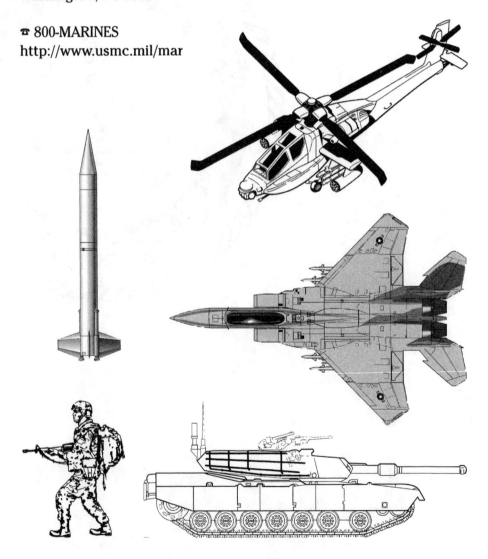

History:	**Established 1775 by Continental Congress**
Mottos:	**Semper Fidelis** or **Semper Fi** (Always Faithful) **One Shot, One Kill**
Elite Forces:	**Marine Expeditionary Unit (MEU)**
Recruiting Slogan:	**The Few...the Proud...the Marines** (Recruits 41,000 new personnel each year)

PROFILE OF USMC PERSONNEL

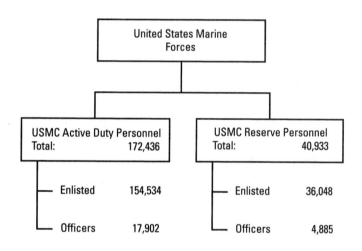

OVERVIEW   The Marine Corps, one of the oldest military services, was established on November 10, 1775 by the Continental Congress to act as landing forces with the naval fleet. On July 11, 1798, the United States Marine Corps was established as a separate service, and in 1834 it was made part of the Department of the Navy. The Marine Corps offers a wide variety of career and educational opportunities. The Marine Corps Reserve offers the same career fields as the active Marine Corps.

MISSION   The Marines are an elite fighting force. Part of the Department of the Navy, they operate in close cooperation with U.S. naval forces at sea. Marines serve on U.S. navy ships, protect naval bases, guard U.S. embassies, and provide a quick, ever-ready strike force to protect U.S. interests anywhere in the world. The Marine Corps is also responsible for developing programs including tactics, techniques, and equipment used by landing forces.

Special Operations Forces—Marine Expeditionary Unit (MEU)

The MEU is a small tactical unit of the Marine Corps Air/Ground Task Force. The elite MEU has approximately 2,200 members. Its mission is to serve as an "expeditionary intervention force with the ability to rapidly organize for combat operations in virtually any environment. Naval Special Warfare encompasses operations generally accepted as being unconventional in nature and clandestine in character, including use of specially trained and equipped forces."

WHERE THEY SERVE   Total of personnel assigned ashore (bases):   169,431
Total of personnel assigned afloat (ships):   5,208

MAJOR U.S. MARINE CORPS COMMANDS AND BASES

U.S. Marine Corps Headquarters
2 Navy Annex
Washington, DC 20380–1775

California
I Marine Expeditionary Force, MCB Camp Pendleton
1st Marine Division, MCB Camp Pendleton
1st Force Service Support Group, MCB Camp Pendleton
3rd Marine Aircraft Wing, MCAS El Toro

Hawaii
Marine Forces Pacific, Camp Smith

Louisiana
Marine Reserve Forces, New Orleans

North Carolina
II Marine Expeditionary Force, MCB Camp Lejeune
2nd Marine Division, MCB Camp Lejeune
2nd Marine Aircraft Wing, MCAS Cherry Point
2nd Force Service Support Group, MCB Camp Lejeune

Virginia
Marine Forces Atlantic, Norfolk

Japan
III Marine Expeditionary Force, MCB Camp Courtney, Okinawa
3rd Marine Division, MCB Camp Smedley D. Butler, Okinawa
1st Marine Aircraft Wing, MCB Camp Butler, Okinawa
3rd Force Service Support Group, Camp Kinser, Okinawa

Enlisted Opportunities

☐ **U.S. Marine Corps Enlisted Career Fields**
☐ **Special Enlisted Opportunities and Programs**

Enlisted Entrance Overview

Age: 17 to 28 years
Enlistments: 3, 4, and 5 years

Recruit (Basic or Boot Camp) Training

Duration: 11 weeks
Location: Parris Island, SC
               San Diego, CA
Instruction: physical fitness, weapons handling/firing and marks-
               manship, field skills, close order drill, Marine Corps
               history, customs and courtesies, and related subjects

Required Combat Training

Due to the overall mission of the Marine Corps, immediately following recruit training, male Marines attend four weeks of combat training, which is follow-up instruction in advanced field and combat
skills. This training is conducted at the School of Infantry at either
Camp Lejeune, NC, or Camp Pendleton, CA. Although both males and
females receive intense periods of instruction in defensive combat,
only males receive instruction in offensive combat. Female Marines
receive a combined package of recruit training and follow-up field
skills training while at Parris Island over a 12-week period.

Enlisted Promotion Path

E-1 *Recruit*—(Basic or Boot) Training

E-2 *Private First Class*—Six months active duty and commander's recommendation

E-3 *Lance Corporal*—Eight months active time in grade, nine months time in service (and commander's recommendation)

E-4 *Corporal*—Twelve months active duty service, eight months time in grade (and commander's recommendation)

E-5 *Sergeant*—24 months active duty service, 12 months time in grade (and commander's recommendation)

E-6–E-9 *Staff Sergeant and above*—Must meet various time in grade requirements and Marine Corps selection board criteria

Critical Needs—Enlisted Career Fields

Aviation Maintenance Officer
Cavalry Scout
Combat Engineer
Field Artillery Officer
Infantryman

Special Operations Forces

Marine Expeditionary Unit (MEU)

ENLISTED CAREER FIELDS

Military Occupational Specialties

(See Chapter 12 for more information on Enlisted Career Fields.)

Administration
- ☐ Accounting Clerk
- ☐ Administrative Clerk
- ☐ Drill Instructor
- ☐ Personal Finance Records Clerk
- ☐ Personnel Clerk
- ☐ Postal Clerk
- ☐ Recruiter
- ☐ Subsistence Supply Clerk
- ☐ Travel Clerk
- ☐ Unit Diary Clerk

Aviation
- ☐ Aerial Navigator
- ☐ Air Control Electronics Specialist
- ☐ Air Crew Survival Equipment Specialist
- ☐ Air Support Operations Operator
- ☐ Air Traffic Controller
- ☐ Airborne Radio Operator
- ☐ Aircraft Firefighting/Rescue Specialist
- ☐ Aircraft Recovery Specialist
- ☐ Aviation Machinist Mate (Jet Engine)
- ☐ Aviation Maintenance Administration Specialist
- ☐ Aviation Operations Clerk
- ☐ Aviation Safety Equipment Specialist
- ☐ Aviation Support Equipment Technician

Combat
- ☐ Air Delivery Specialist
- ☐ Amphibian Crewman
- ☐ Antitank Assault Guided Missileman
- ☐ Artillery Meteorologist
- ☐ Assaultman
- ☐ Basic Field Artilleryman
- ☐ Basic Infantryman
- ☐ Basic Logistics Marine

- ☐ Combat Service Support Chief
- ☐ Field Artillery, Cannoneer
- ☐ Field Artillery Operations Man
- ☐ Field Artillery Radar Operator
- ☐ Fire Support Man
- ☐ Hawk Missile Systems Operator
- ☐ Infantry Unit Leader
- ☐ Landing Support Specialist
- ☐ Light Armored Vehicle Crewman
- ☐ Machine Gunner
- ☐ Maintenance Management Specialist
- ☐ Mortarman
- ☐ Reconnaissance Man
- ☐ Red Artillery Fire Controlman
- ☐ Redeye Gunner
- ☐ Rifleman
- ☐ Tactical Air Defense Controller
- ☐ Tank Crewman

Engineering, Science, and Technical
- ☐ Ammunition Storage Specialist
- ☐ Aviation Electrician Mate
- ☐ Aviation Fire Control Technician
- ☐ Aviation Ordnance Munitions Technician
- ☐ Aviation Radio Technician
- ☐ Avionics Technician
- ☐ Basic Engineer
- ☐ Basic Surface/Nuclear Weapon Disposal Specialist
- ☐ Communications Center Operator
- ☐ Computer Operator
- ☐ Construction Wireman
- ☐ Data Control Specialist
- ☐ Field Radio Operator
- ☐ Ground Radar Technician
- ☐ High-Frequency Communication Central Operator
- ☐ Imagery Interpretation Equipment Repairman

☐ Improved Hawk Fire Control Technician
☐ Improved Hawk Missile Technician
☐ Meteorological Equipment Maintenance Technician
☐ Microwave Equipment Operator
☐ Precision Measuring Equipment Technician
☐ Systems Programmer
☐ Tactical Satellite Microwave System Operator
☐ Weather Forecaster

Intelligence
☐ Basic Intelligence Marine Specialist
☐ Counterintelligence Specialist
☐ Electronic Warfare Specialist
☐ Imagery Intelligence Specialist
☐ Intelligence Intercept Specialist
☐ Intelligence Specialist
☐ Interrogation Translation Specialist
☐ Topography Intelligence Specialist
☐ Voice Processing Specialist

Law Enforcement and Security
☐ Corrections Specialist
☐ Criminal Investigations Officer
☐ Marine Security Guard
☐ Military Police

Legal
☐ Legal Services Reporter
☐ Legal Services Specialist

Machinists, Mechanics, and Precision
☐ Assault Amphibian Repairman
☐ Automotive Maintenance Specialist
☐ Aviation Hydraulic Mechanic
☐ Aviation Radio Repairer
☐ Aviation Radio Technician
☐ Aviation Structure Mechanic
☐ Cable Splicing Specialist
☐ Electric Equipment Repair Specialist
☐ Electro-Optical Instrument Repairer

☐ Engineer Equipment Operator
☐ Fuel and Electric Systems Repairer
☐ Ground Radio Repairer
☐ Light Armored Vehicle Repairer
☐ Metal Worker
☐ Meteorological Equipment Specialist
☐ Refrigeration Mechanic
☐ Small Arms Repairer
☐ Small Craft Mechanic
☐ Telephone Switchboard Repairer
☐ Teletype Repairer
☐ Test Instrument Repairer
☐ Tracked Vehicle Repairer
☐ Vehicle Body Repairer

Media and Public Affairs
☐ Apprentice Imagery Production Specialist
☐ Apprentice Visual Information Specialist
☐ Audiovisual Equipment Technician
☐ Basic Broadcaster
☐ Basic Journalist
☐ Basic Offset Printing Specialist
☐ Basic Photographic Process Specialist
☐ Graphics Specialist
☐ Production Specialist
☐ Still Photographer Specialist

Music
☐ Assistant Bandleader
☐ Drum and Bugle Corps Member
☐ Musician

Support Service
☐ Basic Food Service Specialist
☐ Club Management Specialist

Transportation
☐ Motor Vehicle Operator
☐ Tractor Trailer Operator
☐ Traffic Management Coordinator

Special Enlisted Opportunities and Programs

Marine Corps College Enlistment Program

This program offers accelerated promotion to the rank of Lance Corporal (E-3) in high-tech fields. An applicant must possess an associate degree or a postsecondary education equal to an associate degree (minimum of 60 semester hours or 90 quarter hours) from an accredited school.

Marine Corps Quality Enlistment Program

This program offers similar incentives to qualified high school graduates. Applicants may choose their military occupational field and geographic area of assignment.

Marine Corps Enlistment Options Program

This program offers training and assignments in a job skill to qualified applicants who demonstrate interest and aptitude.

Marine Corps Musician Enlistment Option Program

This program offers qualified instrumentalists training and assignment in one of the Marine Corps field bands. Exceptional musicians are eligible for accelerated promotion and guaranteed duty-station assignment.

Marine Corps Enlisted Commissioning Education Program

This provides selected enlisted Marines, ages 20 to 26, with an opportunity to earn a baccalaureate degree by attending a college or university full-time. After obtaining a degree and completing officer candidate school, MECEP graduates are commissioned regular second lieutenants.

Degree Completion Program for Staff Noncommissioned Officers

This program provides selected staff noncommissioned officers with the opportunity to obtain a baccalaureate degree while attending a college or university full-time. Eligibility is limited to Marines in the grades of Staff Sergeant through First Sergeant/Master Sergeant.

The Marine Corps College Fund

This is related to the Montgomery GI Bill. It can provide up to $30,000 in educational benefits to enlistees.

Officer Opportunities

☐ **Standard Officer Commissioning Programs**
☐ **Officer Career Fields**
☐ **Special Officer Opportunities and Programs**

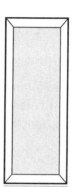

Standard Officer Commissioning Programs

☐ **U.S. Naval Academy**
☐ **Direct Commissions**
☐ **Naval Academy Preparatory School**
☐ **NROTC**
☐ **Platoon Leaders Class**
☐ **BOOST**
☐ **Officer Candidate Class**

U.S. Naval Academy

This program accepts Marine Corps candidates as midshipmen. The academy offers bachelor of science degrees and reserve commissions as second lieutenants to graduates.
(See Chapter 10—Military Academies.)

Direct Commissions

There are several direct commissioning programs. Programs exist for prior trained military officers, aviators, lawyers, medical and health professionals, engineers, and others who possess a four-year degree from a college or university.

Naval Academy Preparatory School
This program accepts applications from active duty and inactive reserve members of the Marine Corps.
(See Chapter 10—Military Preparatory Schools.)

Reserve Officer Training Corps (NROTC)

Navy/Marine Corps ROTC programs are offered at more than 65 colleges and universities across the country. College students who complete four years of naval science study may receive Marine Corps commissions as second lieutenants. The Navy ROTC offers several options to earn an Marine Corps commission:

>Four-Year Program
>Two-Year Program
>One-Year Program
>NROTC Three- and Four-Year Scholarships
>NROTC Pre-Health Professions Program
>NROTC Nurse Program

(See Chapter 11—ROTC Opportunities.)

Platoon Leaders Class

The Platoon Leaders Class (PLC) Program is for those college freshmen, sophomores, and juniors who have made the decision to pursue a Marine Corps officer commission.

Broadened Opportunity for Officer Selection and Training (BOOST)

BOOST offers active duty enlisted men and women the opportunity to receive up to 12 months of extensive academic preparation in order to become more competitive for selection to the Naval Academy, Marine Corps Enlisted Commissioning Education Program (MECEP), and Navy/Marine Corps ROTC scholarship programs.

Officer Candidate Class

Under the officer candidate programs, male and female graduates of an accredited four-year college or university and graduates of accredited law schools licensed to practice in a state or federal court are eligible for a reserve commission.

Critical Needs—Officer Career Fields

Aviation
Combat
Engineer
Infantry

Special Operations Forces

Marine Expeditionary Unit (MEU)

OFFICER CAREER FIELDS

Military Occupational Specialties

(See Chapter 13 for more information on Officer Career Fields.)

Administrative
- [ ] Basic Personnel and Administration Officer
- [ ] Civil Administration Officer
- [ ] Contracting Officer
- [ ] Instructor
- [ ] International Relations Officer
- [ ] Management Analyst
- [ ] Personnel Officer
- [ ] Postal Officer
- [ ] Procurement Officer
- [ ] Supply Officer
- [ ] Training Officer
- [ ] Warehouse Officer

Aviation
- [ ] Air Traffic Control Manager
- [ ] Airplane Pilot
- [ ] Helicopter Pilot
- [ ] Navigator

Combat
- [ ] Embarkation Officer
- [ ] Field Artillery Officer
- [ ] Infantry Officer
- [ ] Infantry Weapons Officer
- [ ] Light Armored Vehicle Officer
- [ ] Logistics Officer
- [ ] Missile Systems Officer

Engineer, Science, and Technical
- [ ] Astronaut
- [ ] Bulk Fuel Officer
- [ ] Cartographer
- [ ] Construction Officer
- [ ] Electronics Engineer
- [ ] Engineer Equipment Officer
- [ ] Engineering Officer
- [ ] Facilities Management Officer
- [ ] Physicist
- [ ] Space Operations Officer
- [ ] Survey and Meteorological Officer

Human Services
- [ ] Chaplain (Navy)

Intelligence
- [ ] Air Intelligence Officer
- [ ] Basic Intelligence Officer
- [ ] Counterintelligence Officer
- [ ] Ground Electronic Warfare Officer
- [ ] Ground Intelligence Officer

☐ Human Resource Intelligence Officer
☐ Marine Air/Ground Task Force
   Intelligence Officer
☐ Signal Intelligence Officer
☐ Tactical Intelligence Officer
☐ Topographic Intelligence Officer

Law Enforcement
☐ Corrections Officer
☐ Inspector General
☐ Military Police

Legal
☐ Lawyer
☐ Military Judge

Media and Public Affairs
☐ Audiovisual and Broadcast Director
☐ Public Information Officer

Medical
(Navy Personnel)

Music
☐ Band Director

Special Operations Forces
☐ MEU Officer

Support Service
☐ Food Service Officer
☐ Store Manager

Transportation
☐ Aircraft Maintenance Officer
☐ Automotive Maintenance Officer
☐ Aviation Maintenance Officer
☐ Transportation Manager

Special Officer Opportunities and Programs

Special Education Program

This program allows officers to earn master's degrees in designated disciplines by attending the Naval Postgraduate School, the Air Force Institute of Technology, or approved civilian schools.

Advanced Degree Program

Under the Advanced Degree Program, expenses for the cost of a master's degree are partially funded. Officers are selected to study in a particular technical or nontechnical discipline and may attend the accredited school of their choice.

Excess Leave Program—Law

The Excess Leave Program—Law provides qualified Marine Corps officers the opportunity to take time off from active duty to attend an accredited law school at their own expense.

Funded Law Education Program

Under the Funded Law Education Program, Marine Corps officers attend an accredited law school of their choice, with the Marine Corps paying their tuition and expenses. Full pay and allowances are provided to these officers.

U.S. Marine Corps Reserve

☎ 1-800-MARINES

Special Opportunities and Programs

U.S. Marine Corps Reserve

Provides most of the same special training and education opportunities as regular enlistment and can provide enlistment bonuses for certain specialties.

Inventory of U.S. Marine Corps Aircraft, Tanks, and Vehicles

- ☐ **Aircraft**
- ☐ **Armored Vehicles**
- ☐ **Helicopters**
- ☐ **Missiles**
- ☐ **Tracked Vehicles**
- ☐ **Additional Vehicles**

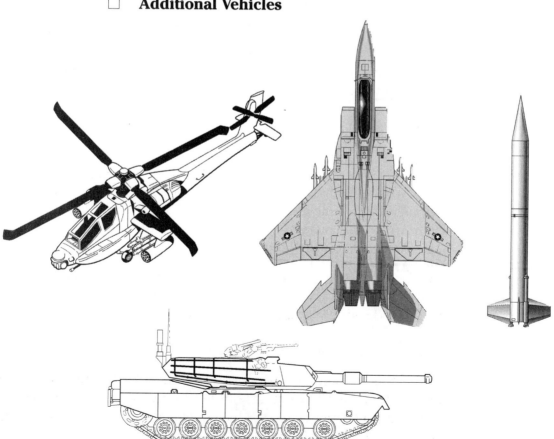

OVERVIEW The Marine Corps, by way of its combat mission, has a wide assortment of aircraft, tanks, and weapons. In the Desert Storm war, the AV-8B Harrier II Jet, the first Marine Corps tactical strike platform, was deployed from navy ships and land bases. The Marine Corps works closely with the Army in tank operations.

Aircraft—Fixed Wing

AV-8B	Harrier II
EA-6B	Prowler
F/A-18A/C/CN	Hornet
F/A-18D	Hornet
KC-130	Hercules

Special Profile	**AV-8B Harrier II**
Purpose:	attack Jet
Power:	Rolls Royce turbofan engine
Speed:	subsonic to transonic
Crew:	1

Aircraft—Rotary Wing

AH-1W	Super Cobra Helicopter
CH-46E	Sea Knight Helicopter
CH-53E	Super Stallion Helicopter
CH/RH-53D	Sea Stallion Helicopter
UH-1N	Huey Helicopter

Aircraft—Tilt Rotor

MV-22	Osprey

Armor

Light Armored Vehicle—25 (LAV-25)
Light Armored Vehicle—Anti-Tank (LAV-AT)
Light Armored Vehicle—Command and Control (LAV-C2)
Light Armored Vehicle—Logistics (LAV-L)
Light Armored Vehicle—Mortar (LAV-M)
Light Armored Vehicle—Recovery (LAV-R)

Missiles

AGM-45	Shrike Missile
AGM-65E	Maverick Missile
AIM-7	Sparrow III Missile
AIM-9	Sidewinder Missile

Hawk Surface-to-Air Missile System

Tracked Vehicles

Assault Amphibian Vehicle Command Model 7A1
Assault Amphibian Vehicle Personnel Model 7A1
Assault Amphibian Vehicle Recovery Model 7A1
M1A1 Main Battle Tank
M60A1 Armored Vehicle Launched Bridge
M88A1E1 Hercules Recovery Vehicle

Special Profile	**M1A1 Main Battle Tank**
Purpose:	main battle tank (MBT)
Power plant:	AGT-1500 turbine engine
Weight fully armed:	67.7 tons (61.4 metric tons)
Speed:	42 mph (67.72 kms)
Crew:	driver, loader, gunner, and tank commander

Additional Vehicles

High Mobility Multipurpose Wheeled Vehicle (HMMWV)
(M998 Truck)

KLR 250-D8	Marine Corps Motorcycle
MK48-14	Container Transporter Rear Body Unit
MK48-15	Recovery/Wrecker Rear Body Unit
MK48-16	5th Wheel Semitrailer Adapter Rear Body Unit
MK48-17	Dropside Cargo Rear Body Unit
MK48-18	Self-loading Container and Ribbon Bridge Transporter

ADDITIONAL RESOURCES

Videos:
"Heritage of Glory: The U.S. Marine Corps Story"
"Marine Corps Silent Drill Team"
"Marines: A Few Good Women"
"Pageantry of the Corps Marching Band"
"The Making of a Marine"
"U.S.M.C.: Bootcamp"
"U.S.M.C. Scout/Sniper"

Books:

First to Fight: An Inside View of the U.S. Marine Corps by Victor Krulak (1991)

Making the Corps by Thomas Ricks (1997)

Marine: A Guided Tour of a Marine Expeditionary Unit by Tom Clancy (1997)

One Shot, One Kill by Charles Sasser and Craig Roberts (1997)

Semper Fidelis: The History of the U.S. Marine Corps by Allan Millett (1991)

Magazines:

Marines

Navy Times—Marine Corps Edition

Popular Movies:

Sands of Iwo Jima (1949: John Wayne) Classic WWII Drama

Flying Leathernecks (1951: John Wayne) Classic WWII Saga

Tribes (1969: Jan Michael Vincent) Vietnam/ Boot Camp Drama

Boys in Company C (1978: Andrew Stevens) Vietnam War Saga

Heartbreak Ridge (1986: Clint Eastwood) Grenada Conflict Drama

Full Metal Jacket (1987: Matthew Modine) Boot Camp/Vietnam War Drama.

Advisory

You should not make a career decision based on a popular movie or television show. Remember: They are, for the most part, based loosely on facts or truths. Your final decision should be based on research into what will be good for you; however, popular movies and films can provide fine entertainment dealing with the military service.

Chapter 9

U.S. NAVY

U.S. Navy

- [ ] Overview
- [ ] Mission
- [ ] Where They Serve
- [ ] Major U.S. Navy Commands and Bases
- [ ] **Enlisted Opportunities**
- [ ] **Officer Opportunities**
- [ ] **U.S. Navy Reserve**
- [ ] **Inventory of U.S. Navy Aircraft, Guns, Missiles, Submarines, and Ships**
- [ ] Additional Resources

Navy Recruiting Command
801 North Randolph Street
Arlington, VA 22203

☎ 800-327-Navy
http://www.navy.job

Famous Service Sayings:	**I Have Not Yet Begun to Fight!** **Don't Give Up the Ship!** **Damn the Torpedoes! Full Speed** **Ahead!**
Elite Forces:	**Navy SEALS** (Sea-Air-Land teams) **The Blue Angels** (Navy Flight Demonstration Squadron)
Recruiting Slogans:	**It's Not a Job, It's an Adventure** **You and the Navy. Full Speed Ahead** **Let the Journey Begin** (Recruits 60,000 new personnel per year)

PROFILE OF U.S. NAVY PERSONNEL

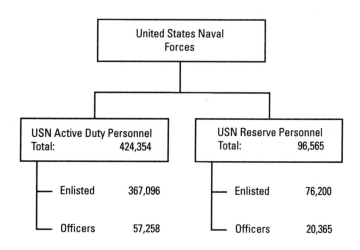

OVERVIEW   The Navy, one of the oldest military services, was established in 1775 by the Continental Congress. Throughout American history, wars were decided by the Navy's sea power. The Department of the Navy is responsible for the Marine Corps and, in a time of war or if the president directs, the U.S. Coast Guard as well. The Navy offers a wide variety of career and educational opportunities, especially in the nuclear and engineering fields. The Navy Reserve offers the same career fields as the active Navy.

MISSION   The Navy maintains freedom on the seas. It defends the rights of our country and its allies to travel and trade freely on the world's oceans and helps protect our country during times of international conflict. Navy sea and air power make it possible for our country to use the oceans when and where our national interests require it. Navy personnel serve on ships, on submarines under the sea, in aviation positions on land, and at shore bases around the world.

Special Operations Forces—Sea-Air-Land (SEAL)

Formally known as the "Underwater Demolition Teams," the Navy SEALs are lightly armed units that operate with stealth, concealment, and surprise to accomplish their operations. Navy SEALs conduct search and destroy missions, clear underwater mine fields, and go behind enemy lines.

WHERE THEY SERVE

Total of personnel assigned ashore (bases):   272,410
Total of personnel assigned afloat (ships and submarines):   162,207

MAJOR U.S. NAVY COMMANDS AND BASES

U.S. Atlantic Fleet Headquarters—Norfolk, VA
Atlantic, Mediterranean, Indian Ocean areas

U.S. Pacific Fleet Headquarters—Pearl Harbor, HI
Pacific Ocean regions

MAJOR U.S. NAVY BASES

United States

California
San Diego
San Francisco

Connecticut
Groton

Florida
Jacksonville
Orlando
Pensacola

Georgia
Kings Bay

Hawaii
Pearl Harbor

Illinois
Great Lakes

Louisiana
New Orleans

Rhode Island
Newport

Tennessee
Memphis

Texas
Corpus Christi

Virginia
Norfolk
Virginia Beach

Washington
Bremerton
Seattle

Foreign Ports

Bermuda

England
London

Germany
Stuttgart

Iceland
Keflavik

Italy
Greta
Naples

Japan
Yokosuka

Mariana Islands
Guam

Puerto Rico
San Juan

Sicily
Sigonella

Enlisted Opportunities————————————

- ☐ **U.S. Navy Enlisted Career Fields**
- ☐ **Special Enlisted Opportunities and Programs**

Enlisted Entrance Overview

Age: 17 to 34 years of age
Enlistments: 2 to 6 years (Regular Active Duty)

Recruit Training

Duration: 8 weeks
Location: Great Lakes
Instruction: full schedule of military and technical subjects; about one-third of the course is devoted to seamanship, survival-at-sea techniques, ship structures, and firefighting instruction

Enlisted Promotion Path

Promotions occur through a series of written and practical exams that test proficiency in a specialty along time in grade. It is possible to advance from Seaman Recruit to Chief Petty Officer within 14 years.

E-1   *Recruit—(Basic or Boot) Training*
E-2   *Seaman or Fireman Apprentice—*Completion of basic training
E-3   *Seaman or Fireman—*Six months active duty service and commander's recommendation
E-4   *Petty Officer Third Class—*Six months time in grade and commander's recommendation
E-5–E-6   *Petty Officer Second Class to Petty Officer First Class—*Test against peers in job skill and meet promotion criteria
E-7–E-9   *Chief Petty Officer and above—*Must meet selection board criteria

---

Critical Needs—Enlisted Career Fields

Communications Systems Maintenance Technicians
Communications Systems Operations Specialists
Computer Technicians
Electronics Technicians (Electricians and Machinists)
Engineering Technicians (Nuclear Power Field)
Foreign Language Specialists (Arabic, Chinese, French, Hebrew, Korean, Persian, Russian, Spanish, Vietnamese)

Nuclear Field
Radar Signal Systems Technicians

Special Operations Forces

Sea-Air-Land (SEALs)

ENLISTED CAREER FIELDS

Rates/Military Occupational Specialties

(See Chapter 12 for more information on Enlisted Career Fields.)

Administration
- ☐ Legalman (LN)
- ☐ Navy Counselor (NC)
- ☐ Personalman (PN)
- ☐ Postal Clerk (PC)
- ☐ Religious Program Specialist (RP)
- ☐ Yeoman (YN)

Air Traffic Controller
- ☐ Air Traffic Controller (AT)

Aviation Ground Support
- ☐ Aviation Boatswain's Mate (AB)
- ☐ Aviation Support Equipment Technician (AS)

Aviation Maintenance
- ☐ Adminstrationman (AZ)
- ☐ Aerographer's Mate (AG)
- ☐ Aviation Sensor Operations Officer
- ☐ Aviation Systems Warfare Operator

Aviation Maintenance/Weapons Group
- ☐ Aviation Electrician's Mate (AE)
- ☐ Aviation Electronics Technician (AT)
- ☐ Aviation Machinist's Mate (AD)
- ☐ Aviation Survival Equipmentman (PR)

Communications
- ☐ Radioman (RM)

Construction
- ☐ Builder (BU)
- ☐ Construction Electrician (CE)
- ☐ Construction Mechanic (CM)
- ☐ Engineering Aide (EA)
- ☐ Equipment Operator (EO)
- ☐ Steelworker (SW)
- ☐ Utilitiesman (UT)

Data Systems
- ☐ Data Processing Technician (DP)
- ☐ Data Systems Technician (DS)

Health Care
- ☐ Dental Technician (DT)
- ☐ Hospital Corpsman (HM)

Intelligence
- ☐ Intelligence Specialist (IS)
- ☐ Meteorologist

Law Enforcement
- ☐ Master-at-Arms (MA)

Logistics
- ☐ Aviation Storekeeper (AK)
- ☐ Disbursing Clerk (DK)
- ☐ Mess Management Specialist (MS)
- ☐ Ship's Serviceman (SH)
- ☐ Storekeeper (SK)

Marine Engineering
- ☐ Boiler Technician (BT)
- ☐ Electrician's Mate (EM)
- ☐ Engineman (EN)
- ☐ Gas Turbine System Technician (GS)
- ☐ Interior Communications Electrician (IC)
- ☐ Machinist's Mate (MM)

Media
- ☐ Illustrator Draftsman (DM)
- ☐ Journalist (JO)
- ☐ Lithographer (LI)
- ☐ Photographer's Mate (PH)

Musician
- ☐ Musician (MU)

Ordnance Systems
- [ ] Gunner's Mate (GM)
- [ ] Mineman (MN)
- [ ] Missile Technician (MT)
- [ ] Torpedoman's Mate (TM)

Seamanship
- [ ] Boatswain's Mate (BM)
- [ ] Signalman (SM)

Sensor Operations
- [ ] Electronics Warfare Technician (EW)
- [ ] Ocean Systems Technician (OT)
- [ ] Sonar Technician

Ship's Maintenance
- [ ] Damage Controlman (DC)
- [ ] Hull Maintenance Technician (HT)

- [ ] Instrumentman (IM)
- [ ] Machinery Repairman (MR)
- [ ] Molder (ML)
- [ ] Opticalman (OM)
- [ ] Patternmaker (PM)

Ship's Operation
- [ ] Operations Specialist (OS)
- [ ] Quartermaster (QM)

Special Warfare Career (non-rating)
- [ ] Navy SEAL Team

Weapons Control
- [ ] Electronics Technician (ET)
- [ ] Fire Control Technician (FT)
- [ ] Fire Controlman (FC)

Special Enlisted Opportunities and Programs

- [ ] **Nuclear Power Program**
- [ ] **Navy Campus**
- [ ] **Program for Afloat College Education**
- [ ] **Enlisted Commissioning Program**

Nuclear Power Program

This program offers qualified people training in operating nuclear propulsion systems. Nuclear-trained officers and enlisted personnel man the nuclear-powered ships that comprise more than 40 percent of the Navy's combat fleet. Enlisted candidates can receive advanced rate, enlistment bonuses, special duty pay, and special education benefits.

Navy Campus

Personnel can earn the same academic degrees and vocational certificates earned by students at civilian institutions, whether they are stationed on land or on board a ship or submarine. Tuition assistance may be used for courses taken at accredited colleges and universities, vocational/technical schools, or independent study courses.

Program for Afloat College Education

This tuition-free program offers college courses to crewmembers serving aboard ships at sea. The majority of the courses are at the freshman and sophomore level and are taught by college professors traveling with the Navy.

Enlisted Commissioning Program

In this program, enlisted men and women with previous college credit can complete their baccalaureate degrees in 36 months or less at any NROTC host university and earn a Navy commission upon graduation.

Warrant Officer (W-1 to W-3)

The rank of Warrant Officer in the Navy is restricted to members who have demonstrated a potential for greater responsibility than normally expected of petty officers. This is not an entry-level position. They are assigned responsibilities and have authority commensurate with their rank, including assignments as commanding officers and engineering officers aboard many types of units. Warrant Officer example: CWO3—Chief Warrant Officer Boatswain's Mate.

Officer Opportunities

- ☐ **Standard Officer Commissioning Programs**
- ☐ **Officer Career Fields**
- ☐ **Special Officer Opportunities and Programs**

Standard Officer Commissioning Programs

- ☐ **U.S. Naval Academy**
- ☐ **U.S. Naval Academy Preparatory School**
- ☐ **Direct Commissions**
- ☐ **BOOST**
- ☐ **Navy Officer Candidate School**
- ☐ **Naval Reserve Officer Training Corps (NROTC)**

U.S. Naval Academy

This program offers four years of college education leading to a bachelor of science degree. Candidates or Midshipmen earn a commission in the Navy or Marine Corps Reserve upon graduation. Competition to enter the academy is fierce.
(See Chapter 10—Military Academies.)

U.S. Naval Academy Preparatory School

This school accepts qualified civilian applicants and applicants from the regular and reserve components of the Navy, Coast Guard, and Marine Corps.
(See Chapter 10—Military Preparatory School.)

Direct Commissions

There are several direct commissioning programs. Programs exist for prior trained military officers, aviators, lawyers, medical and health professionals, engineers, and others who possess a four-year degree from a college or university.

Broadened Opportunity for Officer Selection and Training (BOOST)

BOOST offers the opportunity to receive up to 12 months of extensive academic preparation in order to be offered appointments to the Naval Academy or NROTC scholarship programs.

Navy Officer Candidate School

Qualified graduates of regionally accredited colleges receive 13 weeks of basic naval science and indoctrination at Pensacola, FL. Successful candidates are commissioned as ensigns in the Naval Reserve.

- 19 to $26\frac{1}{2}$ weeks for nuclear propulsion programs
- 19 to 28 weeks for unrestricted line and supply corps officers
- 19 to 34 weeks for restricted line and civil engineer corps officers
- 19 to 26 weeks for naval aviators and flight officers

Naval Reserve Officer Training Corps (NROTC)

NROTC scholarship programs lead to officer commissions in the Naval Reserve or Marine Corps Reserve. NROTC scholarships allow candidates to attend one of more than 50 civilian colleges around the country. The Navy pays for tuition, fees, and required textbooks for NROTC scholarship students. Standard NROTC programs:

Four-Year Program
Two-Year Program
One-Year Program
NROTC Three- and Four-Year Scholarships
NROTC Pre-Health Professions Program
NROTC Nurse Program

(See Chapter 11—ROTC.)

Critical Needs—Officer Career Fields

Engineers
Medical Personnel
Nuclear Occupational Specialists
Nursing Specialties

Special Operations Forces

Sea-Air-Land (SEAL)

OFFICER CAREER FIELDS

Military Occupational Specialties

(See Chapter 13 for more information on Officer Career Fields.)

Officer Career Classifications

Unrestricted Line Officers—Not restricted to the performance of duties in one field.
Restricted Line Officers—Specialists restricted to performing duties only in their areas of expertise, which could be any of those listed below.
Staff Corps Officers—Those assigned to one of the staff.

Administrative
☐ Accounting Officer
☐ Financial Specialist
☐ Fiscal Officer
☐ Fleet Support Officer
☐ Instructor
☐ International Relations Officer
☐ Logistics/Inventory Officer
☐ Personnel Officer
☐ Postal Officer
☐ Procurement and Recruiting Officer
☐ Supply Officer
☐ Training Officer
☐ Warehouse Officer

Aviation
☐ Air Traffic Control Manager
☐ Airplane Pilot
☐ Aviation Maintenance Manager
☐ Helicopter Pilot
☐ Naval Aviator
☐ Naval Flight Officer

Combat
☐ Missile Systems Officer
☐ Special Operations Officer
☐ Submarine Warfare Officer

Engineering, Science, and Technical
☐ Aeronautical Engineer
☐ Astronaut
☐ Chemist
☐ Civil Engineer
☐ Computer Systems Officer
☐ Cryptology Officer
☐ Electronics Engineer Officer
☐ Engineering Duty Officer
☐ Environmental Health and Safety
 Officer
☐ Industrial Engineer
☐ Life Scientist
☐ Marine Engineer
☐ Meteorologist
☐ Nuclear Reactor Instructor
☐ Oceanographer
☐ Physicist
☐ Space Operations Officer
☐ Surveying and Mapping Officer

Human Services
☐ Chaplain
☐ Social Worker

Intelligence
☐ Intelligence Officer
☐ Operational Intelligence Officer
☐ Psychology Officer
☐ Tactical Intelligence Officer

Law Enforcement
☐ Inspector General
☐ Security Officer
☐ Shore Patrol Officer

Legal
☐ Judge
☐ Lawyer

Media and Public Affairs
☐ Motion Picture and Television Officer
☐ Public Information Officer

Medical and Health Care
☐ Administrator
☐ Dietitian
☐ Nurse
☐ Pharmacist
☐ Physical and Occupational Therapist
☐ Physician's Assistant
☐ Speech Therapist

**Medical Diagnosing/
Treatment Practitioner**
☐ Dentist
☐ Optometrist
☐ Physician
☐ Psychologist
☐ Surgeon

Music
☐ Music Director

Ship and Submarine
☐ Nuclear Reactor Engineer
☐ Ship Engineer
☐ Ship Officer
☐ Submarine Officer
☐ Supply Officer

Special Operations Forces
☐ Special Warfare Officer

Support Service
☐ Food Service Manager
☐ Store Manager

Transportation
☐ Aircraft Maintenance Manager
☐ Automotive Maintenance Manager
☐ Aviation Maintenance Manager
☐ Transportation Manager

Special Officer Opportunities and Programs

- ☐ **Intelligence Program**
- ☐ **Medical Field Program**
- ☐ **Naval Flight Officer Training**
- ☐ **Navy Aeronautical Engineer**
- ☐ **Navy Postgraduate School**
- ☐ **Nuclear Power Program**
- ☐ **Pilot Training**

Intelligence Program

Special Duty Intelligence is a program for training as an intelligence special duty officer in a non-flying assignment. After 13 weeks at OCS, candidates are commissioned ensigns in the Naval Reserve.

Medical Field Program

The Navy offers financial assistance to students in medical and dental school and for certain medical corps specialties in return for specified periods of military service. Medical students who qualify receive tuition, books, fees, and a monthly allowance.

Naval Flight Officer Training

Naval Flight Officer (NFO) training is available to qualified commissioned officers of the OCS, U.S. Naval Academy, or NROTC. After the completion of basic NFO Ground School, officers have the opportunity to specialize and receive advanced training in one of the following categories: antisubmarine warfare, electronic countermeasures evaluation, radar interception, airborne early warning, or bombardier/navigator. NFO wings are received upon completion of advanced training.

Navy Aeronautical Engineer (Aviation Maintenance)

This is a program for those who desire to become specialists in the aviation maintenance management field. Selected candidates receive orders to OCS. Upon completion of 13 weeks of indoctrination training, they are commissioned ensigns in the Naval Reserve. As commissioned officers, they undergo about 16 weeks of instruction at the Aviation Maintenance Officer School.

Navy Postgraduate School

The Naval Postgraduate School offers studies in advanced engineering disciplines. Candidates can also earn advanced degrees in programs accepted by leading accrediting and professional associations.

Nuclear Power Program

This program offers qualified candidates training in operating nuclear propulsion systems. Nuclear-trained officers man the nuclear-powered ships that comprise more than 40 percent of the Navy's combat fleet. Officers who volunteer for submarine duty will be assigned to three months of training at the Submarine School. Officers assigned to surface ships will be assigned to four months of training at Surface Warfare Officer School.

Pilot Training

Naval pilot training is available to qualified commissioned officers of the OCS, U.S. Naval Academy, or NROTC. Upon completion of primary flight training, candidates may be accepted for one of three aviation fields: jet, prop, or helo. After successful completion of advanced flight training, student pilots receive their wings and are designated as naval aviators.

U.S. Navy Reserve

☎ 800-USA-USNR

SPECIAL OPPORTUNITIES AND PROGRAMS

☐ Advanced Paygrade Program
☐ Navy Veteran Program
☐ Other Service Veteran Program
☐ (Reserve) Direct Commission
☐ Training and Administration of Reserves Program

Advanced Paygrade Program

Candidates who have work experience or training in a field needed by the Navy may be qualified to enter the Naval Reserve in a higher pay grade. Non-prior service applicants must be at least 26 years old and not have reached their 36th birthday. Recruit training may not be required for this program.

Navy Veteran Program

Qualified veterans discharged from the Navy within four years or less can be reenlisted in the same pay grades they held at the time of separation through the NAVET program, depending upon Naval Reserve needs in particular ratings.

Other Service Veteran Program

The OSVET Program provides for enlistment in the Naval Reserve by people who have been in the Army, Air Force, Coast Guard, or Marine Corps. These individuals must have now or have had in the past job classifications in other services similar to those in the Navy.

(Reserve) Direct Commission

Candidates with specific college degrees and applicable work experience may receive direct commissions in the Naval Reserve as officers in such fields as engineering, cryptology, intelligence, public affairs, oceanography, medicine, nursing, supply, and chaplaincy.

Training and Administration of Reserves Program

This special program is open to qualified Navy veterans to serve on full-time active duty to manage, train, and administer to Naval Reserve personnel in accordance with policies prescribed by Naval Operations. TAR assignments for officers and enlisted personnel are at air squadrons or aboard Naval Reserve Force ships.

Inventory of U.S. Navy Aircraft, Guns, Missiles, Submarines, and Ships

☐ **Planes**
☐ **Helicopters**
☐ **Gun Systems**
☐ **Missiles**
☐ **Submarines**
☐ **Surface Ships**

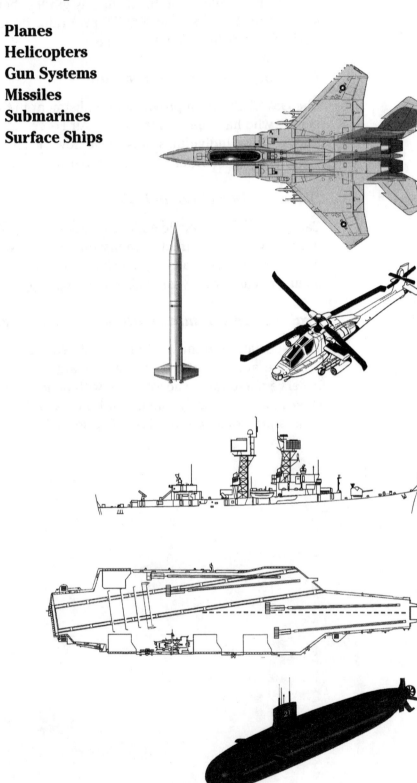

OVERVIEW The Navy operates two of the modern-day wonders of the world: the aircraft carrier and the nuclear submarine. Navy aircraft carriers are the largest craft in the world, and are literally floating cities of military personnel, aircraft, and equipment. The Navy's newest nuclear submarine, the "Seawolf class," claims to be so silent underway that it is "less detectable at high speed than a Los Angeles-class submarine sitting at pier."

Aircraft—Fixed Wing

A6E	Intruder medium attack aircraft
C2A	Greyhound logistics aircraft
C9	Skytrain logistics aircraft
C130	Hercules logistics aircraft
E2C	Hawkeye early warning and control aircraft
E6A	Tacamo airborne command post
EA6B	Prowler electronic warfare aircraft
F14	Tomcat fighter
F/A18	Hornet strike fighter
P3C	Orion long-range ASW aircraft
S3	Viking multimission and ASW aircraft
T45A	Goshawk training aircraft

Aircraft—Rotary Wing

CH46	Sea Knight helicopter
CH53	Sea Stallion helicopter
H3H	Sea King helicopter
SH2	Seasprite helicopter
SH60	Sea Hawk helicopter
TH57	Sea Ranger helicopter
V22A	Osprey tilt rotor aircraft

Guns—Weapons Systems

5-inch gun
Aegis weapons system
Mark 25 gun
Mark 75 gun
Mines ·
Phalanx weapons system
Torpedoes

Missiles

AMRAAM missile
Harpoon/SLAM missile
Harm missile
Maverick missile
Penguin missile
Phoenix missile
Sea Sparrow missile
Sidewinder missile
Standard missile
Tomahawk cruise missile
Trident II D5 ballistic missile

Submarines

Attack Submarines SSN
Ballistic Missile Submarines SSBN
Deep Submergence Craft NR1
Deep Submergence Rescue Vehicle DSRV
Research Submarine AGSS

Special Profile	**Seawolf Class**
Purpose:	advanced nuclear-powered attack submarine
Displacement:	9,150 tons (submerged)
Length:	353 ft
Hull Diameter:	40 ft
Speed:	25+ kt
Diving Depth:	800+ ft
Weapons:	antisubmarine torpedoes, Harpoon missiles, Tomahawk cruise missiles
Crew:	130 members

Surface Ships

Aircraft Carriers CV/CVN
Air-Cushioned Landing Craft
Ammunition Ships AE
Amphibious Assault Ships LHA, LHD, LPH
Amphibious Command Ships LCC
Amphibious Transport Dock LPD
Coastal Mine Countermeasures Ship
Command Ships AGE
Cruisers CG/CGN
Destroyers DD/DDG
Dock Landing Ships LSD
Fast Combat Support Ships ACE

Fleet Oilers AO
Frigates FFG
Hospital Ships TAH
Landing Craft
Mine Countermeasures Ship MCS
Missile Range Instrumentation Ships TAGM
Navigation and Acoustic Research Ships TAG
Oceanographic Ships TAGS
Patrol Coastal
Rescue and Salvage Ships ARS
Sea Shadow Experimental Ship
Submarine Tender AS
Surveillance Ships TAGOS
Tank Landing Ships LST
USS Constitution (the oldest commissioned ship in the Navy)

Special Profile	**Nimitz Class Carrier**
Power Plant:	two nuclear reactors
	four geared steam turbines
Length:	1,040 ft
Flight Deck Width:	252 ft
Beam:	134 ft
Displacement:	97,000 tons full load
Speed:	30+ kt (34.5 mph)
Aircraft:	85
Crew:	3,200 ship's company
	2,480 air wing
	(total 5,680)
Armament:	four NATO Sea Sparrow launchers, 20mm Phalanx CONS mounts

Military Sealift Command

Cable Repair Ship TARC
Combat Stores Ships TAFS
Fast Sealift Ships TAKR
Fleet Ocean Tugboats TATF

ADDITIONAL RESOURCES

Videos:

"Ambush: Navy Seals in Deadly Action"
"Anchors Aweigh, The U.S. Navy Story"
"Naval Academy—150 years at Annapolis"
"Navy SEAL Buds Training"
"Navy SEALs: The Tides of Specwar"
"Sea of Honor, The U.S. Navy Story 1775–1945"
"Wings of Gold, U.S. Naval Aviation"

Books:

A Day in the Life of a Midshipman by the Naval Institute for Young Readers (1996)

Inside the US Navy SEALs by Gary Stubblefield, Hans Halberstadt (1995)

SSN: Strategies of Submarine Warfare by Tom Clancy (1997)

Submarine: A Guided Tour inside a Nuclear Warship by Tom Clancy (1997)

U.S. Navy SEALs in Action by Hans Halberstadt (1995)

Official Magazine:

All Hands (official magazine of the U.S. Navy)

Popular Movies:

Navy Blue and Gold (1937: James Stewart) Army-Navy Football Story
The Fighting Seabees (1944: John Wayne) Classic WWII Drama
You're in the Navy Now (1951: Gary Cooper) Navy Crew Comedy
The Caine Mutiny (1954: Humphrey Bogart) Classic Drama
Mister Roberts (1955: Henry Fonda) WWII Ship Comedy-Drama
Run Silent, Run Deep (1958: Clark Gable) WWII Submarine Drama
McHale's Navy (1964: Ernest Borgnine) PT Boat Comedy
The Bedford Incident (1965: Richard Widmark) Cold War Submarine/ Ship Drama
The Last Detail (1974: Jack Nicholson) Classic Navy Shore Patrol Drama
Gray Lady Down (1977: Charlton Heston) Nuclear Submarine Drama
An Officer and a Gentleman (1982: Richard Gere) Naval Academy Drama
Das Boot (1982: German [The Boat]) Classic WWII Submarine Drama
Top Gun (1986: Tom Cruise) Navy Fighter Pilots Action Story
The Hunt for Red October (1990: Sean Connery) Nuclear Submarine Drama
Navy SEALs (1990: Charlie Sheen) Action Drama
Mission of the Shark (1991: Stacy Keach) USS Indianapolis Story
A Few Good Men (1992: Tom Cruise) Navy Legal Drama

Crimson Tide (1995: Denzel Washington) Nuclear Submarine Drama
Under Siege (1995: Steven Seagal) Aircraft Carrier Saga
Down Periscope (1996: Kelsey Grammer) Submarine Comedy
Hostile Waters (1997: Rutger Hauer) Cold War Submarine Saga

Advisory

You should not make a career decision based on a popular movie or television show. Remember: They are, for the most part, based loosely on facts or truths. Your final decision should be based on research into what will be good for you; however, popular movies and films can provide fine entertainment dealing with the military service.

SECTION

3

MILITARY
COLLEGE
OPPORTUNITIES

Chapter 10

U.S. MILITARY ACADEMIES

MILITARY ACADEMY PREPARATORY SCHOOLS

- ☐ **Overview**
- ☐ **Military Academies**
- ☐ **U.S. Air Force Academy Preparatory School**
- ☐ **U.S. Military Academy Preparatory School**
- ☐ **U.S. Coast Guard Academy Preparatory School**
- ☐ **U.S. Naval Academy Preparatory School**

OVERVIEW The main mission of all U.S. Military Academy Preparatory (prep) schools is to strengthen a candidate's background in mathematics, English, and science for possible entrance into one of the service academies. Many candidates admitted to the military academies need post-high school preparation and are encouraged to attend preparatory schools.

The prep schools (Army, Air Force, Coast Guard, Navy) are 10-month courses that begin in July and end in May of each year. Graduates selected to attend a service academy have a summer break of approximately six weeks before reporting to the academy. Note: Attendance at academy prep schools in no way guarantees acceptance to the service academies.

Selected Marine Corps and Coast Guard candidates may attend the Naval Preparatory School, provided the respective services refer the candidate.

U.S. AIR FORCE ACADEMY PREPARATORY SCHOOL
Director of Admissions
USAFA Preparatory School
2304 Cadet Drive, Suite 200
USAF Academy
Colorado Springs, CO 80840-5025
☎ 800-443-9266 or 719-333-2520

U.S. MILITARY ACADEMY PREPARATORY SCHOOL
Commandant
U.S. Military Academy Preparatory School
ATTN: MAPSADA
Ft. Monmouth, NJ 07703
☎ 800-USA-ARMY

U.S. COAST GUARD ACADEMY PREPARATORY SCHOOL
Director of Admissions
U.S. Coast Guard Academy
15 Mohegan Avenue
New London, CT 06320
☎ 800-GET-USCG

U.S. NAVAL ACADEMY PREPARATORY SCHOOL
Director of Candidate Guidance
U.S. Naval Academy
Annapolis, MD 21402-5018
☎ 800-638-9156

MILITARY ACADEMIES

- ☐ **Overview**
- ☐ **Nomination Process**
- ☐ **U.S. Air Force Academy**
- ☐ **U.S. Military Academy**
- ☐ **U.S. Coast Guard Academy**
- ☐ **U.S. Naval Academy**
- ☐ **Sample Nomination Request Letters**

OVERVIEW The service academies represent the military's most outstanding opportunity. Graduates of a military academy not only receive a free state-of-the-art education, but are considered "elite," not only within the military itself, but also in the private sector. To put it bluntly: There are not many academy graduates on the streets; they do very well in all environments. The education provided is outstanding and personalized. Most classrooms accommodate small class sessions of 12 to 20 students. Not all instruction takes place on the grounds of the academies—training ships, planes, and other military hardware are utilized at various locations as part of the learning process.

Costs

The military academies do not charge for tuition; the cost, including room, board, and medical and dental care, is borne entirely by the U.S. government. In addition, most candidates receive a monthly salary to pay for supplies, clothing, and personal expenses. Prior to admission, most academies require candidates to deposit approximately $2,500 to help defray the initial cost of uniforms and supplies.

Basic Admissions Process

The candidate must:
1. have basic eligibility
2. obtain a nomination
3. qualify scholastically
4. qualify medically
5. qualify physically
6. be selected for an appointment

Basic Eligibility

Age: 17–23
Status: U.S. citizen
            Unmarried
            Not be pregnant or have a legal obligation to support a child or children
Medical: Must be in good physical and mental health
            Must be able to pass a Department of Defense Medical Examination Review Board medical examination
Physical: Must be able to pass the Physical Aptitude Examination (PAE)

NOMINATION PROCESS

Candidates to the military academies are required (by law) to have a nomination to attend a particular academy; the only exception is the U.S. Coast Guard Academy, where entrance is by merit only. Since the nomination process is lengthy, you should seek a nomination as early as possible. To increase your chances of being selected, you should apply for a nomination from your U.S. Representative, your two U.S. Senators, and the Vice-President of the United States. They may nominate up to ten candidates for each vacancy. Vacancies occur when cadets graduate or leave prior to graduation. You also may be eligible for a nomination in one or more of the military-affiliated categories. Most members of Congress do not accept requests for nominations after October, so you should contact them in the spring semester of your junior year (sample letters have been included at the end of this chapter).

Nominations/Appointments Authorized (Cumulative)

The authorized appointments are at maximum strength for each nomination category. Cumulative appointments are the total number available, of which approximately one-third will enter each year.

Category	Military Academy*	Number/Nominations
President	Air Force Army Navy (Marines)	100 100 100
Vice President	Air Force Army Navy (Marines)	5 5 5
100 United States Senators (5 each)	Air Force Army Navy (Marines)	500 500 500
435 United States Representatives (5 each)	Air Force Army Navy (Marines)	2,175 2,175 2,175
District of Columbia (5) Puerto Rico (6) American Samoa (2) Guam (2) Virgin Islands (2)	Air Force Army Navy (Marines)	16 17 10
Regular or Reserve Personnel	Air Force Army Navy (Marines)	85/85 85/85 85/85
Children of Medal of Honor Recipients	Air Force Army Navy (Marines)	Unlimited Unlimited Unlimited
Children of Deceased or Disabled Veterans Children of Persons in a Military Missing Status	Air Force Army Navy (Marines)	65 20 65
Honor Military/Naval School Graduates and Reserve Officer Training Corps (ROTC) Candidates	Air Force Army Navy (Marines)	20 20 20
International	Air Force Army Navy (Marines)	40 40 40

* except for the U.S. Coast Guard Academy, where appointments are based solely on merit.

Testing

All candidates for the military academies must take either the standardized ACT Assessment or the College Board SAT I.

Medical

The Department of Defense Medical Examination Review Board (DODMERB) conducts the medical examination process for all of the medical academies and the four-year ROTC scholarship programs. The exams may be scheduled at a military or civilian facility near your home.

Physical Preparation

The physical demands of military academy life are extreme. You must develop fitness prior to entering the academy by participating in individual and team sports or an individual fitness program, with concentration on upper body strength, running speed, and endurance. Most of the academies require the ability to swim.

U.S. AIR FORCE ACADEMY

U.S.A.F. Academy
HQ USAFA/RRS
Director of Admissions
2304 Cadet Drive, Suite 200
Colorado Springs, CO 80840-5025

☎ 800-443-9266 or 719-333-2520
http://www.usafa.af.mil

Mission

"Develop and inspire air and space leaders with vision for tomorrow"

Overview

About 1,200 fourth-class (freshman) students enter each year.

As with the Air Force itself, the Air Force Academy (established in 1950) is the youngest of all the military academies. It is located in the Colorado Rocky Mountains, eight miles north of Colorado Springs and 70 miles south of Denver. Cadets may select from 29 academic majors. Graduates are awarded a bachelor of science degree and a commission as a second lieutenant in the United States Air Force. All cadets must live in on-campus dormitories and wear uniforms.

Admissions Process

Candidates must:
1. determine whether they meet the requirements or qualifications
2. apply for a nomination
3. start a file at the academy
4. fill out all U.S.A.F.A. forms and return them as soon as possible
5. take the ACT or SAT
6. take the Qualifying Medical Examination
7. take the Physical Aptitude Examination
8. monitor the evaluation and status of their application
9. prepare for entrance to the Air Force Academy

General Qualifications

Age: 17–22
Status: U.S. citizen
Unmarried
Not be pregnant or have a legal obligation to support a child or children
Medical: Must be in good physical and mental health
Must be able to pass a Department of Defense Medical Examination Review Board medical examination
Physical: Must be able to pass the Physical Aptitude Examination (PAE)

Major Fields of Study

Aeronautical Engineering
Astronautical Engineering
Basic Sciences
Behavioral Sciences
Biology
Chemistry
Civil Engineering

Computer Science
Economics
Electrical Engineering
Engineering
Engineering Mechanics
Engineering Sciences
English
Foreign Area Studies
Geography
History
Humanities
Legal Studies
Management
Mathematical Sciences
Mechanical Engineering
Meteorology
Military Doctrine
Operations and Strategy
Operations Research
Physics
Political Science
Social Sciences
Space Operations

Minors

The Academy also offers minors in:
Foreign Languages
Mathematics
Military Operations
Philosophy
Strategy

Testing

All candidates must take either the standardized American College Testing (ACT) Assessment Program exam or the College SAT I.

ACT American College Testing Assessment Program
English, Reading, Mathematics, and Science Reasoning

SAT I College Board Exam
Verbal and Mathematics

Hours	Activities
0600	Start of day call to quarters
0610–0650	Physical training
0655	Day call to quarters
0705	Breakfast formation
0715	Reveille
0800–1150	Academic classes or individual study time
1205	Noon formation
1300–1530	Academic classes, military training, or individual study time
1500–1930	Intercollegiate practice
1600–2000	Unscheduled time
1600	Retreat/end of day call to quarters
1620–1820	Intramural sports
1700–1945	Evening meal
1730–2000	Squadron, chaplain time, or evening lectures
1900–2330	Academic call to quarters
2330	Taps/night call to quarters

TYPICAL COLORADO DAILY SCHEDULE

Obligation

Service commitment is five years after graduation.

U.S. Military Academy

U.S.M.A.
Director of Admission
600 Thayer Road
West Point, NY 10996-9902

☎ 914-938-4041
http://www.usma.edu

Motto

"Duty, Honor, Country"

Mission

"To educate and train the Corps of Cadets so that each graduate shall have the attributes essential to professional growth throughout a career as an officer of the regular Army and to inspire each to a lifetime of service"

OVERVIEW Each year the United States Military Academy admits approximately 1,200 candidates.

West Point is the oldest of all the military academies (established 1802). The academy is located in West Point, New York, 50 miles north of New York City. Cadets may select from 25 fields of study. Upon graduation, cadets are awarded a bachelor of science degree and a commission as a second lieutenant in the United States Army. All cadets must live in on-campus dormitories and wear uniforms.

Admissions Process

Candidates must:
1. determine whether they meet the requirements or qualifications
2. apply for a nomination
3. start a file at West Point
4. fill out all U.S.M.A. forms and return them as soon as possible
5. take the ACT or SAT
6. take the Qualifying Medical Examination
7. take the Physical Aptitude Examination
8. monitor the evaluation and status of their application
9. prepare for entrance to West Point

General Qualifications

Age: 17–23
Status: U.S. citizen
           Unmarried
           Not be pregnant or have a legal obligation to support a child or children
Medical: Must be in good physical and mental health
           Must be able to pass a Department of Defense Medical Examination Review Board medical examination
Physical: Must be able to pass the Physical Aptitude Examination (PAE)

Major Fields of Study

American Legal System
Applied Sciences and Engineering
Basic Sciences Interdisciplinary
Behavioral Sciences
Chemistry and Life Science
Civil Engineering Computer Science
Economics
Electrical Engineering
Engineering Management
Engineering Physics
Environmental Engineering
Environmental Science
Foreign Area Studies
   (East Asia, Latin America, Eastern Europe, Western Europe, or the Middle East)
Foreign Languages
   (Arabic, Chinese, French, German, Portuguese, Spanish, and Russian)
General Management
Geography (Physical Geography and Human/Regional Geography)

History
Mathematical Science
Mechanical Engineering
Military Art and Science
Nuclear Engineering
Operations Research
Physics
Political Science
Studies in Philosophy and Literature
Systems Engineering

Testing

All candidates must take either the standardized ACT (American College Testing) Assessment Program exam or the SAT I (College Board).

ACT American College Testing Assessment Program
English, Reading, Mathematics, and Science Reasoning

SAT I College Board
Verbal and Mathematics

TYPICAL WEST POINT DAILY SCHEDULE	
Hours	**Activities**
0630–0710	Breakfast
0715–1125	Class or study
1145–1230	Lunch
1230–1325	Commandant/Dean time
1335–1540	Class or study
1540–1800	Intramural; club, or intercollegiate athletics, or free time
1730–1900	Optional dinner
1905–1930	Cadet duties
1930–2030	Study conditions
2030–2330	Study time only
2330	Taps
2400	Lights out

Obligation

Service commitment is five years after graduation.

U.S. Coast Guard Academy

U.S.C.G.A.
Director of Admissions
15 Mohegan Avenue
New London, CT 06320-4195

☎ 800-883-USCG
http://www.dot.gov/dotinfo/uscg/hq/uscga

OVERVIEW About 250 cadets enter the Coast Guard Academy each year.

The academy is located in New London, Connecticut, on the Atlantic Ocean. U.S. Coast Guard cadets may select from several academic majors. The Coast Guard Academy is the largest source of U.S. Coast Guard officers. Graduates are awarded a bachelor of science degree and a commission as an ensign in the United States Coast Guard. All must live in on-campus dormitories and wear uniforms.

Admissions Process

The Coast Guard does not accept nominations. Entrance is based solely on merit and background.

Candidates must:
1. determine whether they meet the requirements or qualifications
2. fill out all U.S.C.G. forms and return them as soon as possible
3. take the ACT or SAT
4. take the Qualifying Medical Examination
5. take the Physical Aptitude Examination
6. monitor the evaluation and status of their application

General Qualifications

Age: 17–23
Status: U.S. citizen
           Unmarried
           Not be pregnant or have a legal obligation to support a child or children
Medical: Must be in good physical and mental health
           Must be able to pass a Department of Defense Medical Examination Review Board medical examination
Physical: Must be able to pass the Physical Aptitude Examination (PAE)

Major Fields of Study

Civil Engineering
Electrical Engineering
Government
Management
Marine Science
Mathematical and Computer Sciences
Mechanical Engineering
Naval Architecture and Marine Engineering

Testing

All candidates must take either the standardized American College Testing (ACT) Assessment Program exam or the College Entrance Examination Board (CEEB) Scholastic Assessment Test (SAT I).

ACT American College Testing Assessment Program
English, Reading, Mathematics, and Science Reasoning

SAT College Board Admissions Testing Program
Verbal and Mathematics

TYPICAL NEW LONDON DAILY SCHEDULE	
Hours	**Schedule**
0600	Reveille
0620	Formation and breakfast
0700–0745	Military training/administrative period
0800–1150	Morning classes
1200–1245	Noon meal
1250–1540	Afternoon classes
1600–1835	Sports, extracurricular activities, time to meet with academic instructors
1840	Formation and dinner
1930–2000	Optional meeting period
1930–2200	Evening study period
2200	Taps

Obligation

Service commitment is five years after graduation.

U.S. Naval (Marine Corps) Academy

U.S.N.A.
Candidate Guidance Office
United States Naval Academy
117 Decatur Road
Annapolis, MD 21402-5018

☎ 800-638-9156
http:www.nadn.navy.mil

Motto

"From Knowledge, Seapower"

Mission

"To develop midshipmen morally, mentally, and physically and to imbue them with the highest ideals of duty, honor, and loyalty in order to provide graduates who are dedicated to a career of naval service and have potential for future development in mind and character to assume the highest responsibilities of command, citizenship, and government."

OVERVIEW Each year the United States Naval Academy admits approximately 1,200 candidates.

The Naval Academy, one of the oldest military academies, was established in 1842. It is located in Annapolis, the state capital of Maryland, 33 miles east of Washington, DC, and 30 miles southeast of Baltimore. Cadets may select from 18 fields of study. Graduates are awarded a bachelor of science degree and a commission either as an ensign in the U.S. Navy or a second lieutenant in the U.S. Marine Corps.

General Qualifications

Age:	17–23
Status:	U.S. citizen
	Unmarried
	Not be pregnant or have a legal obligation to support a child or children
Medical:	Must be in good physical and mental health
	Must be able to pass a Department of Defense Medical Examination Review Board medical examination
Physical:	Must be able to pass the Physical Aptitude Examination (PAE)

Admission Process

Candidates must:

1. apply for admission between April 1 of their junior year in high school and February 28 of their senior year in high school
2. fill out and return a Precandidate Questionnaire to the academy
3. apply for a nomination
4. take the SAT or ACT college admission tests
5. complete the candidate application packet as early as September of their senior year of high school
6. take the Physical Aptitude Examination
7. take the Qualifying Medical Examination
8. interview with a Naval Academy Information Officer in their area

Major Fields of Study

Aerospace Science
Chemistry
Computer Science
Economics
Electrical Engineering
English
General Engineering
General Science
History
Marine Engineering
Mathematics
Mechanical Engineering
Naval Architecture
Nuclear Engineering
Ocean and Systems Engineering
Oceanography
Physics
Political Science

Testing

All candidates must take either the standardized American College Testing (ACT) Assessment Program exam or the College Entrance Examination Board (CEEB) Scholastic Assessment Test (SAT I).

ACT American College Testing Assessment Program
English, Reading, Mathematics, and Science Reasoning

SAT College Board Admissions Testing Program
Verbal and Mathematics

_TYPICAL ANNAPOLIS DAILY SCHEDULE	
Hours	**Schedule**
0530	Reveille
0545–0630	Physical training
0700–0720	Breakfast
0730–1215	Morning workshops
1225–1300	Lunch
1345–1600	Afternoon workshops
1600–1800	Sports or drill competition
1830–1900	Evening meal
2000–2245	Special events
2300	Taps

Obligation

Service commitment is five years after graduation.

SAMPLE NOMINATION REQUEST LETTER

For a Congressional or Vice-Presidential Nomination
(This is intended as a guide. Each military academy will provide a sample with its application material. A separate letter must be sent to the Vice-President and to each senator and representative to whom you apply.)

Honorable (Name)
House of Representatives [or] United States Senate
Washington, DC 20515 or Washington, DC 20510
[or]
The Vice-President
The White House
Washington, DC 20501

Date

Dear Mr./Mrs./Ms. (Name) [or] Dear Senator (Name) [or] Mr. Vice-President:

It is my desire to attend the [Air Force or Army or Marine Corps or Navy] Academy and to serve in the United States [Air Force or Army or Marine Corps or Navy]. I respectfully request that I be considered as one of your nominees for the class that enters the Academy in [June or July].

In order to assist you in your selection, I am supplying the following pertinent information:

Name [print as recorded on birth certificate]
Social Security Number
Date of Birth [spell out month]
Place of Birth
Permanent Address [street, city, county, state, zip]
Permanent Phone Number [include area code]
High School Attended [with address]
Date of Graduation
Rank in Class [if known]
Approximate grade point average (GPA), and PSAT, PACT, SAT I and ACT scores if you have taken these tests. Include verbal and math scores for the PSAT and SAT I exams, the composite for the PACT, and English, reading, math, and science reasoning scores for the ACT exam.
Extracurricular Activities [list]

[Your reasons for wanting to enter the Air Force or Army or Navy Academy]

Thank you for considering me as one of your nominees to the [Air Force or Army or Navy] Academy.

Sincerely,

[Your Signature]

SAMPLE NOMINATION REQUEST LETTER

Format of Request for Military Affiliated Nomination

(This is intended as a guide: Each military academy will provide a sample with its application material. Categories are: Presidential, Children of Deceased or Disabled Veterans, Children of Military Personnel in Missing Status, Children of Medal of Honor Recipients, or Current Members applying themselves.)

Director of Admissions
[Air Force or Army or Navy] Academy
[Complete Address]

Date

Dear Sir:

I want to attend the [Air Force or Army or Navy] Academy and to serve in the United States [Air Force or Army or Marine Corps or Navy]. I request a nomination under the [name of appropriate category] for the class that enters the Academy in [Month] 19_.

Name [print as recorded on birth certificate]
Social Security Number
Date of Birth [spell out month]
Place of Birth
Permanent Address [street, city, county, state, zip]
Permanent Phone Number [include area code]
High School Attended [with address]
Date of Graduation
Rank in Class [if known]
Information on parents:
Name, rank, social security numbers, branch of service:
Parent's active duty: attach statement of service dated and signed by current personnel officer specifying all duty and any breaks therein, parent retired or deceased [attach copy of retirement orders or casualty report: Department of Veteran Affairs (VA) claim number, if appropriate. Include brief statement with date and circumstances of Medal of Honor award, if appropriate].
Enlisted applicant's rank, serial number, component, and branch of service.
[check with your command's personnel officer for procedures]

[Your reasons for wanting to enter the Air Force or Army or Navy Academy]
Thank you for considering me as one of your nominees to the [Air Force or Army or Navy] Academy.

Sincerely,

[Your Signature]

Chapter 11

U.S. RESERVE OFFICER TRAINING CORPS (ROTC)

ROTC Opportunities

- ☐ **ROTC Opportunities**
- ☐ Overview

- ☐ **U.S. Air Force ROTC**
- ☐ Overview
- ☐ Colleges and Universities That Offer AFROTC

- ☐ **U.S. Army ROTC**
- ☐ Overview
- ☐ Colleges and Universities That Offer AROTC
- ☐ Army-Approved ROTC Courses

- ☐ **U.S. Navy/Marine Corps ROTC**
- ☐ Overview
- ☐ Colleges and Universities That Offer NROTC

OVERVIEW   Largest single source of military officers.

If college is your main interest, you should shop around with each branch for the best deal. If you are looking for a career in nuclear engineering, the Navy may have the best options; however, if you live in Alaska and would like to attend college close to home, the Air Force or Army may be better for you.

ROTC cadets or midshipmen make their own arrangements for college enrollment and room and board, and take the normal course load required by the college or university for degree completion. They live just like other students, the only difference is that ROTC candidates participate in weekly drill instruction, summer training periods, and military science classes. During drills, cadets or midshipmen wear uniforms furnished by the government and must conduct themselves in a military manner.

The military commander of an NROTC unit is a senior officer, works as a professor of military science, and may also be a member of the college faculty. The ROTC commander also serves as a counselor and advisor to the cadets or midshipmen on personal and academic matters.

ROTC PROGRAMS		
Program	**Overview**	**Branch**
Four Years	Most ROTC candidates go through the four-year program. The program is geared for college students with three or more years to go. It consists of: General Military Course (two hours a week) Field Training (weeks during breaks) Professional Officer Course (three hours per week) Once the POC is completed, the student can receive a military allowance of $150/month.	Air Force Army Navy (Marine Corps)
Two Years	*Competitive* Students with two years left in college or transfers join the two-year ROTC program.	Air Force Army Navy (Marine Corps)
One Year	*Very Competitive* This program is usually earmarked for students who are in a field the branch has a critical need of (nursing, medicine, and so on).	Air Force Army Navy (Marine Corps)

ROTC PROGRAMS (continued)		
Program	**Overview**	**Branch**
Scholarships	*Very Competitive* The majority of scholarships pay full college tuition and most laboratory, textbook, and incidental fees, plus a $150 monthly non-taxable allowance during the school year.	Air Force Army Navy (Marine Corps)
Nursing	*Critical Need Area* Candidates need to be enrolled in an accredited National League of Nursing school. Nursing scholarship candidates must be in pursuit of a four-year degree—bachelor of science in nursing.	Air Force Army Navy (Marine Corps)
Basic or General Military Course Professional Officer Course/ Advanced Course Field Training	BC or GMC is the first half of the four-year program and is usually taken during the freshman and sophomore years. POC/AC takes place during the last half of the four-year program, is competitive, and includes successful completion of a four-week field training encampment. Courses cover leadership skills and national defense policy. POC candidates receive a tax-free allowance of $150 a month. FT is a rigorous program of physical conditioning, weapons practice, and survival training.	Air Force Army Navy (Marine Corps)
General Qualifications	Must be a full-time student at a school offering ROTC or at a crosstown school with an enrollment agreement. Must be a U.S. citizen. Must be in good physical condition. Must have good moral character. Must be at least 14 years old (17 to receive a scholarship appointment).	Air Force Army Navy (Marine Corps)
Application Process	1. Request and fill out the Preliminary Application. 2. Take the SAT or the ACT as early as possible and authorize the testing agency to release your scores directly to the ROTC Scholarship Program or ROTC Programs. 3. Apply to the ROTC colleges or universities you are interested in attending. 4. Take the Qualifying Medical Examination. 5. Take the Physical Aptitude Examination. 6. Enroll.	Air Force Army Navy (Marine Corps)

ROTC PROGRAMS (continued)		
Program	**Overview**	**Branch**
College Testing	All candidates must take either the standardized American College Testing (ACT) Assessment Program exam or the College Board Admissions Testing Program Scholastic Assessment Tests (SAT). ***ACT*** ***American College Testing Assessment Program*** English, Reading, Mathematics, and Science Reasoning ***SAT College Board Admissions Testing Program*** Verbal and Mathematics	Air Force Army Navy (Marine Corps)
Current Military Members/Prior Service	Active duty members and veterans who are eligible may enroll in ROTC programs while in college, complete degree requirements, and earn an officer's commission. Veterans may use the G.I. Bill or veterans' benefits, receive the nontaxable allowance, and compete for other scholarships and financial aid programs.	Air Force Army Navy (Marine Corps)

U.S. AIR FORCE ROTC

551 East Maxwell Boulevard
Maxwell Air Force Base, AL 36112-6663

☎ 800-522-0033 ext 2091
http://www.usaf.mil

OVERVIEW Largest single source of Air Force officers.

The Air Force Reserve Officers' Training Corps (AFROTC) is an outstanding educational program designed to provide candidates with the opportunity to become Air Force officers while completing their bachelor's degree programs. The Air Force is in current need of candidates with degrees in engineering, architecture, mathematics, computer science, meteorology, physics, and nursing. Upon graduation, AFROTC cadets are commissioned as second lieutenants in the U.S. Air Force Reserve.

Programs

Four years
Two years
One year
Nursing Programs
Scholarships

Admissions Process

Candidates must:
1. request and fill out the Preliminary Application.
2. take the SAT or the ACT as early as possible and authorize the testing agency to release their scores directly to the ROTC Scholarship Program or ROTC Programs.

3. apply to the ROTC colleges or universities they are interested in attending.
4. be interviewed and selected by a board of military officers.
5. take the Qualifying Medical Examination.
6. take the Physical Aptitude Examination.
7. enroll in the ROTC program.

General Qualifications

Age: 17–23
- Pilot/navigator candidate before age $26\frac{1}{2}$
- Waived through age 29 if candidate had prior service
- Scholarship recipient—before age 25 as of June 30 in the year of commissioning
- Nonscholarship recipient—before age 30

Status: U.S. citizen
Must be a full-time student at a school offering ROTC

Medical: Must be in good physical and mental health
Must be able to pass a Department of Defense Medical Examination Review Board medical examination

Physical: Must be able to pass the Physical Aptitude Examination (PAE)

Testing

All candidates must take either the standardized American College Testing (ACT) Assessment Program exam or the College Board Admissions Testing Program Scholastic Assessment Tests (SAT I).

ACT American College Testing Assessment Program
English, Reading, Mathematics, and Science Reasoning

SAT College Board Admissions Testing Program
Verbal and Mathematics

Candidates must also successfully pass the Air Force Officer Qualifying Test.

Obligation

Must enlist in the U.S. Air Force Reserve for a period of eight years.

COLLEGES AND UNIVERSITIES THAT OFFER AFROTC (AND THOSE WITH CROSSTOWN ENROLLMENT AGREEMENTS)

Many of the AFROTC colleges or universities listed below have crosstown agreements with other colleges and universities located nearby (as of March 1993). These crosstown agreements establish a formal relationship between the host AFROTC university and the crosstown university, which permits students to attend the crosstown school and still participate in the AFROTC program at the AFROTC school. You are advised to obtain a current list of crosstown agreements from the AFROTC.

State/AROTC Unit or Crosstown University

Italics indicate host AFROTC unit.

Alabama
Alabama State University, Montgomery
Auburn University, Auburn
Auburn University at Montgomery
Birmingham Southern College, Birmingham
Bishop State Community College, Mobile
Huntington College, Montgomery
Jefferson State Junior College, Birmingham
Miles College, Birmingham
Sanford University, Birmingham
Shelton State Community College, Tuscaloosa
Southern Union State Junior College, Wadley
Spring Hill College, Mobile
Stillman College, Tuscaloosa
Troy State University, Montgomery
Troy State University, Troy
Tuskegee University, Tuskegee
University of Alabama in Birmingham, Birmingham
University of Alabama in Huntsville, Huntsville
University of Alabama, Tuscaloosa
University of Mobile, Mobile
University of Montevallo, Montevallo
University of South Alabama, Mobile
University of West Alabama, Livingston

Arizona
Arizona State University, Tempe
DeVry Institute of Technology, Phoenix
Embry-Riddle Aeronautical University, Prescott
Glendale Community College, Glendale
Grand Canyon University, Phoenix
Mesa Community College, Mesa
Northern Arizona University, Flagstaff
Paradise Valley Community College, Phoenix
Phoenix College, Phoenix
Pima Community College, Tucson
Scottsdale Community College, Scottsdale
South Mountain Community College, Phoenix
University of Arizona, Tucson
University of Phoenix, Phoenix
Yavapai Community College, Prescott

Arkansas
John Brown University, Siloam Springs
University of Arkansas, Fayetteville

California
American River College, Sacramento
Antelope Valley College, Lancaster

Azusa Pacific University, Azusa
Biola University, La Mirada
California Lutheran University,
    Thousand Oaks
California State Polytechnic University,
    Pomona
California State University,
    Dominguez Hills
California State University, Fresno
California State University, Fullerton
California State University, Hayward
California State University, Long Beach
California State University, Los Angeles
California State University, Northridge
California State University, Sacramento
California State University, San Marcos
Canada College, Redwood City
Chaffey College, Rancho Cucamonga
Chapman University, Orange
Christian Heritage College, El Cajon
Citrus College, Glendora
City College of San Francisco,
    San Francisco
Claremont McKenna College, Claremont
College of Alameda, Alameda
College of the Canyons, Valencia
College of Notre Dame, Belmont
College of San Mateo, San Mateo
College of the Sequoias, Visalia
Compton Community College, Compton
Contra Costa College, San Pablo
Cuyamaca Community College, El Cajon
Cypress College, Cypress
DeAnza College, Cupertino
Delta College, Stockton
Diablo Valley College, Pleasant Hill
Dominican College, San Rafael
East Los Angeles College, Monterey Park
El Camino College, Torrance
Evergreen Valley College, San Jose
Foothill College, Los Altos Hills
Fresno City College, Fresno
Fullerton College, Fullerton
Glendale Community College, Glendale
Golden West College, Huntington Beach

Grossmont Community College, El Cajon
Harvey Mudd College, Claremont
Holy Names College, Oakland
Kings River Community College, Reedley
Laney College, Oakland
Las Positas College, Livermore
Loma Linda University, Loma Linda
Los Angeles City College, Los Angeles
Los Angeles Harbor College, Wilmington
Los Angeles Mission College,
    San Fernando
Los Angeles Pierce College,
    Woodland Hills
Los Angeles Southwest College,
    Los Angeles
Los Angeles Training Technical College,
    Los Angeles
Los Angeles Valley College, Van Nuys
Los Medanos College, Pittsburg
Loyola Marymount University,
    Los Angeles
Merced College, Merced
Merritt College, Oakland
Mills College, Oakland
Mira Costa College, Oceanside
Mission College, Santa Clara
Moorpark College, Moorpark
Mount St. Mary's College, Los Angeles
Mount San Antonio College, Walnut
Mount San Jacinto College, San Jacinto
National University, Los Angeles
Occidental College, Los Angeles
Ohlone College, Fremont
Orange Coast College, Costa Mesa
Palomar College, San Marcos
Pasadena City College, Pasadena
Pepperdine University, Malibu
Pitzer College, Claremont
Point Loma Nazarene College, San Diego
Pomona College, Claremont
Rancho Santiago College, Santa Ana
Rio Hondo College, Whittier
Riverside Community College, Riverside
Sacramento City College, Sacramento
Saddleback College, Mission Viejo

Saint Mary's College of California,
  Moraga
San Bernardino Valley College,
  San Bernardino
San Diego City College, San Diego
San Diego Mesa College, San Diego
San Diego Miramar College, San Diego
San Diego State University, San Diego
San Francisco State University,
  San Francisco
San Jose City College, San Jose
San Jose State University, San Jose
Santa Monica College, Santa Monica
Santa Rosa Junior College, Santa Rosa
Scripps College, Claremont
Siena City College, Rocklin
Sonoma State University, Rohnert Park
Southwestern College, Chula Vista
Stanford University, San Jose
University of California at Berkeley,
  Berkeley
University of California, Davis
University of California, Irvine
University of California, Los Angeles
University of California, Riverside
University of California, San Diego,
  La Jolla
University of California, San Francisco
University of California, Santa Barbara
University of California, Santa Cruz
University of La Verne, La Verne
University of the Pacific, Stockton
University of Redlands, Redlands
University of San Diego, San Diego
University of Santa Clara, Santa Clara
University of Southern California,
  Los Angeles
University of San Francisco,
  San Francisco
Ventura College, Ventura
Victor Valley College, Victorville
West Valley College, Saratoga
Westmont College, Santa Barbara
Whittier College, Whittier
Yuba College, Marysville

Colorado
Arapahoe Community College, Littleton
Colorado School of Mines, Golden
Colorado State University, Fort Collins
Front Range Community College,
  Westminster
Regis College, Denver
University of Colorado, Boulder
University of Colorado, Denver
University of Denver, Denver
University of Northern Colorado,
  Greeley

Connecticut
Central Connecticut State University,
  New Britain
Eastern Connecticut State, Willimantic
Fairfield University, Fairfield
Quinnipiac College, Hamden
Southern Connecticut State, New Haven
Trinity College, Hartford
University of Connecticut, Storrs
University of Hartford, West Hartford
University of New Haven, West Haven
Wesleyan University, Middletown
Western Connecticut State University,
  Danbury
Yale University, New Haven

Delaware
Delaware State University, Dover
University of Delaware, Newark
Wilmington College, New Castle

District of Columbia
American University
Catholic University of America
George Washington University
Georgetown University
Howard University
Trinity College
University of the District of Columbia

Florida
Barry University, Miami Shores
Bethune Cookman College,
    Daytona Beach
Brevard Community College, Cocoa
    Beach
Daytona Beach Community College,
    Daytona Beach
Eckerd College, Saint Petersburg
Embry-Riddle Aeronautical University,
    Daytona Beach
Florida A&M University, Tallahassee
Florida Atlantic University, Boca Raton
Florida College, Temple Terrace
Florida International University, Miami
Florida State University, Tallahassee
Hillsborough Community College,
    Tampa
Lake Sumter Community College,
    Leesburg
Miami Dade Community College, Miami
Saint Leo College, Saint Leo
Saint Petersburg Junior College,
    St. Petersburg
Santa Fe Community College, Gainesville
Seminole Community College, Sanford
Tallahassee Community College,
    Tallahassee
University of Central Florida, Orlando
University of Florida, Gainesville
University of Miami, Coral Gables
University of South Florida, Tampa
University of Tampa, Tampa
Valencia Community College, Orlando

Georgia
Agnes Scott College, Decatur
Atlanta College of Art, Atlanta
Clark Atlanta University, Atlanta
Clayton State College, Morrow
Columbia Theological Seminary,
    Decatur
Emory University, Atlanta
Georgia State University, Atlanta
Georgia Institute of Technology, Atlanta

Institute of Paper Science and
    Technology, Atlanta
Kennesaw State College, Marietta
Medical College of Georgia, Augusta
Mercer University, Atlanta
Morehouse College, Atlanta
Morris Brown College, Atlanta
Oglethorpe University, Atlanta
Southern College of Technology,
    Marietta
Spelman College, Atlanta
University of Georgia, Athens
Valdosta State College, Valdosta

Hawaii
Brigham Young University of Hawaii,
    Honolulu
Chaminade University of Honolulu,
    Honolulu
Hawaii Pacific College, Honolulu
Honolulu Community College, Honolulu
Kapiolani Community College, Honolulu
Leeward Community College, Pearl City
University of Hawaii at Manoa, Honolulu
West Oahu College, Pearl City
Windward Community College, Kaneohe

Illinois
Chicago State University, Chicago
College of Dupage, Glen Ellyn
Elmhurst College, Elmhurst
Governors State University,
    University Park
Illinois Institute of Technology, Chicago
John A. Logan College, Caterville
Lewis University, Romeoville
Loyola University, Chicago
North Central College, Naperville
North Park College, Chicago
Northeastern Illinois University, Chicago
Northern Illinois University, DeKalb
Northwestern University, Evanston
Parkland College, Champaign
Southeastern Illinois College, Harrisburg
Southern Illinois University, Carbondale

University of Chicago, Chicago
University of Illinois, Urbana-Champaign
University of Illinois, Chicago
Wheaton College, Wheaton
Xavier College, Chicago

Indiana
Belleville Area College, Belleville
Bethel College, Mishawaka
Butler University, Indianapolis
De Pauw University, Greencastle
Holy Cross Junior College, Notre Dame
Indiana State University, Terre Haute
Indiana University at South Bend,
  South Bend
Indiana University, Bloomington
Lewis and Clark Community College,
  Godfrey
McKendree College, Lebanon
Purdue University at Indianapolis,
  Indianapolis
Purdue University, West Lafayette
*Rose-Hulman Institute of Technology,
  Terre Haute*
Saint Mary's College, Notre Dame
*Southern Illinois University at
  Edwardsville*
University of Notre Dame, Notre Dame
Vincennes University, Vincennes

Iowa
Drake University, Des Moines
Grand View College, Des Moines
Iowa State University, Ames
University of Iowa, Iowa City

Kansas
Baker University, Baldwin City
Kansas State University, Manhattan
Manhattan Christian College, Manhattan
MidAmerica Nazarene College, Olathe
University of Kansas, Lawrence
Washburn University, Topeka

Kentucky
Bellarmine College, Louisville

Centre College, Danville
Eastern Kentucky University, Richmond
Georgetown College, Georgetown
Jefferson Community College, Louisville
Kentucky State University, Frankfort
Louisville Presbyterian Theological
  Seminary, Louisville
Southern Baptist Theological Seminary,
  Louisville
Spalding University, Louisville
Transylvania University, Lexington
University of Kentucky, Lexington
University of Louisville, Louisville

Louisiana
Delgado Community College,
  New Orleans
Dillard University, New Orleans
Grambling State University, Grambling
*Louisiana State University and A&M
  College, Baton Rouge*
Louisiana State University Medical
  Center, New Orleans
Louisiana Tech University, Ruston
Loyola University, New Orleans
Our Lady of Holy Cross College,
  New Orleans
Southern University and A&M College,
  Baton Rouge
Southern University in New Orleans,
  New Orleans
Tulane University, New Orleans
University of New Orleans, New Orleans
William Carey College, New Orleans
Xavier University, New Orleans

Maine
University of Southern Maine, Portland

Maryland
Bowie State University, Bowie
Johns Hopkins University, Baltimore
Loyola College, Baltimore
Prince George's Community College,
  Largo
Towson State University, Towson

University of Maryland, Baltimore
University of Maryland, College Park

Massachusetts
American International College,
    Springfield
Anna Maria College, Paxton
Assumption College, Worcester
Becker College, Worcester
Bentley College, Waltham
Boston University, Boston
Bradford College, Bradford
Bridgewater State College, Bridgewater
Clark University, Worcester
College of the Holy Cross, Worcester
College of Our Lady of the Elms,
    Chicopee
Endicott College, Beverly
Fitchburg State College, Fitchburg
Gordon College, Wenham
Harvard University, Cambridge
Massachusetts Institute of Technology,
    Cambridge
Merrimack College, North Andover
Middlesex Community College, Bedford
Montserrat College of Visual Art,
    Beverly
Nichols College, Dudley
North Shore Community College,
    Beverly
Northeastern University, Boston
Northern Essex Community College,
    Haverhill
Quinsigamond Community College,
    Worcester
Springfield College, Springfield
Tufts University, Medford
University of Massachusetts, Amherst
University of Massachusetts, Lowell
University of Massachusetts Medical
    School, Worcester
Western New England College,
    Springfield
Westfield State College, Westfield
Worcester Polytechnic Institute,
    Worcester

Worcester State College, Worcester

Michigan
Eastern Michigan University, Ypsilanti
Michigan State University, East Lansing
Michigan Technological University,
    Houghton
University of Michigan, Ann Arbor
University of Michigan at Dearborn

Minnesota
Bethel College, St. Paul
College of Saint Scholastica, Duluth
Concordia College, Moorhead
Concordia College, St. Paul
Moorhead State College, Moorhead
North Central Bible College,
    Minneapolis
University of Minnesota, Duluth
University of Minnesota, Minneapolis
University of St. Thomas, St. Paul

Mississippi
Mississippi State University,
    Mississippi State
Mississippi University for Women,
    Columbus
Mississippi Valley State University,
    Itta Bena
University of Mississippi, University
University of Southern Mississippi,
    Hattiesburg
William Carey College, Hattiesburg

Missouri
Parks College of Saint Louis University,
    St. Louis
Saint Louis University, St. Louis
Southeast Missouri State University,
    Cape Girardeau
University of Missouri-Columbia
University of Missouri, St. Louis
University of Missouri-Rolla
Washington University, St. Louis
Westminister College, Fulton

Montana
Montana State University, Bozeman

Nebraska
Bellevue University, Bellevue
College of St. Mary's, Omaha
Creighton University, Omaha
Dana College, Blair
Midland Lutheran College, Fremont
University of Nebraska, Lincoln
University of Nebraska Medical Center, Omaha
University of Nebraska, Omaha

New Hampshire
Colby Sawyer, New London
Daniel Webster College, Nashua
Franklin Pierce College, Rindge
Keene State College, Keene
Notre Dame College, Manchester
Plymouth State College, Plymouth
Saint Anselm's College, Manchester
University of New Hampshire, Durham

New Jersey
Fairleigh Dickinson College, Teaneck
Jersey City State College, Jersey City
Kean College of New Jersey, Union
Montclair State College, Montclair
New Jersey Institute of Technology, Newark
Princeton University, Princeton
Rutgers University, New Brunswick
Seton Hall University, South Orange
Stevens Institute of Technology, Hoboken
Trenton State College, Trenton
William Paterson College, Wayne

New Mexico
New Mexico State University, Las Cruces
New Mexico University, Albuquerque

New York
Adelphi University, Garden City
Alfred University, Alfred

Clarkson University, Potsdam
College of Saint Rose, Albany
Columbia College, New York
Cornell University, Ithaca
CUNY Brooklyn College, Brooklyn
CUNY Lehman College, Bronx
Fordham University, Bronx
Hofstra University, Hempstead
Houghton College, Houghton
Iona College, New Rochelle
Ithaca College, Ithaca
Lemoyne College, Syracuse
Long Island University/C.W. Post Campus, Brookville
Manhattan College, Riverdale
Mercy College, Dobbs Ferry
New York Institute of Technology, Old Westbury
Pace University, New York
Polytechnic University, Brooklyn
Rensselaer Polytechnic Institute, Troy
Roberts Wesleyan College, Rochester
Rochester Institute of Technology, Rochester
Russell Sage College, Troy
Saint John Fisher College, Rochester
St. Lawrence University, Canton
Siena College, Loudonville
SUNY at Albany
SUNY at Stony Brook, Stony Brook
SUNY/College at Brockport
SUNY/College of Environmental Science and Forestry, Syracuse
SUNY/College at Geneseo
SUNY/College at Old Westbury
SUNY/College at Potsdam
Union College, Schenectady
University of Rochester
Utica College of Syracuse, Utica

North Carolina
Davidson College, Davidson
Duke University, Durham
East Carolina University, Greenville
Fayetteville State, Fayetteville
Johnson C. Smith University, Charlotte

Methodist College, Fayetteville
North Carolina A&T State University,
    Greensboro
North Carolina Central University,
    Durham
North Carolina State University, Raleigh
Pembroke State University, Pembroke
Shaw University, Raleigh
St. Augustine's College, Raleigh
University of North Carolina, Chapel Hill
University of North Carolina at Charlotte

North Dakota
North Dakota State University, Fargo
University of North Dakota, Grand Forks

Ohio
Baldwin Wallace College, Berea
*Bowling Green State University,
    Bowling Green*
Cedarville College, Cedarville
Central State University, Wilberforce
Cleveland State University, Cleveland
College of Mount St. Joseph, Cincinnati
Kent State University, Kent
Miami University, Oxford
Ohio Northern University, Ada
Ohio State University, Columbus
Ohio University, Athens
University of Akron, Akron
University of Cincinnati, Cincinnati
University of Dayton, Dayton
Wilberforce University, Wilberforce
Wittenberg University, Springfield
Wright State University, Dayton
Xavier University, Cincinnati

Oklahoma
Oklahoma State University, Stillwater
University of Oklahoma, Norman

Oregon
Concordian College, Portland
Lewis and Clark College, Portland
Marylhurst College, Marylhurst

Oregon Health Science University,
    Portland
Oregon State University, Corvallis
Pacific University, Forest Grove
Reed College, Portland
University of Oregon, Eugene
University of Portland, Portland
Warner Pacific College, Portland

Pennsylvania
Carnegie Mellon University, Pittsburgh
Chatham College, Pittsburgh
Drexel University, Philadelphia
Duquesne University, Pittsburgh
East Stroudsburg University of
    Pennsylvania, East Stroudsberg
King's College, Wilkes Barre
Mercy Hurst College, Erie
Penn State University/Worthington,
    Dunmore
Temple University, Philadelphia
University of Pittsburgh, Pittsburgh
University of Pennsylvania, Philadelphia
University of Scranton, Scranton
Valley Forge Military Academy,
    Valley Forge
Villanova University, Villanova
West Chester University, West Chester
Wilkes University, Wilkes Barre

Puerto Rico
University of Puerto Rico, Mayaguez
University of Puerto Rico, Rio Piedras

South Carolina
Clemson University, Clemson
Medical University of South Carolina,
    Charleston
The Citadel, Charleston
University of South Carolina, Columbia

South Dakota
South Dakota State University, Brookings

Tennessee
Christian Brothers University, Memphis
David Lipscomb University, Nashville
Fisk University, Nashville
Free Will Baptist Bible College, Nashville
Middle Tennessee State University,
   Murfreesboro
Rhodes College, Memphis
Tennessee State University, Nashville
University of Tennessee, Knoxville
Vanderbilt University, Nashville

Texas
Our Lady of the Lake University,
   San Antonio
Saint Mary's University, San Antonio
Southern Methodist University, Dallas
Texas A&M University, College Station
Texas Christian University, Fort Worth
Texas Tech University, Lubbock
Texas Woman's University, Denton
University of the Incarnate Word,
   San Antonio
University of Texas at Austin, Austin
University of Texas at Dallas,
   Richardson
University of Texas at El Paso, El Paso
University of Texas at San Antonio

Utah
Brigham Young University, Provo
Salt Lake Community College,
   Salt Lake City
University of Utah, Salt Lake City
Utah State University, Logan
Utah Valley State College, Orem
Weber State University, Ogden
Westminster College, Salt Lake City

Vermont
Norwich University, Northfield

Virginia
George Mason University, Fairfax
Marymount University, Arlington

Piedmont Community College,
   Charlottesville
University of Virginia, Charlottesville
Virginia Military Institute, Lexington
Virginia Polytechnic Institute,
   Blacksburg

Washington
Bellevue Community College, Bellevue
Central Washington University,
   Ellensburg
Edmonds Community College,
   Lynnwood
Everett Community College, Everett
Highline Community College, Midway
North Seattle Community College,
   Seattle
Seattle Central Community College,
   Seattle
Seattle Pacific University, Seattle
Seattle University, Seattle
Shoreline Community College, Seattle
South Seattle Community College,
   Seattle
University of Washington, Seattle
Washington State University, Pullman

West Virginia
Fairmont State College, Fairmont
West Virginia University, Morgantown

Wisconsin
Alverno College, Milwaukee
Carthage College, Milwaukee
Marquette University, Milwaukee
Milwaukee School of Engineering,
   Milwaukee
Mount Mary College, Milwaukee
University of Wisconsin, Madison
University of Wisconsin, Milwaukee
University of Wisconsin, Whitewater

Wyoming
Laramie County Community College,
   Laramie
University of Wyoming, Laramie

U.S. ARMY ROTC

U.S. Army Gold QUEST Center
PO Box 3279
Warminster, PA 18974-0218

☎ 800-USA-ROTC
http://www-tradoc.army.mil/rotc/index.html.

OVERVIEW   Largest single source of Army officers.

The Army ROTC provides an outstanding program designed to provide candidates the opportunity to become officers in the Regular Army, Army Reserve, and Army National Guard, and is offered at more than 600 colleges and universities. Upon successful completion of ROTC and baccalaureate degree requirements, graduates will be commissioned as second lieutenants in the Active Army, Army Reserve, or the National Guard.

Programs

Four years
Two years
One year
Nursing Programs
Scholarships

Admissions Process

Candidates must:
1. request and fill out the Preliminary Application.
2. take the SAT or the ACT as early as possible and authorize the testing agency to release their scores directly to the ROTC Scholarship Program or ROTC Programs.

3. apply to the ROTC colleges or universities they are interested in attending.
4. be interviewed and selected by a board of military officers.
5. take the Qualifying Medical Examination.
6. take the Physical Aptitude Examination.
7. enroll in the ROTC Program.

General Qualifications

Age: 17–21
- In addition, candidates must not reach their 25th birthday by June 30 of the year in which they will graduate from college and receive their commission.
- If they have prior active duty military service, they may be eligible for extension of the age requirement (age is extended one year for each one year of military service).

Status: U.S. citizen
              Must be a full-time student at a school offering ROTC

Medical: Must be in good physical and mental health
              Must be able to pass a Department of Defense Medical Examination Review Board medical examination

Physical: Must be able to pass the Physical Aptitude Examination (PAE)

Testing

All candidates must take either the standardized American College Testing (ACT) Assessment Program exam or the College Board Admissions Testing Program Scholastic Assessment Tests (SAT I).

ACT American College Testing Assessment Program
English, Reading, Mathematics, and Science Reasoning

SAT College Board Admissions Testing Program
Verbal and Mathematics

Obligation

Must enlist in the U.S. Army Reserve for a period of eight years.

COLLEGES AND UNIVERSITIES THAT OFFER AROTC

Many of the AROTC colleges or universities listed below have crosstown agreements with other colleges and universities located nearby. These crosstown agreements establish a formal relationship between the host AROTC university and the crosstown university, which permits students to attend the crosstown school and still participate in the AROTC program at the AROTC school. A current list should be requested from the AROTC.

Alabama
Alabama A&M University, Normal
Alabama State University, Montgomery
Athens State, Athens
Auburn University, Auburn
Auburn University at Montgomery
Birmingham-Southern, Birmingham
Jacksonville State University,
    Jacksonville
Judson College, Marion
Marion Military Institute, Marion
Miles College, Birmingham
Samford University, Birmingham
Stillman College,Tuscaloosa
Talladega College, Talladega
Troy State University, Montgomery
Troy State University, Troy
Tuskegee Institute, Tuskegee
University of Alabama, Birmingham
University of Alabama, Huntsville
University of Alabama, Tuscaloosa
University of Montevallo, Montevallo
University of North Alabama, Florence
University of South Alabama, Mobile

Alaska
University of Alaska, Fairbanks

Arizona
Arizona State University, Tempe
Embry-Riddle Aeronautical University,
    Prescott
Grand Canyon University, Phoenix

Northern Arizona University, Flagstaff
University of Arizona, Tucson

Arkansas
Arkansas State University,
    State University
Arkansas Tech University, Russellville
Central Baptist College, Conway
Harding University, Searcy
Hendrix College, Conway
John Brown University, Siloam Springs
Ouchita Baptist University, Arkadelphia
Philander Smith College, Little Rock
University of Central Arkansas at
    Conway, Conway
University of Arkansas at Fayetteville
University of Arkansas, at Little Rock
University of Arkansas, at Pine Bluff
University of Arkansas for Medical
    Sciences, Little Rock
Williams Baptist College, Walnut Ridge

California
Art Center College of Design, Pasadena
Azusa Pacific, Azusa
Biola University, La Mirada
California Baptist College, Riverside
California College of Podiatric Medicine,
    San Francisco
California Institute of Technology,
    Pasadena
California Lutheran University,
    Thousand Oaks

California Polytechnic State University,
  San Luis Obispo
California Polytechnic University,
  Pomona
California State University, Chico
California State University,
  Dominguez Hills
California State University, Fresno
California State University, Fullerton
California State University, Hayward
California State University, Los Angeles
California State University, Northridge
California State University, San
  Bernardino
Christian Heritage, El Cajon
Claremont-McKenna College, Claremont
College of Notre Dame, Belmount
DeVry Institute of Technology, Pomona
Dominican College of San Rafael,
  San Rafael
Golden Gate University, San Francisco
Loma Linda University, Loma Linda
Loyola Marymount University,
  Los Angeles
Mills College, Oakland
Mount St. Mary's, Los Angeles
National University, San Diego
Occidental College, Los Angeles
Pepperdine University, Malibu
Point Loma College, San Diego
Samuel Merritt, Berkeley
San Diego State University, San Diego
San Francisco State University,
  San Francisco
Sonomo State University, Rohnert Park
St. Mary's College of California, Moraga
Stanford University, Stanford
United States International University,
  San Diego
University of California, Berkeley
University of California, Davis
University of California, Irvine
University of California, Los Angeles
University of California, Redlands
University of California, Riverside

University of California, San Diego
University of California, Santa Barbara
University of La Verne, La Verne
University of San Diego, San Diego
University of San Francisco,
  San Francisco
University of Santa Clara, Santa Clara
University of Southern California,
  Los Angeles
Westmont College, Santa Barbara
Whittier College, Whittier

Colorado
Beth-el College of Nursing, Colorado
  Springs University of Colorado
  at Denver
Colorado Christian University,
  Lakewood
Colorado College, Colorado Springs
Colorado School of Mines, Golden
Colorado State University, Fort Collins
Colorado Technical University,
  Colorado Springs
Metropolitan State College, Denver
Regis College, Denver
University of Colorado, Boulder
University of Colorado,
  Colorado Springs
University of Colorado, Denver
University of Denver, Denver
University of Northern Colorado,
  Greeley
University of Southern Colorado,
  Pueblo

Connecticut
Central Connecticut State University,
  New Britain
Eastern Connecticut State University,
  Willimantic
Saint Joseph College, West Hartford
Trinity College, Hartford
University of Connecticut, Storrs
University of Hartford, West Hartford

Delaware
Delaware State College, Dover
University of Delaware, Newark

District of Columbia
American University
Catholic University
George Washington University
Georgetown University
Howard University
University of the District of Columbia

Florida
Barry University, Miami
Bethune-Cookman College, Daytona
Eckerd College, Saint Petersburg
Embry Riddle Aeronautical University,
   Daytona
Florida Institute of Technology,
   Melbourne
Florida International University, Miami
Florida Southern College, Lakeland
Florida State University, Tallahassee
Saint Leo College, Saint Leo
Stetson University, Deland
University of Central Florida, Orlando
University of Florida, Gainesville
University of Miami, Coral Gables
University of North Florida, Jacksonville
University of South Florida, Tampa
University of Tampa, Tampa
University of West Florida, Pensacola

Georgia
Albany State College, Albany
Armstrong State College, Savannah
Augusta College, Augusta
Brenau College, Gainesville
Clark Atlanta University, Atlanta
Columbus College, Columbus
DeKalb College, Decatur
Emory University, Atlanta
Fort Valley State College, Fort Valley
Georgia College, Milledgeville
Georgia Institute of Technology, Atlanta
Georgia Military College, Milledgeville

Georgia Southern University, Statesboro
Georgia State University, Atlanta
Medical College of Georgia, Augusta
Mercer University, Macon
Morehouse College, Atlanta
Morris Brown College, Atlanta
North Georgia College, Dahlonega
Paine College, Augusta
Savannah State College, Savannah
Southern Polytechnic State University,
   Marietta
Spelman College, Atlanta
Thomas College, Thomasville
University of Georgia, Athens
West Georgia College, Carrollton

Guam
University of Guam, Agana

Hawaii
Brigham Young University of Hawaii,
   Laie
Chaminade University of Honolulu,
   Honolulu
Hawaii Pacific University, Honolulu
University of Hawaii, Honolulu
University of Hawaii at West Oahu,
   Pearl City

Idaho
Boise State University, Boise
Lewis-Clark State College, Lewiston
Northwest Nazarene College, Nampa
University of Idaho, Moscow

Illinois
Bradley University, Peoria
Chicago State University, Chicago
DePaul University, Chicago
DeVry Institute of Technology, Lombard
Eastern Illinois University, Charleston
Illinois Institute of Technology, Chicago
Illinois State University, Normal
Illinois Wesleyan University,
   Bloomington
Lewis University, Romeoville

Loyola University of Chicago, Chicago
Monmouth College, Monmouth
Northeastern Illinois University, Chicago
Northern Illinois University, DeKalb
Northwestern University, Evanston
Olivet Nazarene College, Kankakee
Purdue University Calumet, Hammon
Saint Xavier College, Chicago
Southern Illinois University at
    Carbondale
Southern Illinois University at
    Edwardsville
University of Chicago, Chicago
University of Illinois at Chicago
University of Illinois at Urbana-
    Champaign
Western Illinois University, Macomb
Wheaton College, Wheaton

Indiana
Bell State University, Muncie
Butler University, Indianapolis
DePauw University, Greencastle
Indiana State University, Terre Haute
Indiana University, Bloomington
Indiana University, Kokomo
Indiana University at South Bend,
    South Bend
Indiana University Southeast,
    New Albany
Marian College, Indianapolis
Purdue University, Indianapolis
Purdue University, West Lafayette
Rose-Hulman Institute of Technology,
    Terre Haute
Saint Mary's College, Notre Dame
University of Indianapolis, Indianapolis
University of Notre Dame, Notre Dame

Iowa
Allen College of Nursing, Waterloo
Coe College, Cedar Rapids
Drake University, Des Moines
Grand View College, Des Moines
Iowa State University, Ames

Simpson College, Indianola
University of Iowa, Iowa City
University of Northern Iowa, Cedar Falls

Kansas
Baker University, Baldwin City
Kansas State University, Manhattan
MidAmerica Nazarene College, Olathe
Pittsburg State University, Pittsburg
Saint Mary College, Leavenworth
University of Kansas, Lawrence
Washburn University, Topeka

Kentucky
Bellarmine College, Louisville
Centre College, Danville
Cumberland College, Williamsburg
Eastern Kentucky University, Richmond
Georgetown College, Georgetown
Kentucky State University, Frankfort
Midway College, Midway
Morehead State University, Morehead
Murray State University, Murray
Northern Kentucky University,
    Highland Heights
Spalding University, Louisville
Thomas More College, Crestview Hills
Transylvania University, Lexington
Union College, Barbourville
University of Kentucky, Lexington
University of Louisville, Louisville
Western Kentucky University,
    Bowling Green

Louisiana
Centenary College of Louisiana,
    Shreveport
Dillard University, New Orleans
East Texas Baptist University, Marshall
Grambling State University, Grambling
Louisiana School of Nursing,
    New Orleans
Louisiana State University and A&M
    College, Baton Rouge
Louisiana Tech University, Ruston

Loyola University, New Orleans
McNeese State University, Lake Charles
Northeast Louisiana University, Monroe
Northwestern State University of
    Louisiana, Natchitoches
Southern University and A&M College,
    Baton Rouge
Tulane University, New Orleans
University of New Orleans, New Orleans
University of Southwestern Louisiana,
    Lafayette

Maine
Colby College, Waterville
Husson College, Bangor
Saint Josephs College, North Windham
University of Maine, Orono
University of Southern Maine, Portland

Maryland
Bowie State University, Bowie
College of Notre Dame of Maryland,
    Baltimore
Coppin State College, Baltimore
Frostburg State University, Frostburg
Johns Hopkins University, Baltimore
Loyola College, Baltimore
Maryland Institute College of Art,
    Baltimore
Morgan State University, Baltimore
Mount Saint Mary's College, Emmitsburg
Salisbury State College, Salisbury
Towson State University, Towson
University of Maryland, Baltimore
    County, Baltimore
University of Maryland at College Park
Western Maryland College, Westminster

Massachusetts
American International College,
    Springfield
Assumption College, Worcester
Babson College, Babson Park
Bentley College, Waltham
Boston College, Chestnut Hill
Boston University, Boston

Brandeis University, Waltham
Bridgewater State College, Bridgewater
Clark University, Worcester
College of the Holy Cross, Worcester
College of Our Lady of the Elms,
    Chicopee
Fitchburg State College, Fitchburg
Harvard University, Cambridge
Massachusetts Institute of Technology,
    Cambridge
Massachusetts Maritime College,
    Buzzards Bay
Mount Holyoke College, South Hadley
Nichols College, Dudley
North Adams State College,
    North Adams
Northeastern University, Boston
Smith College, North Hampton
Springfield College, Springfield
Stonehill College, North Easton
Tufts University, Medford
University of Lowell, Lowell
University of Massachusetts, Amherst
University of Massachusetts, Boston
University of Massachusetts, Dartmouth
Wentworth Institute of Technology,
    Boston
Western New England College,
    Springfield
Westfield State College, Westfield
Worcester Polytechnic Institute,
    Worcester
Worcester State College, Worcester

Michigan
Central Michigan University,
    Mount Pleasant
Davenport College, Kalamazoo
Eastern Michigan University, Ypsilanti
Ferris State University, Big Rapids
Grand Valley State College, Allendale
Hope College, Holland
Kalamazoo College, Kalamazoo
Michigan State University, East Lansing
Michigan Technological University,
    Houghton

Northern Michigan University,
    Marquette
Saginaw Valley State, University Center
University of Detroit, Detroit
University of Michigan/Ann Arbor
University of Michigan/Dearborn
Western Michigan University,
    Kalamazoo

Minnesota

Augsburg College, Minneapolis
Bethel College, St. Paul
College of Saint Benedict, St. Joseph
College of Saint Catherine, St. Paul
College of Saint Scholastica, Duluth
Concordia College, St. Paul
Gustavus Adolphus College, St. Peter
Macalester College, St. Paul
Mankato State University, Mankato
North Central Bible College,
    Minneapolis
Northwestern College, St. Paul
Saint Cloud State University, St. Cloud
Saint John's University, Collegeville
University of Minnesota/Duluth
University of Minnesota/Minneapolis
University of Saint Thomas, St. Paul

Mississippi

Alcorn State University, Lorman
Jackson State University, Jackson
Mississippi College, Clinton
Mississippi State University,
    Mississippi State
Mississippi University for Women,
    Columbus
Mississippi Valley State University,
    Itta Bena
Tougaloo College, Tougaloo
University of Mississippi, University
University of Mississippi School
    of Nursing, Jackson
University of Southern Mississippi,
    Hattiesburg
William Carey College, Hattiesburg

Missouri

Central Bible College, Springfield
Central Methodist College, Fayette
Central Missouri State University,
    Warrensburg
College of the Ozarks, Point Lookout
Drury College, Ft. Leonard Wood
Evangel College, Springfield
Fontbonne College, St. Louis
Kemper Military School and College,
    Boonville
Lincoln University, Jefferson City
Missouri Southern State College, Joplin
Missouri Western State College,
    St. Joseph
Northeast Missouri State University,
    Kirksville
Park College, Parkville
Parks College of Saint Louis University,
    Saint Louis
Rockhurst College, Kansas City
Saint Louis University, St. Louis
Southwest Missouri State University,
    Springville
University of Missouri/Columbia
University of Missouri/Kansas City
University of Missouri/Rolla
Washington University, St. Louis
Wentworth Military Academy and Junior
    College, Lexington
Westminister College, Fulton

Montana

Montana State University, Bozeman
University of Montana, Missoula

Nebraska

Bellevue University, Bellevue
Bishop Clarkson College, Omaha
College of Saint Mary's, Omaha
Concordia College, Seward
Creighton University, Omaha
Dana College, Blair
Doane College, Crete

Methodist College of Nursing, Omaha
Midland Lutheran College, Fremont
Peru State College, Peru
University of Nebraska at Lincoln
University of Nebraska Medical Center,
    Omaha

Nevada
University of Nevada/Reno

New Hampshire
Colby-Sawyer College, New London
Dartmouth College, Hanover
Plymouth State College, Plymouth
Saint Anselm College, Manchester
University of New Hampshire, Durham

New Jersey
Bloomfield College, Bloomfield
Caldwell College, Caldwell
Drew University, Madison
Fairleigh Dickinson College, Teaneck
Jersey City State College, Jersey City
Kean College of New Jersey, Union
Montclair State College, Montclair
New Jersey Institute of Technology,
    Newark
Princeton University, Princeton
Ramapo College of New Jersey, Mahwah
Rider College, Lawrenceville
Rowan College of New Jersey, Glassboro
Rutgers University/Camden
Rutgers University/New Brunswick
Saint Peter's College, Jersey City
Seton Hall University, South Orange
Stevens Institute of Technology,
    Hoboken
Trenton State College, Trenton
Upsala College, East Orange
William Paterson College, Wayne

New Mexico
Eastern New Mexico University, Portales
New Mexico Military Institute, Roswell
New Mexico State University, Las Cruces

New York
Adelphi University, Garden City
Alfred University, Alfred
Buffalo State College, Buffalo
Canisius College, Buffalo
Clarkson University, Potsdam
Colgate University, Hamilton
College of Mount Saint Vincent,
    Riverdale
College of New Rochelle, New Rochelle
College of Saint Rose, Albany
Columbia College, New York
Cornell University, Ithaca
CUNY/Baruch College, New York
CUNY/Brooklyn College, Brooklyn
CUNY/City College, New York
CUNY/John Jay College, New York
CUNY/Lehman College, Bronx
CUNY/Medgar Evers College, Brooklyn
CUNY/Queens College, Flushing
CUNY/York College, Jamaica
D'Youville College, Buffalo
Daemon College, Amherst
Dominican College, Orangeburg
Elmira College, Elmira
Fordham University, Bronx
Hamilton College, Clinton
Hartwick College, Oneonta
Hofstra University, Hempstead
Houghton College, Houghton
Hunter College, New York
Iona College, New Rochelle
Ithaca College, Ithaca
Lemoyne College, Syracuse
Long Island University/C.W. Post
    College, Brookville
Manhattan College, Riverdale
Marymount College, Tarrytown
Mercy College, Dobbs Ferry
New York Institute of Technology,
    Old Westbury
New York University, New York
Niagara University, Niagara
Pace University, New York
Polytechnic University, Brooklyn
Pratt Institute, Brooklyn

Rensselaer Polytechnic Institute, Troy
Roberts Wesleyan College, Rochester
Rochester Institute of Technology,
    Rochester
Russell Sage College, Troy
Saint Bonaventure University,
    St. Bonaventure
Saint Francis College, Brooklyn
Saint John Fisher College, Rochester
Saint John's University, Jamaica
Saint Lawrence University, Canton
Siena College, Loudonville
SUNY at Albany
SUNY at Stony Brook
SUNY/College at Binghamton
SUNY/College at Brockport
SUNY/College at Buffalo
SUNY/College of Environmental Science
    and Forestry, Syracuse
SUNY/College at Geneseo
SUNY/College at Old Westbury
SUNY/College at Oneonta
SUNY/College at Oswego
SUNY/College at Potsdam
SUNY/College at Purchase
SUNY/College of Technology, Alfred
SUNY/College of Technology,
    Farmingdale
Syracuse University, Syracuse
Union College, Schenectady
University of Rochester, Rochester
Utica College of Syracuse University,
    Utica
Wagner College, Staten Island

North Carolina
Appalachian State University, Boone
Campbell University, Buies Creek
Davidson College, Davidson
Duke University, Durham
East Carolina University, Greenville
Elizabeth City State University,
    Elizabeth City
Fayetteville State, Fayetteville
Johnson C. Smith University, Charlotte
Methodist College, Fayetteville

North Carolina A&T State University,
    Greensboro
North Carolina Central University,
    Durham
North Carolina State University, Raleigh
Pembroke State University, Pembroke
Saint Augustine's College, Raleigh
Shaw University, Raleigh
University of North Carolina at
    Chapel Hill
University of North Carolina at
    Charlotte
Wake Forest University, Winston-Salem
Western Carolina University, Cullowhee
Winston-Salem State University,
    Winston-Salem

North Dakota
North Dakota State University, Fargo
University of North Dakota, Grand Forks

Ohio
Baldwin Wallace College, Berea
Bowling Green State University
Capital University, Columbus
Case Western Reserve University,
    Cleveland
Cedarville College, Cedarville
Central State University, Wilberforce
Cleveland State University, Cleveland
College of Mount Saint Joseph,
    Cincinnati
Columbus College of Art and Design,
    Columbus
DeVry Institute of Technology,
    Columbus
Dyke College, Cleveland
Franklin University, Columbus
John Carroll University, Cleveland
Kent State University, Kent
Lourdes College, Sylvania
Miami University, Oxford
Mount Union College, Alliance
Notre Dame College of Ohio,
    South Euclid
Ohio Northern University, Ada

Ohio State University, Columbus
Ohio University, Athens
Otterbein College, Westerville
University of Akron, Akron
University of Cincinnati, Cincinnati
University of Dayton, Dayton
University of Rio Grande, Rio Grande
University of Toledo, Toledo
Ursuline College, Cleveland
Wilberforce University, Wilberforce
Wittenberg University, Springfield
Wright State University, Dayton
Xavier University, Cincinnati
Youngstown State University,
    Youngstown

Oklahoma
Cameron University, Lawton
East Central University, Ada
Langston University, Langston
Oklahoma Christian College,
    Oklahoma City
Oklahoma City University,
    Oklahoma City
Oklahoma State University, Stillwater
Southern Nazarene University, Bethany
University of Central Oklahoma,
    Edmond
University of Oklahoma, Norman
University of Tulsa, Tulsa

Oregon
Columbia Christian College, Portland
Concordia College, Portland
Lewis and Clark State College, Portland
Marylhurst College, Marylhurst
Oregon Health Science University,
    Portland
Oregon State University, Corvallis
Pacific University, Forest Grove
Portland State University, Portland
Reed College, Portland
University of Oregon, Eugene
University of Portland, Portland
Warner Pacific College, Portland
Western Oregon State College, Monmouth

Pennsylvania
Allentown College of Saint Francis,
    Center Valley
Bloomsburg University of Pennsylvania,
    Bloomsburg
Bucknell University, Lewisburg
Cabrini College, Radnor
Carnegie Mellon University, Pittsburgh
Cedar Crest College, Allentown
Chatham College, Pittsburgh
Cheyney College, Cheyney
Dickinson College, Carlisle
Drexel University, Philadelphia
Duquesne University, Pittsburgh
East Stroudsburg University of
    Pennsylvania, East Stroudsburg
Eastern College, St. Davids
Edinboro University of Pennsylvania,
    Edinboro
Franklin and Marshall College, Lancaster
Gannon University, Erie
Indiana University of Pennsylvania,
    Indiana
King's College, Wilkes Barre
Kutztown University, Kutztown
Lafayette College, Easton
LaSalle University, Philadelphia
Lebanon Valley College, Annville
Lehigh University, Bethlehem
Lock Haven University of Pennsylvania,
    Lock Haven
Lycoming College, Williamsport
Marywood College, Scranton
Mercy Hurst College, Erie
Millersville University of Pennsylvania,
    Millersville
Moravian College, Bethlehem
Muhlenberg College, Allentown
Penn State University Fayette Campus,
    Uniontown
Penn State University at Harrisburg
Penn State University/Hazleton
Penn State University/Ogontz, Abington
Penn State University/University Park
Penn State/Worthington, Dunmore

Philadelphia College of Pharmacy and
  Science, Philadelphia
Saint Joseph's University, Philadelphia
Shippensburg University of
  Pennsylvania, Shippensburg
Slippery Rock University, Slippery Rock
Susquehanna University, Selinsgrove
Temple University, Philadelphia
University of Pennsylvania, Philadelphia
University of Pittsburgh at Bradford
University of Pittsburgh, Pittsburgh
University of Scranton, Scranton
Valley Forge Military Academy,
  Valley Forge
Villanova University, Villanova
West Chester University, West Chester
Widener University, Chester
Wilkes University, Wilkes-Barre
York College of Pennsylvania, York

Puerto Rico
Catholic University, Ponce
Interamerican University Metro,
  Hato Rey
Metropolitan University, Rio Piedras
University of Puerto Rico, Cayeh
  Campus, Cayeh
University of Puerto Rico, Mayaguez
University of Puerto Rico, Rio Piedras

Rhode Island
Brown University, Providence
Bryant College, Smithfield
Johnson and Wales University,
  Providence
Providence College, Providence
Rhode Island College, Providence
Roger Williams University, Bristol
Salve Regina University, Newport
University of Rhode Island, Kingston

South Carolina
Clemson University, Clemson
Converse College, Spartanburg
Francis Marion College, Florence
Furman University, Greenville

Lander College, Greenwood
Medical University of South Carolina,
  Charleston
Morris College, Sumter
Presbyterian College, Clinton
South Carolina State College,
  Orangeburg
Spartanburg Methodist College,
  Spartanburg
The Citadel, Charleston
University of Charleston, Charleston
University of South Carolina, Columbia
University of South Carolina at
  Spartanburg, Spartanburg
Wofford College, Spartanburg

South Dakota
Black Hills State College, Spearfish
Mount Marty College, Yankton
South Dakota School of Mines and
  Technology, Rapid City
South Dakota State University,
  Brookings
University of South Dakota, Vermillion

Tennessee
American Baptist College, Nashville
Austin-Peay State University, Clarksville
Belmont College, Nashville
Carson-Newman College, Jefferson City
Christian Brothers University, Memphis
David Lipscomb University, Nashville
East Tennessee State University,
  Johnson City
Fisk University, Nashville
Free Will Baptist Bible College, Nashville
Knoxville College, Knoxville
Lemoyne-Owen College, Memphis
Middle Tennessee State University,
  Murfreesboro
Milligan College, Milligan
Rhodes College, Memphis
Tennessee State University, Nashville
Tennessee Technological University,
  Cookerville
University of Memphis, Memphis

University of Tennessee at Chattanooga
University of Tennessee at Knoxville
University of Tennessee at Martin
Vanderbilt University, Nashville

Texas
Abilene Christian University, Abilene
Concordia Lutheran College, Austin
Dallas Baptist University, Dallas
East Texas State University, Commerce
Houston Baptist University, Houston
Howard Payne University, Brownwood
Lamar University, Beaumont
Lubbock Christian University, Lubbock
McMurray University, Abilene
Our Lady of the Lake University,
    San Antonio
Prairie View A&M University,
    Prairie View
Saint Edwards University, Austin
Saint Mary's University, San Antonio
Sam Houston State University,
    Huntsville
Southern Methodist University, Dallas
Southwest Texas State University,
    Canyon
Stephen F. Austin State University,
    Nagdoches
Tarleton State University, Stephensville
Texas A&M University, College Station
Texas A&M University at Corpus Christi
Texas A&M University at Kingsville
Texas Christian University, Ft. Worth
Texas Southern University, Houston
Texas Tech University, Lubbock
Texas Wesleyan University, Ft. Worth
Texas Woman's University, Denton
University of Central Texas, Illeen
University of Dallas, Irving
University of Houston—Clear Lake,
    Houston
University of Houston—Downtown,
    Houston
University of Houston, Houston
University of Northern Texas, Denton
University of Saint Thomas, Houston

University of Texas at Arlington
University of Texas at Austin
University of Texas at Brownsville
University of Texas at Dallas,
    Richardson
University of Texas at El Paso
University of Texas at San Antonio
University of Texas Health Science
    Center, Houston
University of Texas–Pan American,
    Edinburg
University of the Incarnate Word,
    San Antonio
William Marsh Rice University, Houston

Utah
Brigham Young University, Provo
Southern Utah State College, Cedar City
University of Utah, Salt Lake City
Utah State University, Logan
Weber State College, Ogden
Westminister College, Salt Lake City

Vermont
Castleton State College, Castleton
Middlebury College, Middlebury
Norwich University, Northfield
Saint Michael's College, Colchester
Trinity College, Burlington
University of Vermont, Burlington
Vermont College, Montpellier

Virginia
Christopher Newport University,
    Newport News
College of William and Mary,
    Williamsburg
George Mason University, Fairfax
Hampden-Sydney College, Hampden-
    Sydney
Hampton University, Hampton
James Madison University, Harrisonburg
Longwood College, Farmville
Mary Baldwin College, Staunton
Norfolk State University, Norfolk
Old Dominion University, Norfolk

Radford University, Radford
Saint Paul's College, Lawrenceville
University of Richmond, Richmond
University of Virginia, Charlottesville
Virginia Commonwealth University,
    Richmond
Virginia Military Institute, Lexington
Virginia Polytechnic Institute,
    Blacksburg
Virginia State University, Petersburg
Washington and Lee University,
    Lexington

Washington
Central Washington University,
    Ellensburg
Eastern Washington University, Cheney
Gonzaga University, Spokane
Pacific Lutheran University, Tacoma
Saint Martins College, Lacey
Seattle Pacific University, Seattle
Seattle University, Seattle
University of Puget Sound, Tacoma
Washington State University, Pullman
Whitworth College, Spokane

West Virginia
Fairmont State University, Fairmont
Marshall University, Huntington

West Virginia Institute of Technology,
    Montgomery
West Virginia State College, Institute
West Virginia University, Morgantown

Wisconsin
Bellon College of Nursing, Green Bay
Marian College of Fond du Lac,
    Fond du Lac
Marquette University, Milwaukee
Milwaukee School of Engineering,
    Milwaukee
Ripon College, Rippon
Saint Norbert College, De Pere
University of Wisconsin/Eau Claire
University of Wisconsin/Green Bay
University of Wisconsin/LaCrosse
University of Wisconsin/Madison
University of Wisconsin/Milwaukee
University of Wisconsin/Oshkosh
University of Wisconsin/Stevens Point
University of Wisconsin/Stout,
    Menomonie
University of Wisconsin/Whitewater
Viterbo College, LaCrosse

Wyoming
University of Wyoming, Laramie

ARMY-APPROVED ROTC COURSES
This diverse and comprehensive class listing gives a sense of the opportunities available.

General
Abnormal Psychology
Administration
Agriculture
Animal Husbandry
Anthropology
Applied Psychology
Arabic
Arabic (Eastern)
Arabic (Egyptian)
Arabic (Iraqi)
Arabic (Jordanian)
Arabic (Lebanese)
Arabic (Libyan)
Arabic (Saudi)
Arabic (Syrian)
Arabic (Western)
Art, Commercial
Art, General
Arts, Classic
Arts, Industrial
Bengali
Broadcasting
    (Announcer)
Child Psychology
Chinese (Cantonese)
Chinese (Mandarin)
Church Management
Civil Government
Classical Language/
    Literature
Cognitive Science
College Administration
Commercial (Marketing)
Corrections
Counseling Psychology
Criminal Justice
Criminology
Cultural Foundations
Dramatics
Dutch

Educational Psychology
English
Ethnology
Experimental Psychology
Food Distribution
Foreign Affairs
Foreign Language/
    Literature
Foreign Trade
Forensic Science
French
General Education
General Psychology
General Social Science
Geopolitics
German
Hindi
History
Home Economics
Homiletic
    Communications
Horticulture
Hotel-Restaurant
Human Resources
Indonesian
Industrial Psychology
Institutional
    Management
Interdisciplinary Studies
International Relations
Italian
Japanese
Journalism-Writing
Korean
Labor Relations
Liberal Arts
Library Science/Archives
Malaysian
Merchandising
Military Government
Military Science

Mortuary Science
Motion Picture
    Production
Music
Norwegian
Organizational Behavior
Organizational
    Effectiveness
Personnel Management
Philosophy
Photography
Physical Education
Police Science
Political Science
Portuguese (Brazilian)
Portuguese (European)
Poultry Husbandry
Public Affairs
Public Relations
Public Safety
Public Speaking
Recreation and Parks
Russian
Safety
Serbo-Croatian
Social Psychology
Social Work
Social Work
    Administration
Sociology
Spanish
Spanish (Castilian)
Special Education
Swedish
Technology
Television Production
Thai
Turkish
Urdu

Analytical Physical Science

Acoustics
Aerodynamics
Analytical Chemistry
Applied Science
Astrodynamics
Astronomy
Astrophysics
Bacteriology
Biology
Biometry
Ceramics/Glass Chemistry
Chiropractic
Computer Science
Economic Geology
Electricity/Magnetism
Electrochemistry
Embryology
Endodontics
Entomology
General Biochemistry
General Botany
General Chemistry
General Geography
General Geology
General Mathematics
General Nursing
General Physical Sciences
Geodetic Science
Geophysics
Glass Technology
Health Physics
Histology
Immunology
Industrial Chemistry
Inorganic Chemistry
Jet Propulsion Technology
Laser/Microwave Physics
Material Science
Mathematics/Ballistics
Mathematics/ Cryptanalysis
Medical Microbiology
Medical Technology
Metallurgy
Meteorology/ Climatology
Mineralogy/Petrology
Nautical Sciences
Nuclear Chemistry
Nuclear Medicine
Nuclear Physics
Nuclear Reactor
Oceanography/ Hydrology
OPNS Research Analysis
Organic General Chemistry
Paleontology
Paper Chemistry
Parasitology
Pharmacology
Pharmacy
Physical General Chemistry
Physician's Assistant
Physics
Physics/Astrodynamics
Physics, Biophysics, and Radiology
Physics/Optic Light
Physiology
Polymer Science
Premedicine
Radiation/Biology
Radiochemistry
Radiological Hygiene
Radiological Physics
Seismology
Serology
Space Physics
Space Systems Operations
Statistics
Superficial Geology
Taxonomy
Technology
Terrestrial Geology
Textile Chemistry
Thermal Physics
Tissue Pathology
Toxicology
Virology
Zoology

Engineering

Aeronautical Engineering
Aerospace Engineering (Space Travel)
Agricultural Engineering
Air Conditioning
Architectural Engineering
Architecture
Architecture Landscape
Artificial Intelligence
Astronautical Engineering
Automotive Engineering
Biomedical Engineering
Cartography
Ceramic Engineering
Chemical Engineering
Civil Engineering
Civil Engineering (Safety)
Composite Materials
Computer Science
Diesel Engineering
Electrical Engineering
Electronics Engineering
Energy Resource Engineering
Engineering/ Administration
Engineering/Heating
Engineering/Petroleum
Engineering/Physics
Engineering Structural
Electrical Engineering
Electronics Engineering

Electronic Warfare
Energy Resource
Environmental
  Engineering
Environmental Health
  Science
Environmental Science
Explosive Engineering
Fuel Technology
General Engineering
Geological Engineering
Guided Missiles
Human Factors
Hydraulics Engineering
Industrial Engineering
Maintainability
  Engineering
Marine Engineering
Material Engineering
Mechanical Engineering
Metallurgical Engineering
Mining Engineering
Missiles and Munitions
  Studies
Naval Architecture
Nuclear Engineering
Ordnance Engineering
Pipeline Engineering
Plastics Engineering
Polymer Engineering
Power Engineering
Production Design
Radio Engineering
Radiological Engineering
Railway Engineering
  Reactor Engineering
Refrigeration Engineering
Robotics Engineering
Safety Engineering
Sanitary Engineering
Software Engineering
Space Engineering

Space Facilities
  Engineering
Space Systems
  Engineering
Space Travel
Structural Engineering
Systems Engineering
Textile Engineering
Urban Planning
Vertical Lift Technology

Technical /Management
Accounting/Auditing
Administrative Dietitian
Advertising
Aerospace Management
Agriculture/Forestry
Anatomy
Archeology
Audiology
Aviation Maintenance
Aviation Safety
Banking and Financing
Business Administration
Business Economics
Celestial Navigation
City Planning
Clinical Dietitian
Clinical Optometry
  Management
Clinical Psychology
Commerce
Commercial Aviation
Communications
Communications Science
Comptrollership
Computer Science
Design Technology
Dietetics
Environmental Health
Fish Resources
Food Technology

General Business
General Economics
General Finance
General Law
Health Services
  Administration
Industrial Education
Industrial Management
Information Systems
Instructional Technology
Laboratory Science
Management Logistics
Nuclear Pharmacy
Occupational Therapy
Physical Geography
Physical Therapy
Plant Pathology
Podiatry (Chiropody)
Procurement and
  Contract Systems
  Management
Psychometrics
Psychophysics
  Psychology (Artificial
  Intelligence)
Public Health
Regional Planning
Sanitary Science
Soil Science
Speech Pathology
Strategic Intelligence
Sugar Technology
Technical Management
Telecommunications
Terrestrial Navigation
Therapeutic Dietitian
Topography
  Photogrammetry
Transportation Research
Transportation and
  Traffic Studies
Wildlife Resources

U.S. NAVY/MARINE CORPS ROTC

Navy Recruiting Command
4015 Wilson Boulevard
Arlington, VA 22203-1991

☎ 800-327-NAVY
http://www.navyjobs.com/money/html

OVERVIEW   Largest single source of Navy and Marine Corps officers.

The Naval Reserve Officers Training Corps (NROTC) is an outstanding program that provides candidates with the opportunity to become commissioned officers in the Naval Reserve or Marine Corps Reserve while attending college. The NROTC Program is available at more than 100 colleges and universities that host NROTC units or have cross-enrollment agreements with a host university. Upon graduation, NROTC midshipmen are commissioned as ensigns in the Naval Reserve or as second lieutenants in the Marine Corps Reserve.

Programs

Four years
Two years
One year
Nursing Programs
Scholarships

Admissions Process

Candidates must:
1. request and fill out the Preliminary Application
2. take the SAT or the ACT as early as possible and authorize the testing agency to release their scores directly to the ROTC Scholarship Program or ROTC Programs
3. apply to the ROTC colleges or universities they are interested in attending
4. be interviewed and selected by a board of military officers
5. take the Qualifying Medical Examination
6. take the Physical Aptitude Examination
7. enroll in the ROTC Program

General Qualifications

Age: 17–21
- Candidates must not have reached their 25th birthday by June 30 of the year in which college graduation and commissioning are anticipated.
- Candidates who have prior active duty military service may be eligible for age waivers for the amount of time they served on active duty.

Status: U.S. citizen
Must be a full-time student at a school offering ROTC.

Medical: Must be in good physical and mental health.
Must be able to pass a Department of Defense Medical Examination Review Board medical examination.

Physical: Must be able to pass the Physical Aptitude Examination (PAE).

Testing

All candidates must take either the standardized American College Testing (ACT) Assessment Program exam or the College Board Admissions Testing Program Scholastic Assessment Tests (SAT I)

ACT American College Testing Assessment Program
English, Reading, Mathematics, and Science Reasoning

SAT College Board Admissions Testing Program
Verbal and Mathematics

Obligation

Candidates incur obligations of eight years of commissioned service, of which three years will be on active duty.

COLLEGES AND UNIVERSITIES THAT OFFER NROTC

> Many of the NROTC colleges or universities listed below have crosstown agreements with other colleges and universities located nearby. These agreements establish a formal relationship between the host NROTC university and the crosstown university that permits students to attend the crosstown school and still participate in the NROTC program at the NROTC school. A current list of schools should be obtained from the NROTC.

Alabama
Auburn University, Auburn

Arizona
University of Arizona, Tucson

California
San Diego State University, San Diego
University of California at Berkeley
University of California at Los Angeles
University of San Diego, San Diego
University of Southern California,
   Los Angeles

Colorado
University of Colorado at Boulder

District of Columbia
George Washington University

Florida
Florida A&M University, Tallahassee
Jacksonville University, Jacksonville
University of Florida, Gainesville

Georgia
Georgia Institute of Technology, Atlanta
Morehouse College, Atlanta
Savannah State College, Savannah

Idaho
University of Idaho, Moscow

Illinois
Illinois Institute of Technology, Chicago
Northwestern University, Evanston
University of Illinois, Champaign

Indiana
Purdue University, West Lafayette
University of Notre Dame, Notre Dame

Iowa
Iowa State University, Ames

Kansas
University of Kansas, Lawrence

Louisiana
Southern University and A&M College,
   Baton Rouge
Tulane University, New Orleans

Maine
Maine Maritime Academy, Castine

Massachusetts
Boston University, Boston
College of the Holy Cross, Worcester
Massachusetts Institute of Technology

Michigan
University of Michigan, Ann Arbor

Minnesota
University of Minnesota, Minneapolis

Mississippi
University of Mississippi

Missouri
University of Missouri, Columbia

Nebraska
University of Nebraska, Lincoln

New Mexico
University of New Mexico, Albuquerque

New York
Cornell University, Ithaca
Rensselaer Polytechnic Institute, Troy
SUNY Maritime College, Bronx
University of Rochester, Rochester

North Carolina
Duke University, Durham
North Carolina State University, Raleigh
University of North Carolina, Chapel Hill

Ohio
Miami University, Oxford
Ohio State University, Columbus

Oklahoma
University of Oklahoma, Norman

Oregon
Oregon State University, Corvallis

Pennsylvania
Carnegie Mellon University, Pittsburgh
Pennsylvania State University,
    University Park
University of Pennsylvania, Philadelphia
Villanova University, Villanova

South Carolina
The Citadel, Charleston
University of Southern Carolina,
    Columbia

Tennessee
University of Memphis, Memphis
Vanderbilt University, Nashville

Texas
Prairie View A&M University,
    Prairie View
Rice University, Houston
Texas A&M University, College Station
University of Texas, Austin

Utah
University of Utah, Salt Lake City

Vermont
Norwich University, Northfield

Virginia
Hampton University, Hampton
Norfolk State University, Norfolk
Old Dominion University, Norfolk
University of Virginia, Charlottesville
Virginia Military Institute, Lexington
Virginia Polytechnic Institute,
    Blacksburg

Washington
University of Washington, Seattle

Wisconsin
Marquette University, Milwaukee
University of Wisconsin, Madison

SECTION

4

MILITARY
CAREER FIELDS

Chapter 12

ENLISTED CAREERS

Career Field Comparison/Conversion Charts ——————

    ☐ Overview
    ☐ **Occupational Categories**

OVERVIEW   Each year the military recruits more than 200,000 enlisted personnel.

The purpose for this special section is simple. Candidates who are interested in a particular military occupation can compare the various branches for the same occupation. In addition, the federal government has civil service occupations that military personnel can qualify for based on their military occupational specialty experience. Current military members or those with prior service who are looking at other branches or the federal government for civilian jobs should also find this section of special interest.

OCCUPATIONAL CATEGORIES

ADMINISTRATION OCCUPATIONS		
Occupational Category/Duties	**Branch/MSO**	**Related Titles**
Administrative Support Specialists Record keeping of information; office support; prepare reports, official letters, and military forms.	**Air Force** Administrative Specialist **Army** Administrative Specialist **Coast Guard** Yeoman **Marine Corps** **Navy** Personnel Specialist	**Federal** Clerk Secretary Administrative Assistant **Civilian** Clerk Secretary Administrative Assistant
Computer Systems Specialists Install, maintain, problem solve computer programs; provide customer and user services.	**Air Force** Computer Systems Operator **Army** Computer Operator **Coast Guard** Data Processing Technician **Marine Corps** Computer Operator **Navy** Data Processing Technician	**Federal** Computer Systems Specialist **Civilian** Computer Systems Specialist
Finance and Accounting Specialists Maintain records of financial transactions; conduct audits of financial records; prepare statements, accounts, and reports.	**Air Force** Finance Specialist **Army** Finance Specialist **Coast Guard** Yeoman **Marine Corps** Financial Clerk **Navy** Disbursing Clerk	**Federal** IRS Officer **Civilian** Bookkeeper Accounting Specialist

ADMINISTRATION OCCUPATIONS (continued)		
Occupational Category/Duties	**Branch/MSO**	**Related Titles**
Legal Specialists and Court Reporters The military maintains it own legal system. Legal specialists and court reporters perform legal research and documentation of court cases and assist military judges and lawyers.	**Air Force** Paralegal Specialist **Army** Legal Specialist Court Reporter **Coast Guard** Yeoman **Marine Corps** Legal Services **Navy** Legalman	**Federal** Court Reporter Paralegal **Civilian** Court Reporter Paralegal

Personnel Specialists
 Assist military members with their career, training, and health information; maintain personnel records.
	Air Force
	 Personnel
	    Specialist
	 Army
	 Personnel
	    Specialist
	 Administration
	    Specialist
	 Coast Guard
	 Yeoman
	 Marine Corps
	 Personnel
	    Specialist
	 Administration
	    Specialist
	 Navy
	 Yeoman
		Federal
		 Personnel Clerk
		
		 Civilian
		 Personnel Manager

Postal Specialists Process military and civilian mail.	**Air Force** Postal Specialist **Army** Postal Specialist **Coast Guard** Yeoman **Marine Corps** Postal Clerk **Navy** Postal Clerk	**Federal** U.S. Postal Service **Civilian** Private Courier Express Mail Courier
Recruiting Specialists Recruiters attract civilians to join the military. They are also charged with retaining active-duty military personnel.	**Air Force** Recruiter **Army** Recruiter **Coast Guard** Recruiter **Marine Corps** Recruiter **Navy** Recruiter	**Federal** Recruiter **Civilian** Personnel Generalist

ADMINISTRATION OCCUPATIONS (continued)		
Occupational Category/Duties	**Branch/MSO**	**Related Titles**
Sales and Stock Specialists Operate military stores, retail facilities, snack bars; responsible for record keeping and stock accounting.	**Air Force** Subsistence Specialist **Army** Supply Specialist **Coast Guard** Storekeeper **Marine Corps** Exchange Supply Specialist Marine Supply Specialist **Navy** Ship's Serviceman Storekeeper	**Federal** Store Manager **Civilian** Salesclerk
Supply and Warehousing Specialists Maintain inventory of equipment, supplies, food, weapons, parts, and a variety of other items; load and unload new stock; maintain logs and records on movement.	**Air Force** Supply Service Specialist **Army** Supply Service Specialist **Coast Guard** Storekeeper **Marine Corps** Supply Clerk **Navy** Storekeeper	**Federal** General Supply Technician Purchasing Specialist Inventory Clerk **Civilian** Control Clerk Warehouse Clerk
Training Specialists and Instructors Train and instruct military personnel in the classroom and in the field on a wide variety of subject matters. For most of the branches the title "instructor" is a subsequent duty attached to the main MOS.	**Air Force** Instructor **Army** Instructor **Coast Guard** Instructor **Marine Corps** Instructor **Navy** Instructor	**Federal** Instructor **Civilian** Teacher Instructor

AVIATION-RELATED OCCUPATIONS

Occupational Category/Duties	Branch/MSO	Related Titles
Air Crew Members Operate a variety of equipment on military aircraft, including communication, radar, and weapons systems. In helicopters, air crew members may operate hoists to lift equipment and personnel.	**Air Force** Airman Aerial Gunner Pararescue Specialist **Army** Airman **Coast Guard** Aviation Survivalman **Marine Corps** Pararescue Specialist **Navy** Airman Aviation Boatswain's Mate	**Federal** Airman **Civilian** Flight Crew Member
Air Traffic Controllers Operate air traffic control systems and control towers; direct the takeoffs and landings of military airplanes and helicopters; monitor radar systems.	**Air Force** Air Traffic Controller **Army** Air Traffic Controller **Coast Guard** Air Traffic Controller **Marine Corps** Air Traffic Controller **Navy** Air Traffic Controller	**Federal** F.A.A. Air Traffic Controller **Civilian** Air Traffic Controller
Aircraft Launch and Recovery Specialists Navy aircraft carriers and Coast Guard cutters need specialists to control and assist in the launch and safe landing aboard ships.	**Coast Guard** Aviation Survivalman **Marine Corps** Pararescue Specialist **Navy** Aviation Boatswain's Mate	**Federal** NASA Launch Specialist NASA Recovery Specialist **Civilian** Firefighter Aircraft Launch Technician

AVIATION-RELATED OCCUPATIONS (continued)		
Occupational Category/Duties	**Branch/MSO**	**Related Titles**
Flight Engineers Inspect aircraft, monitor fuel and electrical and key systems; supervise the loading of cargo, fuel, and passengers; conduct fuel consumption projections and assist the pilot in operation of the aircraft.	**Air Force** Flight Engineer **Coast Guard** Aviation Survivalman **Marine Corps** Flight Engineer **Navy** Flight Engineer	**Federal** Flight Engineer **Civilian** Flight Engineer
Flight Operations Specialists Act as planners and coordinators for military flights; maintain records, logs; act as flight dispatchers.	**Air Force** Airfield Management Specialist **Army** Aviation Operations Specialist **Marine Corps** Aviation Operations Specialist **Navy** Aviation Support Technician	**Federal** Aviation Operations Specialist **Civilian** Flight Operation Specialist Flight Dispatcher
Survival Equipment Specialists Inspect, maintain, and repair survival equipment, such as parachutes and aircraft life support systems.	**Air Force** Aircrew Life Support Specialist **Army** Parachute Rigger **Coast Guard** Aviation Survivalman **Marine Corps** Flight Equipment Marine **Navy** Aircrew Survival Equipment Specialist	**Federal** Parachute Packer **Civilian** Survival Equipment Company Worker

COMBAT SPECIALTY OCCUPATIONS

Occupational Category/Duties	Branch/MSO	Related Titles

Artillery/Missile Crew Members
Fire cannons, howitzers, missiles, and rockets; use specialized equipment to locate targets. Artillery is used to protect ground troops and sea forces from air attack.
 	
Restricted:
At the present time this combat occupation is restricted to male military members only.
 	
Field Artillery
Basic Field Artilleryman
Cannoneer
Radar Operator
Fire Controlman, Red Artillery
Meteorologist
Operationsman
Fire Supportman
 	
Air Defense Artillery
Hawk Missile System Crewmember
Patriot Fire Control Enhanced
   Operator
Air Defense Command Control
   Computer Operator
Communication and Intelligence
   Tactical Operations Center
   Enhanced Operator
Command and Control Systems
   Operator
Air Defense System Crewman
Avenger Crewmember
Patriot Launching Station Operator
Enhanced Operator/Maintainer
Chaparral Crewmember
	Air Force
	Nuclear Weapons
	   Specialist
	Missile Systems
	   Specialist
	Army
	Field Artillery
	   Specialist
	Air Defense Artillery
	   Specialist
	MLRS
	   Crewmember
	Coast Guard
	Gunner's Mate
	Fire Controlman
	Marine Corps
	Field Artillery
	   Specialist
	Air Defense Artillery
	   Specialist
	—Hawk
	Navy
	Gunner's Mate
	Fire Controlman
	—Tomahawk
	—Aegis
	—Seasparrow
	—Trident
	—Harpoon
		Federal
		Weapons Engineer
		
		Civilian
		Weapons Engineer
		Gunsmith

Combat Engineers
Build and construct roads, bridges, airfields, fortifications, and bunkers to move military equipment; lay and clear mine fields; assist infantrymen in combat operations.
 	
Restricted:
At the present time this combat occupation is restricted to male military members only.
 	
Engineering Specialties
Bridge Crewmember
	Army
	Combat Engineer
	Bridge
	   Crewmember
	Marine Corps
	Combat Engineer
	Navy
	Warfare Engineer
		Federal
		Construction
		   Worker
		
		Civilian
		Construction
		   Worker
		Shipping Worker

COMBAT SPECIALTY OCCUPATIONS (continued)		
Occupational Category/Duties	**Branch/MSO**	**Related Titles**
Infantryman The infantry is the backbone of the military. Infantry personnel are specially trained to destroy enemy ground forces, operate and fire a variety of weapons, parachute from transport planes, and conduct extended patrol missions. *Restricted:* At the present time this combat occupation is restricted to male military members only. *Infantry Specialties* Basic Infantryman Rifleman Light Armored Vehicle Crewman Reconnaissanceman Machine Gunner Mortarman Assaultman Antitank Assault Guided Missileman Infantry Unit Leader	**Army** Infantryman **Marine Corps** Infantryman	**Federal** Security Guard **Civilian** Police Officer Security Officer

Tank Crew Members
Drive state-of-the-art tanks in combat; operate weapons systems; support and defend ground infantry troops.
 	
Restricted:
At the present time this combat occupation is restricted to male military members only.
 	
Tank Crew Specialties
Bradley Linebacker Crewmember
Engineer Tracked Vehicle Crewman
	Army
	Tank Crew Member
	Marine Corps
	Tank Crew Member
		Federal
		Equipment
		  Operator
		
		Civilian
		Heavy Equipment
		  Operator

ELECTRONIC AND ELECTRICAL EQUIPMENT REPAIR

Occupational Category/Duties	Branch/MSO	Related Titles
Aircraft Electricians Maintain and repair electrical systems on aircraft; replace or repair instruments.	**Air Force** Aircraft Electrical Systems Specialist **Army** Aircraft Electrician **Coast Guard** Aviation Electronics Mate Electronics Technician **Marine Corps** Aircraft Electrical Systems Technician **Navy** Aviation Electrician's Mate	**Federal** Aircraft Electrical Systems Specialist **Civilian** Aircraft Electrician
Communications Equipment Repairers Maintain, test, and repair communications systems.	**Air Force** Communications Specialist **Army** Communications Repair Specialist **Coast Guard** Electronics Technician **Marine Corps** Communications Repair Specialist **Navy** Electronics Technician	**Federal** Communications Repair Specialist **Civilian** Communications Equipment Repairer
Computer Equipment Repairers Install, repair, and maintain computer equipment.	**Air Force** Computer Systems Repairer **Army** Computer Systems Repairer **Marine Corps** Computer Systems Repairer **Navy** Data Systems Technician	**Federal** Computer Systems Repairer **Civilian** Computer Equipment Repairer

ELECTRONIC AND ELECTRICAL EQUIPMENT REPAIR (continued)		
Occupational Category/Duties	**Branch/MSO**	**Related Titles**

Radar and Sonar Equipment Repairers
Install, repair, and operate the sonar and radar equipment that are critical to the many missions of the military.
	Air Force
	Airborne Radar
	  Operator
	Ground Radar
	  Operator
	Army
	Radar Repairer
	Coast Guard
	Electronics
	  Technician
	Marine Corps
	Ground Radar
	  Operator
	Aviation Radar
	  Operator
	Navy
	Radar Technician
		Federal
		Radar Repairer
		
		Civilian
		Avionics Technician
		Electronics
		  Mechanic
		Field Service
		  Technician

Ship Electricians The electrical systems are critical to operating ships and submarines. Ship electricians install, repair, and maintain the systems. Some systems are nuclear.	**Coast Guard** Electrician's Mate **Navy** Electrician's Mate	**Federal** Electrician **Civilian** Ship Electrician

Weapons Maintenance Technicians
Many of the military weapon systems require specialized technicians to maintain, repair, test, and adjust equipment.
	Air Force
	Armament Systems
	  Specialist
	Army
	Armament/Missile
	  Systems Repairer
	Coast Guard
	Fire Control
	  Technician
	Marine Corps
	Ordnance
	  Munitions
	  Technician
	Navy
	Fire Control
	  Technician
		Federal
		Ordnance Systems
		  Mechanic
		Missile Facilities
		  Repairer
		
		Civilian
		Fire Fighter
		Gunsmith
		Field Service
		  Technician

ENGINEERING, SCIENCE, AND TECHNICAL OCCUPATIONS

Occupational Category/Duties	Branch/MSO	Related Titles
Chemical Laboratory Technicians Test and analyze fuels, oils, chemicals, and other materials for purity and durability.	**Air Force** Applied Sciences Technician **Army** Materials Quality Specialist **Coast Guard** Marine Science Technician **Marine Corps** Spectrometric Oil Analysis Technician **Navy** Spectrometric Oil Analysis Technician Damage Control Specialist	**Federal** Chemical Laboratory Technician **Civilian** Chemical Laboratory Technician Manufacturing Technician
Communications Equipment Operators Utilize communications equipment to transmit, receive, encode, and decode messages.	**Air Force** Communications Specialist **Army** Communications Specialist **Coast Guard** Telecommunications Specialist **Marine Corps** Telephone Technician **Navy** Radioman	**Federal** Communications Specialist **Civilian** Cable Installer Line Repairer Communications Technician
Compressed Gas Technicians Fill storage tanks; maintain a variety of compressed gases for use including breathing oxygen and fuels for missiles.	**Army** Materials Quality Specialist **Marine Corps** Cryogenic Equipment Operator **Navy** Cryogenic Technician	**Federal** Gas Generating Plant Operator **Civilian** Industrial and Processing Companies

ENGINEERING, SCIENCE, AND TECHNICAL OCCUPATIONS (continued)		
Occupational Category/Duties	**Branch/MSO**	**Related Titles**

Computer Programmers
Install, maintain, update, and organize computer programs.
	Air Force
	Computer Systems
	  Programmer
	Army
	Computer Systems
	  Programmer
	Coast Guard
	Data Processing
	  Technician
	Marine Corps
	Programmer
	Navy
	Data Processing
	  Technician
		Federal
		Computer
		  Programmer
		
		Civilian
		Computer
		  Programmer

Emergency Management Specialists
Plan and maintain disaster operations; train military personnel and civilians on disaster preparedness.
	Air Force
	Disaster
	  Preparedness
	  Specialist
	Army
	Disaster
	  Preparedness
	  Specialist Safety
	  Inspector
	Navy
	Damage Control
	  Technician
		Federal
		Emergency
		  Management
		  Specialist
		
		Civilian
		Emergency
		  Management
		  Specialist

Environmental Health and Safety Specialists
Inspect military facilities, work locations, housing areas, and food and water supplies for the presence of disease, germs, and hazardous materials.
	Air Force
	Safety Specialist
	Army
	Safety Inspector
	Marine Corps
	Safety Specialist
	Navy
	Hospital Corpsman
		Federal
		Health and Safety
		  Inspector
		
		Civilian
		Health and Safety
		  Inspector

Meteorological Specialists
Collect information on the weather using a variety of equipment and instruments for planning military operations.
	Air Force
	Weather Specialist
	Army
	F.A. Meteorological
	  Crewmember
	Coast Guard
	Marine Science
	  Technician
	Marine Corps
	Weather Forecaster
	Navy
	Meteorology
	  Aerographer
	  Mate
		Federal
		Meteorologist
		
		Civilian
		Meteorologist

ENGINEERING, SCIENCE, AND TECHNICAL OCCUPATIONS (continued)

Occupational Category/Duties	Branch/MSO	Related Titles
Nondestructive Testers Inspect metal parts for wear and damage on a variety of military aircraft, vehicles, and ships; take X rays of various sections for examination and documentation.	**Air Force** Aircraft Maintenance Specialist **Army** Aircraft Structural Repairer **Coast Guard** Aviation Structure Mechanic **Marine Corps** Aircraft Nondestructive Testing Specialist **Navy** Hull Maintenance Technician Aviation Structure Mechanic	**Federal** OSHA Inspector **Civilian** Weld Inspector
Nuclear, Biological, and Chemical Warfare and Ordnance Specialists Transport, store, inspect, prepare, and destroy weapons and ammunition, including large shells, missiles, chemicals, and nuclear devices; nuclear, biological, and chemical (NBC) warfare.	**Air Force** Nuclear Weapons Specialist NBC Specialist Munitions Specialist Explosive Ordnance Disposal Specialist **Army** Ammunition Specialist Explosive Ordnance Specialist Nuclear Ordnance Specialist NBC Specialist Disposal Specialist **Coast Guard** Gunner's Mate **Marine Corps** Ammunition Technician Explosive Ordnance Disposal Technician **Navy** Gunner's Mate Mineman	**Federal** Munitions Specialist Nuclear Weapons Specialist **Civilian** Civil Disaster Coordinator Disposal Expert

ENGINEERING, SCIENCE, AND TECHNICAL OCCUPATIONS (continued)		
Occupational Category/Duties	**Branch/MSO**	**Related Titles**
Radar and Sonar Operators Track aircraft, missiles; determine the position of ships and submarines; direct artillery fire; forecast the weather; aid navigation.	**Air Force** Airborne Warning Radar Systems Specialist **Army** Field Artillery Radar Crewmember **Coast Guard** Radarman **Marine Corps** Field Artillery Radar Operator **Navy** Operations Specialist Sonar Technician	**Federal** Air Traffic Controller **Civilian** Ship Navigator
Radio Intelligence Operators Monitor, intercept, and record radio signals from various sources in the field.	**Air Force** Radio Communications Specialist **Army** Emitter-Identifier/ Locator **Coast Guard** Radioman **Marine Corps** Intercept Operator **Navy** Cryptologic Technician Radioman	**Federal** Interpreter **Civilian** Communications Technician
Space Operations Specialists Monitor communications and transmit data to satellites and other space vehicles used for weather forecasting and collecting intelligence information.	**Air Force** Space Systems Operations Specialist	**Federal** NASA Technician **Civilian** Satellite Technician

ENGINEERING, SCIENCE, AND TECHNICAL OCCUPATIONS (continued)

Occupational Category/Duties	Branch/MSO	Related Titles

Surveying, Mapping, and Drafting Technicians
Conduct land surveys, make terrain maps, and prepare plans and diagrams for the construction of a variety of projects to include airstrips, buildings, and docks.
	Air Force
	Geodetic Specialist
	Army
	Cartographer
	Technical Drafting
	  Specialist
	Marine Corps
	Mapping Compiler
	Surveyor
	Construction Drafter
	Navy
	Illustrator Draftsman
		Federal
		Engineering
		  Draftsman
		Surveyor
		Cartographer
		
		Civilian
		Surveyor
		Engineer
		Architectural
		  Engineer

HUMAN SERVICES OCCUPATIONS

Occupational Category/Duties	Branch/MSO	Related Titles

Caseworkers and Counselors
Assist military personnel and their families with personal problems—drug, alcohol, depression, and emotional.
	Air Force
	Social Actions
	  Coordinator
	Army
	Counselor
	Coast Guard
	Personnel
	  Specialist
	Marine Corps
	Counselor
	Navy
	Counselor
		Federal
		Counselor
		
		Civilian
		Caseworker
		Counselor

Religious Program Specialists
Military personnel come from all walks of life and religious backgrounds. Religious Program Specialists assist in providing services, education, and related duties.
	Air Force
	Chapel Services
	Army
	Chaplain Assistant
	Coast Guard
	Religious Program
	  Specialist
	Marine Corps
	Chaplain Assistant
	Navy
	Religious Program
	  Specialist
		Federal
		N/A
		
		Civilian
		Church Manager
		Religious School
		  Instructor

INTELLIGENCE, LAW ENFORCEMENT, AND SECURITY OCCUPATIONS		
Occupational Category/Duties	**Branch/MSO**	**Related Titles**

Intelligence Specialists
Gather information from a variety of sources, including aerial photographs, electronic monitoring, and human observation; analyze and prepare detailed intelligence reports. This position requires clearance.
 	
Intelligence Specialist Specialties
Language Interrogation
Image Interpretation
Operation Intelligence
Psychological Operations
Counterintelligence
Signal Intelligence
Human Intelligence
	Air Force
	OSI Intelligence
	  Specialist
	Army
	Intelligence Analyst
	Imagery Analyst
	Imagery Ground
	  Station Specialist
	Ground
	  Surveillance
	Counterintelligence
	  Specialist
	Assistant
	  Interrogator
	Signal Security
	  Specialist
	Translator/
	  Interpreter
	Coast Guard
	Intelligence
	  Specialist
	Marine Corps
	Intelligence
	  Specialist
	Navy
	Intelligence
	  Specialist
		Federal
		Federal Police
		  Officer
		U.S. Marshall
		U.S. Customs
		  Official
		Border Patrol
		  Officer
		
		Civilian
		State Police Officer
		Sheriff's Deputy
		City Police Officer

Investigation (Law Enforcement)
Investigate criminal conduct involving personnel and property within military jurisdictions.
 	
Military Police
Conduct patrol, maintain law and order on military installations. In addition, they support battlefield activity by conducting prisoner-of-war activities.
	Air Force
	OSI Investigator
	Security Police
	Army
	CID Investigator
	Military Police
	Coast Guard
	CGI Investigator
	Port Security
	  Specialist
	Marine Corps
	Criminal
	  Investigator
	Military Police
	Navy
	NIS Investigator
	Master-At-Arms
		Federal
		Federal Police
		  Officer
		U.S. Marshall
		U.S. Customs
		  Official
		Border Patrol
		  Officer
		
		Civilian
		State Police Officer
		Sheriff's Deputy
		City Police Officer

INTELLIGENCE, LAW ENFORCEMENT, AND SECURITY OCCUPATIONS (continued)		
Occupational Category/Duties	**Branch/MSO**	**Related Titles**

Corrections Officers
Supervise and maintain control of military prisoners in confinement facilities.
 	
Corrections Specialists
Control and counsel military prisoners; manage correctional treatment programs.
	Air Force
	Corrections
	  Specialist
	Corrections Officer
	Army
	Corrections
	  Specialist
	Corrections Officer
	Marine Corps
	Corrections Officer
	Navy
	Corrections
	  Specialist
		Federal
		Corrections
		  Specialist
		Corrections Officer
		
		Civilian
		Corrections
		  Specialist
		Corrections Officer

Security Security specialists or military guards maintain security patrol or posts at installment or specific sensitive locations.	**Air Force** Security Specialist **Army** Guard **Marine Corps** Guard **Navy** Security Guard	**Federal** Federal Guard **Civilian** Security Specialist Security Guard

MECHANIC, MACHINIST, AND PRECISION WORK OCCUPATIONS

Occupational Category/Duties	Branch/MSO	Related Titles
Aircraft Mechanics Inspect and repair helicopter, jet, and propeller engines, wings, landing gears, and a variety of parts.	**Air Force** Aircraft Maintenance Specialist **Army** Aircraft Repairer **Coast Guard** Aviation Machinist Mate **Marine Corps** Aircraft Mechanic **Navy** Aircraft Machinist Mate	**Federal** Aircraft Mechanic **Civilian** Aircraft Mechanic
Automotive and Heavy Equipment Mechanics Maintain and repair a variety of vehicles to include trucks, jeeps, tanks, bulldozers, and other equipment.	**Air Force** Vehicle Mechanic **Army** Vehicle Mechanic **Marine Corps** Vehicle Mechanic **Navy** Equipment Operator	**Federal** Automotive and Heavy Equipment Mechanic **Civilian** Automotive and Heavy Equipment Mechanic
Heating and Cooling Mechanics Install and repair furnaces, boilers, and air conditioners in military buildings and on airplanes and ships.	**Air Force** Heating Systems Specialist Refrigeration Specialist **Army** Plumber **Coast Guard** Machinery Technician **Marine Corps** Refrigeration Mechanic Utilities Technician **Navy** Utilitiesman Boiler Technician	**Federal** Heating and Cooling Mechanic Plumber Boiler Plant Mechanic **Civilian** Heating and Cooling Mechanic

MECHANIC, MACHINIST, AND PRECISION WORK OCCUPATIONS (continued)		
Occupational Category/Duties	**Branch/MSO**	**Related Titles**
Machinists Make and repair metal parts for engines and equipment; operate lathes, drill presses, grinders, and other shop equipment. **Precision Equipment Repairers** Keep precision instruments in good working order. **Dental and Optical Laboratory Technicians** Construct, repair, and align dental devices, such as dentures, braces, and optical devices (eyeglasses) for military personnel.	**Air Force** Machinist **Army** Machinist Topographic Instrument Repairer **Coast Guard** Aviation Machinist Mate **Marine Corps** Shop Machinist Machinist Optical Repairer **Navy** Machinery Repairman Opticalman Instrumentman	**Federal** Instrument Repairer Machinist **Civilian** Instrument Repairer Machinist Dental and Optical Worker Laboratory Technician
Marine Engine Mechanics Repair, maintain, and install gasoline and diesel engines on boats, ships, and watercraft.	**Air Force** Marine Engine Specialist **Army** Watercraft Engineer **Coast Guard** Machinery Technician **Marine Corps** Marine Engine Specialist **Navy** Engineman	**Federal** Engineman **Civilian** Marine Engine Mechanic
Welders and Metal Workers Build and repair a variety of metal parts on vehicles, ships, tanks, aircraft, equipment, and buildings.	**Air Force** Metals Specialist Fabrication Specialist Body Mechanic **Army** Metal Worker **Coast Guard** Damage Control **Marine Corps** Aircraft Welder Metal Worker **Navy** Hull Maintenance Technician	**Federal** Welder Metal Worker **Civilian** Welder Metal Worker Auto Repairer Shipyard Worker

MEDIA AND PUBLIC AFFAIRS OCCUPATIONS

Occupational Category/Duties	Branch/MSO	Related Titles
Audiovisual and Broadcast Technicians The military produces its own television shows and films for training, documentation, and news reporting. These productions require the expertise of technicians, much like their civilian counterparts.	**Air Force** Visual Information Specialist **Army** Audiovisual Information Specialist **Coast Guard** Public Affairs **Marine Corps** Combat Photographer **Navy** Photographer's Mate	**Federal** Broadcast Equipment Operator **Civilian** Camera Operator Technician
Broadcast Journalists and Newswriters The military provides numerous public and service publications, including magazines and newspapers. In addition, the military also produces and broadcasts news and information radio shows to a wide audience. Journalists serve as liaisons between the military and the public and media.	**Air Force** Public Affairs Journalist **Army** Public Affairs Journalist **Coast Guard** Public Affairs Journalist **Marine Corps** Public Affairs Journalist **Navy** Journalist	**Federal** Public Affairs Specialist Journalist **Civilian** Broadcast Journalist Reporter Public Affairs Journalist
Graphic Designers and Illustrators In connection with the numerous publications that the military provides, graphic designers and illustrators are needed to produce artwork, charts, posters, and other visual displays.	**Air Force** Graphic Specialist **Army** Graphic Specialist **Marine Corps** Graphic Specialist **Navy** Illustrator Draftsman	**Federal** Graphic Specialist Exhibit Specialist **Civilian** Graphic Artist Designer

MEDIA AND PUBLIC AFFAIRS OCCUPATIONS (continued)		
Occupational Category/Duties	**Branch/MSO**	**Related Titles**
Interpreters and Translators Perform the critical task of translating written and spoken foreign languages for intelligence analysis and other purposes. In addition, may also be asked to interrogate or interview a variety of people in a foreign language.	**Air Force** Interpreter Translator **Army** Interpreter Translator **Coast Guard** Interpreter Translator **Marine Corps** Interpreter Translator **Navy** Cryptologic Technician	**Federal** Interpreter Translator **Civilian** Interpreter Translator
Photographic Specialists Photographs are used for a variety of purposes, including intelligence gathering, documentation of events, and news reporting. Photographic specialists need to be expert at using and maintaining a wide variety of photographic equipment.	**Air Force** Photographic Specialist **Army** Visual Information Specialist **Coast Guard** Public Affairs Specialist **Marine Corps** Combat Photographer **Navy** Photographer's Mate	**Federal** Photographer **Civilian** Photographer
Printing Specialists Operate printing presses to produce military newspapers, magazines, and other publications.	**Air Force** Reproduction Specialist **Army** Photo and Layout Specialist Printing and Bindery Specialist **Coast Guard** Public Affairs Specialist **Marine Corps** Offset Press Operator **Navy** Lithographer	**Federal** Printer Reproduction Specialist Banknote Engraver Bookbinder **Civilian** Printing Specialists

MEDICAL AND HEALTH CARE OCCUPATIONS

Occupational Category/Duties	Branch/MSO	Related Titles
Cardiopulmonary and EEG Technicians Operate testing equipment to obtain a variety of diagnostic tests of the heart, lungs, blood, and brain.	**Air Force** Cardiopulmonary Specialist **Army** Cardiopulmonary Specialist **Coast Guard** Cardiopulmonary and EEG Technician **Navy** Hospital Corpsman	**Federal** Cardiopulmonary and EEG Technician **Civilian** Cardiopulmonary and EEG Technician
Dental Specialists Assist dentists in examining, treating, and performing surgery on patients; operate dental X-ray and other equipment.	**Air Force** Dental Specialist **Army** Dental Specialist **Coast Guard** Health Services Technician **Navy** Dental Technician	**Federal** Dental Assistant **Civilian** Dental Assistant
Medical Care Technicians Provide medical care to patients; assist doctors and nurses with treatment and prepare hospital and care facility rooms and equipment.	**Air Force** Medical Specialist **Army** Medical Specialist **Coast Guard** Health Services Technician **Navy** Hospital Corpsman	**Federal** Nursing Assistant **Civilian** Nursing Assistant
Medical Laboratory Technicians Conduct clinical tests on body fluids, tissue, and blood that are necessary to diagnosis and identify diseases.	**Air Force** Medical Laboratory Specialist **Army** Medical Laboratory Specialist **Coast Guard** Health Services Technician **Navy** Hospital Corpsman	**Federal** Medical Laboratory Technician **Civilian** Medical Laboratory Technician

MEDICAL AND HEALTH CARE OCCUPATIONS (continued)		
Occupational Category/Duties	**Branch/MSO**	**Related Titles**
Optometric Technicians Assist optometrists in providing eye care to military members.	**Air Force** Optometry Technician **Army** Optometry Technician **Coast Guard** Health Services Technician **Navy** Hospital Corpsman	**Federal** Optometric Technician **Civilian** Optometric Technician
Pharmacy Technicians Assist pharmacists in issuing prescription drugs and treatments.	**Air Force** Pharmacy Specialist **Army** Pharmacy Specialist **Coast Guard** Health Services Technician **Navy** Hospital Corpsman	**Federal** Pharmacy Technician **Civilian** Pharmacy Technician
Physical and Occupational Therapy Specialists Assist in administering treatments and exercises to patients disabled by injury or illness.	**Air Force** Physical Therapy Specialist **Army** Physical Therapy Specialist **Coast Guard** Health Services Technician **Navy** Hospital Corpsman	**Federal** Physical Therapy Specialist **Civilian** Physical Therapy Specialist
Radiologic (X-ray) Technicians Operate X-ray equipment to detect illness or injury in patients.	**Air Force** Radiology Specialist **Army** Radiology Specialist **Coast Guard** Health Services Technician **Navy** Hospital Corpsman	**Federal** X-ray Technician **Civilian** X-ray Technician

MUSIC AND BAND OCCUPATIONS		
Occupational Category/Duties	**Branch/MSO**	**Related Titles**
Musicians All of the branches pride themselves on having outstanding bands for military parades, ceremonies, and national events. Music is an occupation with numerous specific skills. **Specific Military Band Member Skills** Baritone or Euphonium Player Bassoon Player Bugler Clarinet Player Drummer Electric Bass Guitarist Flute or Piccolo Player French Horn Player Guitarist Keyboard Player Oboe Player Percussionist Pianist Saxophone Player Special Bandmember Trombonist Trumpet Player Tuba Player	**Air Force** Band Member **Army** Band Member **Coast Guard** Musician **Marine Corps** Drum and Bugle Musician **Navy** Musician	**Federal** Music Specialist **Civilian** Music Teacher Musician Orchestrator Music Director

NUCLEAR POWER AND POWER PLANT OCCUPATIONS

Occupational Category/Duties	Branch/MSO	Related Titles
Nuclear Power and Power Plant Operators Operate boilers, turbines, nuclear reactors, and portable generators on ships, submarines, bases, and in the field. **Powerhouse Mechanics** Maintain, repair, and install generating equipment that provides electric power for bases, ships, and field stations. Powerhouses range from small gasoline generators to nuclear reactors. **Shipboard Propulsion Specialties** Submarine Nuclear Propulsion Plant Operator Nuclear Propulsion Plant Maintenance Surface Ship Nuclear Propulsion Operator Gas Turbine System Technician	**Air Force** Electric Power Specialist Marine Engine Specialist **Army** Watercraft Engineer Power Generator Specialist **Coast Guard** Electrician's Mate Machinery Technician **Navy** Engineman Gas Turbine Boiler Technician Electrician's Mate Machinist's Mate	**Federal** Nuclear Reactor Operator Engineman **Civilian** Power Mechanic Boiler Operator

SHIP, BOATING, AND DIVING OCCUPATIONS		
Occupational Category/Duties	**Branch/MSO**	**Related Titles**
Boatswain's Mates and Seamen Boatswain's mates have been called the "jacks of all trades" in ship, submarine, and boat operation and maintenance. As the prime "deck force," they handle cargo, ropes, and lines, and seamanship tasks.	**Air Force** Seaman **Army** Watercraft Operator **Coast Guard** Boatswain's Mate **Navy** Boatswain's Mate	**Federal** Boat Operator **Civilian** Able Seaman Marina Operator Merchant Marine
Divers Specialized military personnel who work as scuba divers or deep-sea divers. Divers conduct repairs, construction, salvage, and military operations under the water.	**Army** Diver **Marine Corps** Diver **Coast Guard** Diver **Navy** Diver	**Federal** Diver **Civilian** Commercial Diver
Quartermasters Specialize in navigation of ships and boats. Bridge watch, vessel control, and steering are among the chief duties.	**Coast Guard** Quartermaster **Navy** Quartermaster	**Federal** Ship Pilot **Civilian** Quartermaster Merchant Marine

SPECIAL OPERATIONS FORCES OCCUPATIONS		
Occupational Category/Duties	**Branch/MSO**	**Related Titles**

Special Operations Forces
 	
Restricted:
At the present time these special forces occupations are restricted to male military members only.
 	
SOF are elite combat units that operate with stealth, concealment, and surprise to accomplish their operations. SOF conduct search and destroy missions, clear underwater mine fields, and go behind enemy lines. They provide specialized air power for worldwide deployment and assignment to conduct unconventional warfare, special reconnaissance, counter-terrorism, foreign internal defense, humanitarian assistance, psychological operations, personnel retrieval, and counternarcotics.
 	
Special Comment:
For the most part, Special Operations are not entry-level positions. The military looks for service members who have already proven themselves prior to special operations duty.
	Air Force
	Special Operations
	  Specialist
	Pararescue
	Army
	Green Berets
	SO Weapons
	  Sergeant
	SO Engineer
	SO Medical
	  Sergeant
	SO Communica-
	  tions Specialist
	Marine Corps
	MEU Team Member
	SO Weapons
	  Sergeant
	SO Engineer
	SO Medical
	  Sergeant
	SO Communica-
	  tions Specialist
	Navy
	SEAL Team
	  Member
		Federal
		CIA Employee
		FBI Employee
		ATF Employee
		
		Civilian
		Corporate Security
		  Person

SUPPORT SERVICE OCCUPATIONS

Occupational Category/Duties	Branch/MSO	Related Titles

Firefighters
 Military bases and ships need to maintain their own full-time fire protection. Like their civilian counterparts, military firefighters are responsible for protecting lives and property from fire.
	Air Force
	 Firefighter
	 Army
	 Firefighter
	 Coast Guard
	 Damage
	    Controlman
	 Marine Corps
	 Firefighter
	 Navy
	 Damage
	    Controlman
		Federal
		 Firefighter (DOVA)
		
		 Civilian
		 Firefighter

Food Service Specialists (Cooks)
 One of the key positions. The military needs to feed its personnel every day on bases, ships, submarines, and in remote stations. Cooks prepare meals for small groups up to thousands. They need to plan, order, prepare, and serve a variety of meals.
	Air Force
	 Services Specialist
	 Army
	 Food Services
	    Specialist
	 Coast Guard
	 Subs Specialist
	 Marine Corps
	 Food Services
	    Specialist
	 Navy
	 Mess Management
	    Specialist
		Federal
		 Hospital Cook
		 Prison Cook
		
		 Civilian
		 Restaurant Cook
		 Hospital Cook
		 Prison Cook
		 School Cook

TRANSPORTATION AND MATERIAL HANDLING		
Occupational Category/Duties	**Branch/MSO**	**Related Titles**
Cargo Specialists Load, pack, and secure cargo into a variety of modes of transportation, including trucks, planes, helicopters, and ships.	**Air Force** Matériel Storage Specialist **Army** Cargo Specialist **Coast Guard** Boatswain's Mate **Marine Corps** Warehouse Clerk **Navy** Boatswain's Mate	**Federal** Warehouse Clerk **Civilian** Trucking Specialist Shipping Specialist

Petroleum Supply Specialists
Most military vehicles, aircraft, and ships operate on petroleum products. Specialists plan and handle the safe transfer, storage, and refueling operations.
	Air Force
	Fuel Specialist
	Army
	Petroleum Supply
	  Specialist
	Coast Guard
	Machinery
	  Technician
	Marine Corps
	Fuel Specialist
	Navy
	Boatswain's Mate
		Federal
		Petroleum Supply
		  Specialist
		
		Civilian
		Oil Refinery
		  Specialist
		Pipeline Mechanic

Railroad Operations The military operates its own rail service. Tanks, weapon systems, missiles, and nuclear matériel travel across the United States. Spur tracks and switching areas are located in several military bases. These positions are mostly in the Army Reserve.	**Army** Locomotive —Operator —Repairer Train Crew Railway Car —Repairer —Airbrake Repairer	**Federal** Amtrak Worker **Civilian** Locomotive —Operator —Repairer Train Crew Railway Car —Repairer —Airbrake Repairer

TRANSPORTATION AND MATERIAL HANDLING (continued)		
Occupational Category/Duties	**Branch/MSO**	**Related Titles**
Transportation Specialists Supervise and coordinate the movement of personnel and cargo.	**Air Force** Traffic Manager **Army** Transportation Management Coordinator **Coast Guard** Storekeeper **Marine Corps** Transportation Management Specialist **Navy** Storekeeper	**Federal** Transportation Clerk **Civilian** Transportation Clerk
Vehicle Drivers Operate a variety of military vehicles to move personnel and equipment; must be able to plan routes and handle all kinds of driving conditions.	**Air Force** Vehicle Operator **Army** Motor Transport Operator **Coast Guard** N/A **Marine Corps** Motor Vehicle Equipment Operator	**Federal** Motor Vehicle Operator **Civilian** Truck Operator

CONSTRUCTION OCCUPATIONS

Occupational Category/Duties	Branch/MSO	Related Titles
Building Electricians Install, repair, and maintain electrical systems for a wide variety of buildings, facilities and locations.	**Air Force** Electrician **Army** Electrician **Coast Guard** Electrician's Mate **Marine Corps** Electrician **Navy** Construction Electrician	**Federal** Electrician **Civilian** Electrician

Construction Equipment Operators
Operate construction equipment to move earth and building material. Assist in the building of airfields, roads, buildings, and other projects.
	Air Force
	Construction
	  Equipment
	  Operator
	Army
	Construction
	  Equipment
	  Operator
	Coast Guard
	Equipment
	  Operator
	Marine Corps
	Equipment
	  Operator
	Navy
	Equipment
	  Operator
		Federal
		Equipment
		  Operator
		
		Civilian
		Construction
		  Equipment
		  Operator

Construction Specialists
Build structures, work with lumber, concrete, masonry, and other materials.
	Air Force
	Structural Specialist
	Army
	Carpenters and
	  Masonry
	  Specialists
	Coast Guard
	Boatswain's Mate
	Marine Corps
	Construction
	  Marine
	Navy
	Constructionman
		Federal
		Carpenters
		Bricklayers
		Cement workers
		
		Civilian
		Carpenters
		Bricklayers
		Cement workers

CONSTRUCTION OCCUPATIONS (continued)		
Occupational Category/Duties	**Branch/MSO**	**Related Titles**
Plumbers and Pipe Fitters Construct, maintain, and repair pipe systems for water, steam, gas, and waste.	**Air Force** Plumbing Specialist **Army** Plumber **Coast Guard** Damage Controlman **Marine Corps** Utilitiesman **Navy** Utilitiesman	**Federal** Plumber Pipe Fitter **Civilian** Plumber Pipe Fitter

Chapter 13

OFFICER CAREERS

Career Field Comparison/Conversion Charts

- ☐ Overview
- ☐ **Occupational Categories**

OVERVIEW Each year the military recruits 23,000 commissioned officers.

The purpose for this special section is simple. Candidates who are interested in a particular military occupation can compare the various branches for the same occupation. In addition, the federal government has civil service occupations that military personnel can qualify for based on their military occupational specialty experience. Current military members or those with prior service who are looking at other branches or the federal government for civilian jobs should also find this section of special interest.

OCCUPATIONAL CATEGORIES

ADMINISTRATIVE, EXECUTIVE, AND MANAGERIAL OCCUPATIONS

Occupational Category/Duties	Branch/MSO	Related Titles
Communications Managers Oversee and direct personnel who operate computer systems, telecommunications, and satellite communications equipment. *Education Requirement:* Four-year college degree (engineering, mathematics, computer sciences, or related fields)	**Air Force** Communications Manager **Army** Signal Officer Communications Officer **Coast Guard** Communications Officer **Marine Corps** Communications Officer **Navy** Communications Officer	**Federal** Communications Manager **Civilian** Satellite Communications Manager TV Broadcasting Manager
Finance and Accounting Managers Manage financial affairs of the military branch; direct budgets and accounting, and set financial policies. *Education Requirement:* Four-year college degree in accounting, finance, or related fields	**Air Force** Comptroller **Army** Comptroller **Coast Guard** Accounting Officer **Marine Corps** Accounting Officer Financial Specialist **Navy** Accounting Officer Fiscal Officer	**Federal** Accounting Supervisor Auditing Supervisor IRS Agent Financial Manager **Civilian** Accountant
Food Service Managers The military needs to feed its personnel every day on bases, ships, submarines, and in remote stations. Food Service Managers plan and direct the preparation of meals for small groups to thousands; they also manage food budgets and inventories. *Education Requirement:* Four-year college degree	**Air Force** Food Service Manager **Army** Subsistence Manager **Coast Guard** Food Service Manager **Marine Corps** Food Service Manager **Navy** Food Service Manager	**Federal** Food Program Specialist **Civilian** Hotel Manager Restaurant Manager Cafeteria Manager

ADMINISTRATIVE, EXECUTIVE, AND MANAGERIAL OCCUPATIONS (continued)

Occupational Category/Duties	Branch/MSO	Related Titles

International Relations Officers
Official liaisons between foreign military and government officials; collect, analyze, and report on information concerning military, political, social, and economic matters of foreign countries.
 	
Specialties
Africa
Asia
Eastern Europe
Latin America
Middle East
Western Europe
 	
Education Requirement:
Four-year college degree; language specialty is an advantage
	Air Force
	Civil Affairs
	  Attaché
	Army
	Civil Affairs
	  Attaché
	Coast Guard
	Attaché
	Marine Corps
	International
	  Relations Officer
	Navy
	International
	  Relations Officer
		Federal
		State Department
		  Official
		Foreign Service
		  Official
		
		Civilian
		Political Scientist
		Corporate Advisor

Management Analysts
Analyze and modify workloads involving the best use of human and material resources.
 	
Education Requirement:
Four-year college degree
	Air Force
	Administration
	  Management
	  Officer
	Army
	Administrative
	  Systems Officer
	Coast Guard
	Management
	  Analyst
	Marine Corps
	Personnel Officer
	Navy
	Management
	  Analyst
		Federal
		Management
		  Analyst
		
		Civilian
		Management
		  Analyst

Personnel Managers
Direct programs that assist military members with their career, training, and health care information; plan the hiring and training of personnel in the future.
 	
Specialties
Mobilization Officer
Personnel Performance Officer
Manpower Planning Officer
 	
Education Requirement:
Four-year college degree
	Air Force
	Personnel Officer
	Army
	Personnel Officer
	Coast Guard
	Personnel Officer
	Marine Corps
	Management
	  Officer
	Navy
	Personnel Officer
		Federal
		Personnel Director
		Employment
		  Manager
		
		Civilian
		Personnel Director
		Employment
		  Manager

ADMINISTRATIVE, EXECUTIVE, AND MANAGERIAL OCCUPATIONS (continued)

Occupational Category/Duties	Branch/MSO	Related Titles

Postal Directors
Manage processing of military and civilian mail to military bases and naval fleets.
 	
Education Requirement:
Four-year college degree
	Air Force
	Postal Officer
	Army
	Postal Officer
	Coast Guard
	Postal Officer
	Marine Corps
	Postal Officer
	Navy
	Postal Officer
		Federal
		U.S. Postal Service
		  Official
		
		Civilian
		Postmaster
		Express Mail
		  Official

Purchasing and Contracting Managers
Oversee and control purchasing of goods, equipment, and supplies; prepare formal contracts for services.
 	
Education Requirement:
Four-year college degree
	Air Force
	Acquisition
	  Manager
	Army
	Contracting
	  Manager
	Coast Guard
	Industrial Officer
	Marine Corps
	Contracting Officer
	Navy
	Procurement
	  Officer
		Federal
		Contract and
		  Procurement
		  Official
		
		Civilian
		Manufacturing
		  Supervisor
		Construction
		  Supervisor

Recruiting Managers
Plan and direct recruiting activities to attract civilians to join the military in specialties of critical need; are also charged with retaining active duty military personnel.
 	
Education Requirement:
Four-year college degree
	Air Force
	Recruiting Service
	  Officer
	Army
	Recruiting Officer
	Coast Guard
	Personnel Officer
	Marine Corps
	Management
	  Officer
	Navy
	Procurement and
	  Recruiting Officer
		Federal
		Personnel Manager
		
		Civilian
		Corporate Recruiter

Store Managers Direct operations and personnel of military exchange stores and food and merchandise outlets. *Specialties* Commissary Store Officer Exchange Officer Ship Store Officer *Education Requirement:* Four-year college degree	**Air Force** Services Officer **Army** Store Officer **Coast Guard** Store Officer **Marine Corps** Store Officer **Navy** Store Officer	**Federal** Commissary Store Manager **Civilian** Retail Manager Store Manager

ADMINISTRATIVE, EXECUTIVE, AND MANAGERIAL OCCUPATIONS (continued)

Occupational Category/Duties	Branch/MSO	Related Titles

Supply and Warehousing Managers
Direct supply personnel and inventory of equipment, supplies, food, weapons, parts, and a variety of other items.
 	
Education Requirement:
Four-year college degree
	Air Force
	Supply Officer
	Logistics Officer
	Army
	Quartermaster
	Supply Officer
	Coast Guard
	Supply Officer
	Marine Corps
	Supply Officer
	Logistics Officer
	Warehouse Officer
	Navy
	Supply Officer
	Logistics/Inventory
	   Warehouse
	     Officer
		Federal
		Property Disposal
		   Supply Manager
		Logistics Manager
		
		Civilian
		Storage Company
		   Supervisor
		Manufacturer/
		   Warehouse
		   Manager

Teaching and Instructors
Train and instruct military personnel in classrooms and in the field on a wide variety of subject matters, including college-level academic subjects.
 	
Training and Education Directors
Develop and direct new training courses, supervise instructors, evaluate programs and progress of instructors and students.
 	
Specialties
Academy Administrator
Aviation Program Officer
Educational and Training
   Management
Professor
Ranger Officer
School Administrator
 	
Education Requirement:
Four-year college degree/master's degree
	Air Force
	Instructor
	Training Officer
	Army
	Instructor
	Training Officer
	Coast Guard
	Training Officer
	Marine Corps
	Instructor
	Training Officer
	Navy
	Instructor
	Training Officer
		Federal
		Instructor
		Education
		   Specialist
		
		Civilian
		College Professor
		College Dean

AVIATION OCCUPATIONS

Occupational Category/Duties	Branch/MSO	Related Titles
Airplane Pilots Each branch of the military has pilots for a wide variety of aircraft from Stealth Bombers to small planes. Pilots are officers who are designated by skills or qualifications of a particular type of aircraft they fly (example, B1B Pilot). Pilots operate weapons, deliver troops, cargo, and bombs, and perform search and rescue missions. *Types* Airlift Pilot Bomber Pilot Fighter Pilot Generalist Pilot Special Operations Pilot Tanker Pilot Test Pilot Trainer Pilot *Aeronautical Specialties* Astronaut *Education Requirement:* Four-year college degree *Special Requirement:* 20/20 vision	**Air Force** Pilot **Army** Pilot **Coast Guard** Pilot **Marine Corps** Pilot **Navy** Pilot	**Federal** Pilot **Civilian** Pilot
Helicopter Pilots Perform diverse missions from search and rescue to combat operations. *Education Requirement:* Four-year college degree	**Air Force** Helicopter Pilot **Army** Helicopter Pilot **Coast Guard** Helicopter Pilot **Marine Corps** Helicopter Pilot **Navy** Helicopter Pilot	**Federal** Helicopter Pilot **Civilian** Helicopter Pilot

AVIATION OCCUPATIONS (continued)		
Occupational Category/Duties	**Branch/MSO**	**Related Titles**
Aircraft Navigators Assist and direct pilots via navigation instruments; conduct fuel consumption projections and assist pilots in operation of the aircraft. ***Navigation Specialties*** Airlift Navigator Bomber Navigator Warfare Navigator Fighter Navigator Generalist Navigator Special Operations Navigator Tanker Navigator Test Navigator *Education Requirement:* Four-year college degree	**Air Force** Navigator **Army** Navigator **Coast Guard** Navigator **Marine Corps** Navigator **Navy** Navigator	**Federal** Navigator **Civilian** Navigator
Air Traffic Control Managers Direct operations of air traffic control systems and control towers; direct takeoffs and landings of military airplanes and helicopters; supervise operators of radar systems. *Education Requirement:* Four-year college degree	**Air Force** Air Traffic Control Manager **Army** Air Traffic Control Manager **Coast Guard** Air Traffic Control Manager **Marine Corps** Air Traffic Control Manager **Navy** Air Traffic Control Manager	**Federal** F.A.A. Supervisor **Civilian** Air Traffic Control Manager

COMBAT OCCUPATIONS

Occupational Category/Duties	Branch/MSO	Related Titles
Artillery Officer Direct firing of cannons, howitzers, missiles, and rockets; supervise the use of specialized equipment to locate targets. Artillery is used to protect ground troops and sea forces from air attack. *Air Defense Artillery* Air Defense Artillery, General Short-Range Air Defense Artillery (SHORAD) Hawk Missile ADA Patriot Missile ADA *Field Artillery* Field Artillery General Light Missile Field Artillery Field Artillery Target Acquisition Cannon Field Artillery *Education Requirement:* Four-year college degree	**Air Force** Artillery Officer **Army** Artillery Officer **Coast Guard** Artillery Officer **Marine Corps** Artillery Officer **Navy** Artillery Officer	**Federal** Ordnance Engineer **Civilian** Ammunition 　Storage 　Supervisor
Infantry Officer The infantry is the backbone of the military. Infantry officers lead specially trained units to destroy enemy ground forces, operate and fire a variety of weapons, parachute from transport planes, and conduct extended patrol missions. *Restricted:* At the present time this combat occupation is restricted to male military members only. However, things change. *Education Requirement:* Four-year college degree	**Army** Infantry Officer **Marine Corps** Infantry Officer	**Federal** Security Specialist **Civilian** Police Officer

COMBAT OCCUPATIONS (continued)		
Occupational Category/Duties	**Branch/MSO**	**Related Titles**
Missile Systems Officers Direct and control missile crew and ballistic missile systems that are fired from underground silos, submarines, and land-based launchers. *Missile Officer Specialties* Missile Commander Missile Launch Officer Missile Operations Officer Hawk Missile Air Defense Officer Patriot Missile Air Defense Officer *Education Requirement:* Four-year college degree	**Air Force** Missile Systems Officer **Army** Missile Systems Officer **Marine Corps** Missile Systems Officer **Navy** Missile Systems Officer	**Federal** Ordnance Engineer **Civilian** Electronics Systems Supervisor
Tank Officers Command and drive state-of-the-art tanks in combat; operate weapons systems; support and defend ground infantry troops. *Restricted* At the present time this combat occupation is restricted to male military members only. *Fighting Vehicles* M1A2, Abrams Tank M1/M1 A, Abrams Tank M2 Bradley Infantry Fighting Vehicle M3 Cavalry Fighting Vehicle M60 A1-A3 and M48 Series Tank M551 Armor Reconnaissance Vehicle *Education Requirement:* Four-year college degree	**Army** Tank Officer **Marine Corps** Tank Officer	**Federal** Ordnance Engineer **Civilian** Operating Engineer

ENGINEERING, SCIENCE, AND TECHNICAL OCCUPATIONS		
Occupational Category/Duties	**Branch/MSO**	**Related Titles**
Aerospace Engineers Oversee the production of aerospace equipment, including guidance, propulsion, and weapons systems; examine and analyze new designs for aircraft, missiles, and spacecraft. *Education Requirement:* Four-year college degree in aeronautical, astronautical, or mechanical engineering	**Air Force** Aeronautical Engineer **Coast Guard** Aeronautical Engineer **Marine Corps** Aeronautical Engineer **Navy** Aeronautical Engineer	**Federal** NASA Aerospace Engineer **Civilian** Contractor
Astronauts and Space Operations Officers Manage space flight planning, training, mission control, and other activities involving launching and recovery of spacecraft; astronauts serve as crew members or commanders on space flights. *Education Requirement:* Four-year college degree in science, engineering, mathematics, or related fields.	**Air Force** Astronauts and Space Operations Officer **Marine Corps** Astronauts and Space Operations Officer **Navy** Astronauts and Space Operations Officer	**Federal** NASA Technician **Civilian** Satellite Technician
Chemists Conduct research and experiments in chemistry and biochemistry to develop new materials for military equipment, medicines, and defensive agents. *Specialties* Biochemistry Inorganic Chemistry Organic Chemistry Physical Chemistry *Education Requirement:* Four-year college degree in chemistry, chemical engineering, or biology	**Air Force** Chemical Research Officer **Army** Chemist **Coast Guard** Chemist **Marine Corps** Chemist **Navy** Chemist	**Federal** Chemist **Civilian** Chemist

ENGINEERING, SCIENCE, AND TECHNICAL OCCUPATIONS (continued)		
Occupational Category/Duties	**Branch/MSO**	**Related Titles**
Civil Engineers Plan, design, and direct the construction of airfields, roads, bridges, buildings, power plants, docks, and facilities. *Education Requirement:* Four-year college degree in civil, architectural, sanitary, or environmental engineering	**Air Force** Civil Engineer **Army** Civil Engineer **Coast Guard** Civil Engineer **Marine Corps** Construction Officer **Navy** Civil Engineer	**Federal** Civil Engineer **Civilian** Civil Engineer
Computer Systems Officers The military uses computers for a wide variety of missions. Computer systems officers oversee and maintain complex computer systems and direct computer programs and specialists. *Education Requirement:* Four-year college degree in computer science, computer or industrial engineering, or related science	**Air Force** Computer Systems Officer **Army** Computer Systems Officer **Coast Guard** Computer Systems Officer **Marine Corps** Computer Systems Officer **Navy** Computer Systems Officer	**Federal** Computer Systems Manager **Civilian** Information Systems Manager ADP Manager Computer Engineer
Electrical and Electronics Engineers Design, develop, and test electrical and electronic equipment. *Education Requirement:* Four-year college degree in electrical, electronics, or communications engineering	**Air Force** Electronics Engineer **Army** Electronics Engineer **Coast Guard** Electronics Engineer **Marine Corps** Electronics Engineer **Navy** Electronics Engineering Officer	**Federal** Electrical and Electronics Engineer **Civilian** Electrical and Electronics Engineer

ENGINEERING, SCIENCE, AND TECHNICAL OCCUPATIONS (continued)

Occupational Category/Duties	Branch/MSO	Related Titles
Environmental Health and Safety Officers Study air, ground, and water to identify and analyze sources of pollution; direct programs to control safety and health hazards. *Education Requirement:* Four-year college degree in biomedical or biological science	**Air Force** Health and Safety Officer **Army** Health and Safety Officer **Coast Guard** USPHO **Marine Corps** Health and Safety Officer **Navy** Safety Engineer	**Federal** OSHA Inspector **Civilian** Environmental Scientist Industrial Hygienist Health and Safety Officer
Industrial Engineers Examine and study ways for the military to improve the way work is done and direct quality control and production programs. *Education Requirement:* Four-year college degree in industrial engineering, industrial management or a related field	**Air Force** Industrial Engineer **Army** Industrial Engineer **Coast Guard** Industrial Engineer **Marine Corps** Industrial Engineer **Navy** Industrial Engineer	**Federal** Industrial Engineer **Civilian** Industrial Engineer
Life Scientists Conduct studies of human and animal diseases and bacteria and parasites to understand their causes and find treatments. *Specialties* Biologists Entomologists Immunologists Toxicologists *Education Requirement:* Four-year college degree in related field	**Air Force** Life Scientist **Army** Life Scientist **Navy** Life Scientist	**Federal** Biologist **Civilian** Biologist Entomologist Immunologist Toxicologist
Marine Engineers Design ships, submarines, and other watercraft for the military. *Education Requirement:* Four-year college degree in marine engineering	**Coast Guard** Marine Engineer **Navy** Naval Engineer	**Federal** Naval Architect **Civilian** Marine Engineer

ENGINEERING, SCIENCE, AND TECHNICAL OCCUPATIONS (continued)		
Occupational Category/Duties	**Branch/MSO**	**Related Titles**
Meteorologists Study weather conditions and prepare weather forecasts. *Education Requirement:* Four-year college degree in meteorology	**Air Force** Weather Service Specialist **Army** Meteorology Officer **Marine Corps** Meteorologist **Navy** Meteorologist	**Federal** Meteorologist **Civilian** TV and Radio Weather Reporter
Nuclear Engineers Direct operation and maintenance of nuclear power plants, strategic weapons, and defense systems. *Education Requirement:* Four-year college degree in physics, nuclear engineering, or related fields	**Air Force** Nuclear Engineer **Army** Nuclear Weapons Engineer **Marine Corps** Nuclear Engineer **Navy** Nuclear Engineer Ship Reactor Officer	**Federal** Nuclear Engineer **Civilian** Public Utilities/ Power Plant Contractor
Oceanographers Study ocean tides, currents, weather, and physical features of the ocean floor. *Education Requirement:* Four-year college degree in a related field	**Coast Guard** Oceanography Officer **Navy** Oceanography Officer	**Federal** NOAA Technician **Civilian** Ocean Research Technician
Physicists Direct research and development on new materials for ships, aircraft, and weapons by conducting experiments in aerodynamics, optics, geophysics, biophysics, nuclear physics, and astrophysics. *Education Requirement:* Four-year college degree	**Air Force** Physicist **Army** Physicist **Coast Guard** Physicist **Navy** Physicist	**Federal** Physicist **Civilian** Physicist
Surveying and Mapping Managers Plan and direct surveying and mapmaking operations and teams. *Education Requirement:* Four-year college degree in photographic science, cartography, or related fields	**Air Force** Mapping, Charting, and Geodesy Officer **Army** Topographic Engineer **Marine Corps** Cartography	**Federal** Cartographer Land Surveyor **Civilian** Cartographer Land Surveyor

HUMAN SERVICES OFFICERS OCCUPATIONS

Occupational Category/Duties	Branch/MSO	Related Titles
Chaplains Military personnel come from all walks of life and religious backgrounds. Chaplains hold worship services and provide education and related duties. ***Chaplain-Related Designations*** Chaplain Education and Training Chaplain Resource Manager Chaplain Service School (Instructor) Confinement Ministry Hospital Ministry Marriage and Family Ministry Pastoral Coordinator Pastoral Counselor, Alcohol and Drug Abuse Counselor Religious Education Ministry *Education Special Requirement:* Master's degree in theology and ordination	**Air Force** Chaplain **Army** Chaplain **Coast Guard** Chaplain **Navy** Chaplain	**Federal** Chaplain **Civilian** Clergyman Minister Preacher Priest Rabbi
Social Workers Assist military personnel and their families with personal problems, such as drug and alcohol abuse, depression, and emotional problems. *Education Requirement:* Four-year college degree in social work/sciences	**Air Force** Social Worker **Army** Social Worker **Navy** Social Worker	**Federal** Social Worker **Civilian** Social Worker

INTELLIGENCE AND LAW ENFORCEMENT OFFICERS AND AGENTS

Occupational Category/Duties	Branch/MSO	Related Titles
Inspector General Office Occupations Conduct and supervise investigations of fraud, waste, and abuse of government resources; maintain both investigatory and audit personnel. A large number of federal agencies maintain Inspector General Offices to include the Department of Defense (Pentagon duty). *Education Requirement:* Four-year college degree (numerous fields)	**Air Force** Inspector General **Army** Inspector General **Coast Guard** DOT Inspector General **Marine Corps** Inspector General **Navy** Inspector General	**Federal** Inspector General —Investigator —Auditor FBI Agent **Civilian** Special Investigator
Intelligence The chief mission of Intelligence is gathering information critical to national defense. There are numerous specialties within the Intelligence field. "Intell" officers help plan military missions and direct sea, ground, and human surveillance. ***Intelligence Specialties*** Counterintelligence Human Intelligence Image Interpretation Language Interrogation Operation Intelligence Psychological Operations Signal Intelligence *Education Requirement:* Four-year college degree (numerous fields)	**Air Force** Intelligence Signals Intelligence Imagery Intelligence **Army** Military Intelligence Strategic Intelligence Tactical Intelligence Human Intelligence Signals Intelligence Imagery Intelligence Counterintelligence **Coast Guard** CGI Intelligence **Marine Corps** Intelligence **Navy** ONI Intelligence Psychology Operational Intelligence Tactical Intelligence	**Federal** CIA Agent NSA Agent FBI Agent **Civilian** Corporate Intelligence

INTELLIGENCE AND LAW ENFORCEMENT OFFICERS AND AGENTS (continued)		
Occupational Category/Duties	**Branch/MSO**	**Related Titles**

Law Enforcement and Military Police
Direct and supervise military police officers, much like a chief of police; oversee physical security, criminal investigations, and correction activities.
 	
Education Requirement:
Four-year college degree (numerous fields)
	Air Force
	OSI Security Police
	Army
	CID Military Police
	Corrections Officer
	Coast Guard
	CGI Investigations
	   Officer
	Marine Corps
	NIS Military Police
	Corrections Officer
	Navy
	NIS Security Officer
	Shore Patrol Officer
		Federal
		FBI Agent
		U.S. Customs
		   Agent
		ATF Agent
		Corrections Officer
		
		Civilian
		Chief of Police
		Director of Security
		Warden
		State Trooper
		Police Officer

LEGAL OCCUPATIONS

Occupational Category/Duties	Branch/MSO	Related Titles
Lawyers The military maintains it own legal system. Lawyers conduct legal research, prosecute, and defend court cases and military personnel. In addition, they represent the military in civil and international legal matters. *Legal Related Skills* Claims/Litigation Specialist Government Contract Law Specialist International Law Specialist Military Lawyer Environmental Lawyer *Education Requirement:* Law degree and membership in the bar in either federal court or the highest court in the state	**Air Force** Lawyer **Army** Lawyer **Coast Guard** Lawyer **Marine Corps** Lawyer **Navy** Lawyer	**Federal** Lawyer **Civilian** Lawyer
Military Judges Preside over military legal cases, make judgments based on the Uniform Code of Military Justice, and rule on law. Most military judges have prior experience as military lawyers. *Education Requirement:* Law degree and membership in the bar in either federal court or the highest court in the state	**Air Force** Judge **Army** Judge Advocate General **Coast Guard** Judge **Marine Corps** Judge **Navy** Judge	**Federal** Judge **Civilian** Judge

MEDIA AND PUBLIC AFFAIRS OFFICERS OCCUPATIONS

Occupational Category/Duties	Branch/MSO	Related Titles
Audiovisual and Broadcast Directors Produce motion pictures, videotapes, and television and radio productions for a wide audience. *Education Requirement:* Four-year college degree	**Air Force** Visual Information Officer **Army** Audiovisual Officer **Marine Corps** Audiovisual Officer **Navy** Motion Picture and Television Officer	**Federal** Audiovisual Production Director **Civilian** Television Stations Manager Motion Picture Company Director Advertising Director
Public Information Officers Liaison between the military and the public and media is a key part of this career. PIOs answer questions and inquiries from the public, the media, and government leaders. *Education Requirement:* Four-year college degree	**Air Force** Public Affairs Officer **Army** Public Affairs Officer **Coast Guard** Public Affairs Officer **Marine Corps** Public Affairs Officer **Navy** Public Affairs Officer	**Federal** Public Affairs Officer **Civilian** Corporation Officer College Public Relations Representative
Music and Band Directors All of the branches pride themselves on having an outstanding band for military parades, ceremonies, and national events. Music and band directors supervise musicians for various productions. *Education Requirement:* Four-year college degree in music/music education	**Air Force** Band Officer **Army** Band Officer **Coast Guard** Band Officer **Marine Corps** Band Officer **Navy** Music Director	**Federal** N/A **Civilian** Band Director Music Teacher

MEDICAL AND HEALTH CARE PROFESSIONALS

Occupational Category/Duties	Branch/MSO	Related Titles

Health Care Administrators
Manage military hospitals, clinics, and health care facilities.
 	
Health Care Administration Specialties
Health Care Administrator
Health Services Administrator
Health Services Comptroller
Health Services Systems Manager
Patient Administrator
Health Services Human Resources
   Management
Health Services Material
   Management
 	
Education Requirement:
Four-year college degree in health care, business, nursing administration, or related fields
	Air Force
	Administrator
	Army
	Administrator
	Coast Guard
	Administrator
	Marine Corps
	Administrator
	Navy
	Administrator
		Federal
		Administrator
		Hospital Director
		
		Civilian
		Hospital Director
		Medical
		   Coordinator

Dietitians Manage medical food services facilities and plan special diets for patients and plan budgets. *Education Requirement:* Four-year college degree in food and nutrition or related fields	**Air Force** Dietitian **Army** Dietitian **Coast Guard** USPHSO **Navy** Dietitian	**Federal** Dietitian **Civilian** Dietitian
Pharmacists Manage the purchasing, storing, and dispensing of drugs and medicine. *Education Requirement:* Four-year college degree in pharmacy and a state license to practice pharmacy	**Air Force** Pharmacist **Army** Pharmacist **Coast Guard** USPHSO **Navy** Pharmacist	**Federal** Pharmacist **Civilian** Pharmacist

MEDICAL AND HEALTH CARE PROFESSIONALS (continued)

Occupational Category/Duties	Branch/MSO	Related Titles
Physical and Occupational Therapists Plan and administer treatments and exercise to patients disabled by injury or illness. *Education Requirement:* Four-year college degree in physical and occupational therapy	**Air Force** Physical and Occupational Therapist **Army** Physical and Occupational Therapist **Coast Guard** USPHSO **Navy** Physical and Occupational Therapist	**Federal** Physical and Occupational Therapist **Civilian** Physical and Occupational Therapist
Physician Assistants Examine, diagnose, and treat patients under the supervision of medical doctors. *Education Requirement:* Four-year college degree/Graduation from an accredited physician assistant's program	**Air Force** Physician Assistant **Army** Physician Assistant **Coast Guard** USPHSO **Navy** Physician Assistant	**Federal** Physician Assistant **Civilian** Physician Assistant
Registered Nurses Direct nursing teams and provide care to patients; give injections, assist physicians during surgery, and maintain patient records. ***Nursing Specialties*** Clinical Nurse Community Health Nurse Medical-Surgical Nurse Nurse Administrator Nurse Anesthetist Nurse Practitioner Nurse Recruiting Obstetric and Gynecologic Nurse Operating Room Nurse Pediatric Nurse Psychiatric/Mental Health Nurse *Education Requirement:* Graduation from an accredited nursing program and a nursing license	**Air Force** Registered Nurse **Army** Registered Nurse **Coast Guard** Registered Nurse **Navy** Registered Nurse	**Federal** Registered Nurse **Civilian** Registered Nurse

MEDICAL AND HEALTH CARE PROFESSIONALS (continued)		
Occupational Category/Duties	**Branch/MSO**	**Related Titles**
Speech Therapists Treat patients with hearing and speech problems. *Education Requirement:* Master's degree in audiology or speech therapy	**Air Force** Audiologist **Army** Audiologist **Coast Guard** Speech Therapist **Navy** Audiologist	**Federal** Speech Pathologist **Civilian** Speech Therapist

MEDICAL DIAGNOSING AND TREATMENT PRACTITIONERS

Occupational Category/Duties	Branch/MSO	Related Titles
Physicians and Surgeons Medical doctors and surgeons provide services to military personnel and their dependents. ***Medical Specialties*** Allergist-Clinical Immunologist Anesthesiologist Cardiologist Child Neurologist Clinical Pharmacologist Dermatologist Diagnostic Radiologist Emergency Physician Endocrinologist Family Physician Field Surgeon Flight Surgeon Gastroenterologist General Surgeon Infectious Disease Officer Internist Medical Oncologist/Hematologist Nephrologist Neurologist Neurosurgeon Nuclear Medicine Officer Obstetrician/Gynecologist Occupational Medicine Officer Operational Medicine Ophthalmologist Orthopedic Surgeon Otolaryngologist Pathologist Pediatric Cardiologist Pediatrician Peripheral Vascular Surgeon Physiatrist Plastic Surgeon Rheumatologist Therapeutic Radiologist Thoracic Surgeon Urologist *Education Requirement:* A medical or osteopathy doctoral degree and advanced training in a medical specialty	**Air Force** Physician Surgeon **Army** Physician Surgeon **Coast Guard** USPHSO **Navy** Physician Surgeon	**Federal** Physician Surgeon **Civilian** Physician Surgeon

MEDICAL DIAGNOSING AND TREATMENT PRACTITIONERS (continued)

Occupational Category/Duties	Branch/MSO	Related Titles
Psychiatrists and Psychologists Conduct research and treatment of military personnel involving human behavior and mental illness. *Psychologists* Child Psychologist Clinical Psychologist Neuropsychologist Research Psychologist *Psychiatrist* Child Psychiatrist *Education Requirement:* Four-year college degree in psychology or doctor of psychiatry	**Air Force** Psychiatrist Psychologist **Army** Psychiatrist Psychologist **Coast Guard** USPHSO **Navy** Psychiatrist Psychologist	**Federal** Psychiatrist Psychologist **Civilian** Psychiatrist Psychologist
Optometrists Provide eye care and treat visual problems. *Education Requirement:* Doctor of optometry degree	**Air Force** Optometrist **Army** Optometrist **Coast Guard** USPHSO **Navy** Optometrist	**Federal** Optometrist **Civilian** Optometrist
Dentists Examine, diagnose, and treat diseases and disorders of the mouth. *Dental Specialties* Endodontist Oral and Maxillofacial Surgeon Oral Pathologist Orthodontist Periodontist Prosthodontist Public Health Dentist *Education Requirement:* Doctor of dentistry degree	**Air Force** Dental Officer **Army** Dentist **Coast Guard** USPHO **Navy** Dental Officer	**Federal** Dentist **Civilian** Dentist

MEDICAL DIAGNOSING AND TREATMENT PRACTITIONERS (continued)		
Occupational Category/Duties	**Branch/MSO**	**Related Titles**
Veterinarians Provide medical services to animals. ***Veterinary Services*** Field Veterinary Service Veterinary Comparative Medicine Veterinary Laboratory Animal Medicine Veterinary Microbiology Veterinary Pathology Veterinary Preventive Medicine *Education Requirement:* Doctor of veterinary medicine degree	**Air Force** Veterinary Services Officer **Army** Veterinary Scientist	**Federal** Veterinarian **Civilian** Veterinarian

SHIP AND SUBMARINE OFFICERS OCCUPATIONS

Occupational Category/Duties	Branch/MSO	Related Titles
Ship and Submarine Officers Categorized by department or specialties such as: communi- cations, weapons, supply. *Ship Officer Titles* Commanding Officer, Afloat Search and Rescue Officer Undersea Weapons Project Officer Hull Inspection Officer Flight Deck Officer Submarine Warfare Officer Ship Electric Warfare Officer Diving Officer *Education Requirement:* Four-year college degree (numerous fields)	**Coast Guard** Ship Officer **Navy** Ship Officer Submarine Officer	**Federal** Ship Officer **Civilian** Merchant Marine Ship Officer
Ship Engineering Officers Supervise and control ship or submarine engineering departments that are responsible for the engine operation, gener- ators, heating plants, and air conditioning systems. *Ship Engineer Officer Specialties* General Diesel Gas Turbine Steam Nuclear *Education Requirement:* Four-year college degree (numerous fields)	**Coast Guard** Engineering Officer **Navy** Engineering Officer Nuclear Reactor Engineer	**Federal** Engineer **Civilian** Engineer

SPECIAL OPERATIONS FORCES OFFICERS OCCUPATIONS		
Occupational Category/Duties	**Branch/MSO**	**Related Titles**
Special Operations Forces Officers SOF are elite combat units that operate with stealth, concealment, and surprise to accomplish their operations. SOF conduct search and destroy missions, clear underwater mine fields, and go behind enemy lines. They provide specialized air power for worldwide deployment and assignment to conduct unconventional warfare, special reconnaissance, counter-terrorism, foreign internal defense, humanitarian assistance, psychological operations, personnel retrieval, and counternarcotics.	**Air Force** Special Operations Officer **Army** Green Berets Officer **Marine Corps** MEU Team Officer **Navy** SEAL Team Officer	**Federal** CIA Agent FBI Agent ATF Agent **Civilian** Corporate Security Officer
Special Comment For the most part, Special Operations are not entry-level positions. The military is looking for service members who have already proven themselves prior to special operations duty.		
Restricted: At the present time Special Forces occupations are restricted to male military members only.		
Education Requirement: Four-year college degree		

TRANSPORTATION OFFICERS OCCUPATIONS

Occupational Category/Duties	Branch/MSO	Related Titles
Transportation Managers Direct movement of personnel and matériel by air, road, rail, and water, using aircraft, trucks, trains, and ships. *Transportation Management Specialties* Air Traffic Manager Cargo Officer Households Goods Officer Marine and Terminal Operations Motor/Rail Transportation Passenger Transportation Officer Shipping Operations Officer Traffic Manager *Education Requirement:* Four-year college degree	**Air Force** Transportation Officer **Army** Transportation Manager **Coast Guard** Transportation Manager **Marine Corps** Traffic Manager **Navy** Transportation Officer	**Federal** Transportation Specialist **Civilian** Airline Manager Railroad Manager Shipping Manager
Transportation Maintenance Managers Direct personnel who repair and maintain the military's transportation system, which includes ships, aircraft, trucks, vehicles, and railroad cars. *Specialties* Aircraft Maintenance Aviation Maintenance Automotive Maintenance *Education Requirement:* Four-year college degree	**Air Force** Aircraft Maintenance Manager Automotive Maintenance Manager **Army** Aircraft Maintenance Manager Automotive Maintenance Manager **Coast Guard** Maintenance Manager **Marine Corps** Aircraft Maintenance Manager Automotive Maintenance Manager **Navy** Aviation Maintenance Manager	**Federal** Maintenance Manager **Civilian** Transportation Maintenance Manager

SECTION

5

MILITARY
INFORMATION

Chapter 14

ADDITIONAL INFORMATION

The Pentagon
☐ Overview

The Department of Defense
☐ DOD Organization

The U.S. Military and War
☐ Overview

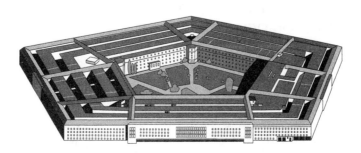

THE PENTAGON

Arlington, VA

One of the greatest opportunities in the military is working at the Pentagon. Not only can the duty be rewarding, it can lead to federal employment in one of the numerous agencies that are housed at this unique military city.

OVERVIEW   The Pentagon, headquarters of the Department of Defense, is one of the world's largest office buildings and virtually a city in itself. Approximately 23,000 employees, both military and civilian, work there in a variety of positions.

Tours

The Pentagon provides walk-in tours to the general public. Tours are given by active-duty military personnel who serve as guides for up to one year. They conduct all tours in ceremonial dress uniforms. The Pentagon tour general information number is (703) 695-1776 or Director, Pentagon Tours, 1400 Defense Pentagon, Washington, DC 20301-1400.

THE DEPARTMENT OF DEFENSE (DOD)

The DOD is a major part of the U.S. government's responsibility for a multitude of missions, including formulating joint military policies and maintaining the branches of the armed forces.

DOD ORGANIZATIONS

American Forces Information Service
Ballistic Missile Defense Organization
Defense Advanced Research Projects Agency
Defense Commissary Agency
Defense Contract Audit Agency
Defense Finance and Accounting Service
Defense Human Resources Agency
Defense Information Systems Agency
Defense Intelligence Agency
Defense Investigative Service
Defense Legal Services Agency
Defense Logistics Agency
Defense Medical Programs Activity
Defense POW/Missing Personnel Office
Defense Security Assistance Agency
Defense Special Weapons Agency
Defense Support Activities
Defense Technology Security Administration
Department of Defense Education Activity
Inspector General Department of Defense
Joint Chiefs of Staff
National Imagery and Mapping Agency
National Security Agency
Office of Civilian Health and Medical Program of the Uniformed
    Services

Office of Economic Adjustment
Office of the Secretary of Defense
On-Site Inspection Agency
Uniformed Services University of the Health Sciences
U.S. Court of Appeals for the Armed Forces
Washington Headquarters Services

THE U.S. MILITARY AND WAR

U.S. Army War College Motto:
Not to Promote War But to Preserve Peace

OVERVIEW One of the realities of military service is the possibility of being sent to participate in a war or armed conflict. The primary mission of all of the services is to prepare for such events but don't fear—fortunately, the United States, through its superior training and technically advanced weaponry, incurs fewer losses of its military forces than other countries. Special Forces and front line units, however, are at greater risk.

THE COSTS OF WAR AND MILITARY CONFLICTS		
Major Wars and Conflicts	**Deaths (total)**	**Wounded**
Revolutionary War (1775-1873)	4,425	6,188
War of 1812 (1812-1815)	2,260	4,505
Mexican War (1846-1848)	13,283	4,152
Civil War (1861-1865)	505,149	281,881
Spanish-American War (1898)	2,446	1,662
World War I (1917-1918)	116,516	204,022
World War II (1941-1945)	405,421	671,846
Korean Conflict (1950-1953)	36,914	103,284
Vietnam Conflict (1964-1973)	59,799	153,303
Lebanon Peacekeeping Mission (1982-1984)	263	n/av
Grenada "Urgent Fury" (1983)	19	n/av
Panama "Operation Just Cause" (1989)	23	n/av

THE COSTS OF WAR AND MILITARY CONFLICTS (continued)		
Major Wars and Conflicts	**Deaths (total)**	**Wounded**
Persian Gulf War "Desert Storm" (1990-1991)	383	n/av
Somalia "Restore Hope" (1992-1994)	43	n/av
Haiti "Uphold Democracy" (1994-1997)	4	n/av

(Source: DOD Defense Almanac issue #5)

Whether you enlist or not, remember to honor our veterans for their sacrifices. If you do join, you may also feel the pride one day of being a United States veteran who served our country.

Memorial Day (last Monday in May):
This day was originally established in 1868 to honor the dead from the Civil War. It is now known as a day to remember all U.S. military members killed or missing in action from all wars.

Veterans Day (November 11):
This is an established holiday to honor all veterans of the armed forces; formerly known as Armistice Day, the anniversary of the World War I armistice.

APPENDICES

GLOSSARY OF MILITARY TERMS

The following selected military terms are provided to assist in understanding the options and opportunities in the military. "Military-speak" is a unique and complex language so additional terms have been provided. The glossary will help you become familiar with words and their meaning.

Note: Definitions were abstracted from the DOD Military Term Dictionary and previously cited official military material.

A

Active Duty Continuous duty on a daily basis, comparable to full-time when referring to a civilian job; full-time duty in the active service of a uniformed service, including duty on the active list, full-time training duty, annual training duty, and attendance while in the active service at a school designated as a service school by law or by the secretary concerned.

Actual Strength The number of personnel in, or projected to be in, an organization or account at a specified point in time.

Allowances Money, other than basic pay, to compensate in certain specified situations for expenses such as meals, rent, clothing, and travel. Compensation is also given for maintaining proficiency in specific skill areas such as flying or parachuting.

Annual Training The minimal period of annual active duty for training or annual field training a serviceman/woman performs each year to satisfy the annual training requirement associated with a Reserve component assignment. It may be performed during one consecutive period or in increments of one or more days, depending upon mission requirements.

Armed Forces of the United States The Army, Navy, Air Force, Marine Corps, and Coast Guard, and all components thereof.

Armed Services Vocational Aptitude Battery (ASVAB) A test that provides students with academic and vocational aptitude scores to assist them in career exploration and decision making. ASVAB scores are used by the military services to determine enlistment eligibility and to assign occupational specialties.

Army National Guard The Army portion of the organized militia of the several states,

Commonwealth of Puerto Rico, and District of Columbia, whose units and members are federally recognized.

Army National Guard of the United States A Reserve component of the Army, all of whose members are also members of the Army National Guard.

Artillery Large cannons or missile launchers used in combat.

Assigned Strength Actual strength of an entire service, not necessarily equal to combined unit actual strengths since individuals may be assigned but not joined.

ASVAB The Armed Services Vocational Aptitude Battery is a group of ten subtests that measures ability in various career areas and provides an indication of academic ability. It is an aptitude test that predicts academic success and eligibility for the Armed Services. It is not a pass-or-fail test.

Authorized Strength The total strength of the service as authorized by Congress.

B

Barracks A building where military personnel live.

Base A locality or installation on which a military force relies for supplies or from where it initiates operations.

Basic Pay The amount of pay a military member receives, as determined by pay grade and length of service. Basic pay does not include other benefits such as allowances and bonuses.

Basic Training A rigorous orientation to the military, which provides a transition from civilian to military life.

BDU Battle Dress Uniform.

Below Downstairs.

Boot Seaman recruit in boot camp; historic slang from the days in which the recruits wore leggings that resembled boots.

Briefing A verbal military communication method used to provide or exchange information, to obtain a decision, or to review important mission details. It should include an introduction, body, conclusion, and an audience question-and-answer period. There are four types of briefing formats: information, decision, staff, and mission. Also, the act of giving in advance specific instructions or information.

Brightwork Brass or shiny metal.

Bulkhead Wall.

Bunk or rack Bed.

C

Chain of Command The succession of commanding officers from a superior to a subordinate through which command is exercised; also called command channel.

Civil Functions Functions primarily associated with the civil works program of the Army Corps of Engineers. This program encompasses planning, programming, designing, constructing, and operating federal water resource projects for navigation, flood control, hydroelectric power, water supply, recreation, and related activities. Civil

Functions also includes cemetery workers (Army) and conservation management employees (Air Force).

Civilian Anyone not on active duty in the military.

Colleges

Community or Junior Colleges: Two-year schools that offer usually freshman- and sophomore-level courses of all subjects, and grant associate's degrees.

Colleges and Universities: Four-year schools that offer all levels of courses required for an undergraduate four-year degree and sometimes courses required for a master's or doctorate degree.

College Entrance Testing Exams The following exams are used by military academies and ROTC programs to determine candidates' aptitude. Most of these exams are given at area high schools or local colleges.

ACT (American College Testing Assessment Program)

SAT (College Board)

GRE (Graduate Record Exam)

College Degrees

Associate's Degree: Two-year course of study, generally 60 hours of credit.

Bachelor's Degree: Four-year course of study, generally 120–130 hours of credit.

Master's Degree: One- or two-year course of study, usually 30–60 hours beyond the bachelor's degree.

Doctorate Degree: The highest academic degree in a discipline or profession; generally requires three or more years of graduate work and completion of a dissertation approved by a faculty committee; 60–100 hours beyond a master's degree.

Degrees are also classified into either arts or science; the difference is the number of credits earned in the major versus the number earned in the liberal arts. Generally, a bachelor of science requires more credits in the major while a bachelor of arts encourages study in the liberal arts.

A *major* is a concentration of specific courses in a chosen field of study.

College Student Classification

Freshman: First-year student (approximately 30 semester hours).

Sophomore: Second-year student (approximately 60 semester hours).

Junior: Third-year student (approximately 90 semester hours).

Senior: Fourth-year student (approximately 120 semester hours for a bachelor's degree).

Colors The raising or lowering of the American flag.

Combat Information Unevaluated data, gathered by or provided directly to the tactical commander that, due to its highly perishable nature or the critical nature of the situation, cannot be processed into tactical intelligence in time to satisfy the user's tactical intelligence requirements.

Command A specifically designated organization.

Commissary A store on a military base that sells groceries and other items at a substantial discount to military personnel.

Commissioned Officer A member of the military holding the rank of second lieutenant, ensign, or above. This role in the military is similar to that of a manager or executive.

Concealment The protection from observation or surveillance. A position that cannot easily be detected from the front or from the air; in other words, it blends well enough with the surroundings that an approaching soldier approximately 35 meters to the front or within hand grenade range cannot detect it.

Continental United States Unless otherwise qualified, this refers to the 48 contiguous states and the District of Columbia.

Cook-Off Functioning of a chambered round of ammunition, initiated by the heat of the weapon.

Cover A natural or man-made protection from enemy observation and fire. An example of this would be a frontal parapet high and thick enough to protect the soldier's head completely while he is firing a weapon. It should afford protection from direct frontal small arms fire and from the effects of indirect fire.

Critical Occupational Specialties (COS) Specialties designated by the Secretary of Defense to maintain an operational level necessary to obtain strategic goals in a conflict.

Cryptomaterial All material, including documents, devices, or equipment, that contains crypto information and is essential to the encryption, decryption, or authentication of telecommunications.

D

Danger Close In artillery and naval gunfire support, information in a call for fire to indicate that friendly forces are within 600 meters of the target.

Dead Space An area within the maximum effective range of a weapon, surveillance device, or observer that cannot be covered by fire or observation from a particular position because of intervening obstacles, the nature of the ground, the characteristics of the trajectory, or the limitations of the pointing capabilities of the weapons.

Deck Floor.

Delayed Entry Program (DEP) A military program that allows an applicant to delay entry into active duty for up to one year for such things as finishing school, and so forth.

Direct Fire Fire directed at a target that is visible to the aimer. To avoid direct fire, the soldier moves from cover to cover, using the "rush" technique.

Direct Hire Civilians Employees hired directly by an agency of DOD; includes foreign nationals hired by DOD to support DOD activities in their home countries.

Drill To train or exercise in military operations; a disciplined, repetitious exercise to teach and perfect a skill or procedure, such as fire, man overboard, abandon ship, lifeboat, and damage control drills on watercraft.

Duty Assigned task or occupation.

E

Enlisted Member A person enlisted, enrolled, or conscripted into the military service; also includes enlisted personnel currently enrolled in an officer training program and military personnel below the rank of warrant or commissioned officers. This role is similar to that of a company employee or supervisor.

Enlistee A service member, not a warrant or commissioned officer, who has been accepted by the military and has taken the Oath of Enlistment.

Enlistment 1. A voluntary entrance into military service under enlisted status, as distinguished from induction through Selective Service, which existed for many years; **2.** a period of time, contractual or prescribed by law, which enlisted members serve between enrollment and discharge.

Enlistment Agreement (Enlistment Contract) A legal contract between the military and an enlistment applicant that contains information such as enlistment date, term of enlistment, and other options such as a training program guarantee or a cash bonus.

F

Field of Fire The area that a weapon or group of weapons may cover effectively with fire from a given position.

Frocked Authorized to pin on the next higher insignia of rank before being officially promoted to that rank.

G

Galley Kitchen.

GI Bill Benefits A program of education benefits for individuals entering the military. This program enables service persons to set aside money to be used later for educational purposes.

H

Head Bathroom.

I

Inactive Reserve Duty Affiliation with the military in a nontraining, nonpaying status after completing the minimum obligation of active duty service.

Infantry Units that are trained, armed, and equipped to fight on foot.

Intelligence (Military) The product resulting from the collection, processing, integration analysis, evaluation, and interpretation of available information concerning foreign countries or areas.

L

Leave Paid time off for vacation, personal reasons, or sick time.

Liberty Time off ashore.

Logistics The science of planning and carrying out the movement and maintenance of forces. In its most comprehensive sense, those aspects of military operations that deal with: **1.** design development, acquisition, storage, movement, distribution, maintenance, evacuation, and disposition of material; **2.** movement, evacuation, and hospitalization of personnel; **3.** acquisition or construction, maintenance, operation, and disposition of facilities; and **4.** acquisition or furnishing of services.

M

Military Academy Status Terms

Appointee: A qualified candidate who has been offered an appointment to the Academy.

Appointment: An offer of admission to a candidate.

Cadet: An appointee who has been admitted to the academy and has taken the oath of allegiance.

Candidate: A precandidate who has a nomination in an authorized category.

Nomination: The selection of a precandidate as an official candidate for admission to the academy by a legal nominating authority.

Precandidate: A student interested in attending a military academy who has returned a completed application/precandidate questionnaire.

Principal Nominee: A nominee whom the member of Congress ranks as first choice for an authorized vacancy.

Qualified Alternate: A qualified candidate not chosen to fill any specific nomination category but placed in a nationwide pool from which additional appointments are made to fill the entering class.

Qualified Candidate: A candidate who has met all admissions requirements.

Tentative Candidate: A precandidate who appears to have the potential to be a qualified candidate, based upon self-reported information.

Military Afloat Navy and Marine Corps military personnel aboard ship; also includes Navy and Marine Corps military personnel who are assigned to afloat and mobile units, such as aircraft squadrons, construction battalions, and fleet and air command staffs, and who are aboard ship.

Military Entrance Processing Stations (MEPS) Located around the country, they are basically one-stop processing stations that conduct attitude testing, medical and physical exams, and provide career counseling to candidates.

Military Functions Activities normally associated with the uniformed services.

Military Occupation Specialty (MOS) A specific job or occupation in one of the five services; a term used to identify a group of duty positions possessing such close occupational or functional relationships that an optimal degree of interchangeability among persons so classified exists at any given level of skill.

Military Occupational Specialty (MOS) Code A fixed number that indicates a given military occupational specialty; also known as Military Occupational Number and Specification Serial Number.

Military Temporarily Shore-Based Navy and Marine Corps military personnel assigned to afloat and mobile units, such as aircraft squadrons, construction battalions, and fleet and air command staffs, and who are temporarily based ashore for a period that will exceed 30 days.

Missing Active-duty military personnel who are not present at their duty station due to apparent involuntary reasons and whose location is not known. Excluded are personnel who are in an absent-without-leave or deserter status, or those who have been dropped from the rolls of their military service.

Musters Groups assembling in formation.

N

Noncommissioned Officer (NCO) An enlisted member in pay grades E-4 or higher.

O

Obligation The period of time one agrees to serve on active duty, in the Reserve, or a combination of both.

Obstacle Any obstruction that stops, delays, or diverts movement. Obstacles may be natural—deserts, rivers, swamps, or mountains—or they may be artificial—barbed wire entanglements, pits, concrete, or metal antimechanized traps; they may be issued ready made or they may be constructed in the field.

Officer Candidate School (OCS) Program for college graduates with no prior military training who wish to become military officers; also, qualified enlisted members who wish to become officers may attend OCS. After successful completion, candidates are commissioned as military officers.

Officer Training School (OTS) See OCS.

Operating Location The geographic location where military or civilian employees of the Department of Defense are physically located for the performance of duties.

Operation Order A directive, usually formal, issued by a commander to subordinate commanders for the purpose of effecting the coordinated execution of an operation.

P

Pay Grade A level of employment, as designated by the military. There are nine enlisted pay grades and ten officer pay grades through which personnel can progress during their career. Pay grade and length of service determine a service member's pay.

Q

Quarters Living accommodations or housing.

R

Rating A job specialty.

Ready Reserve The Selected Reserve and Individual Ready Reserve liable for active duty as prescribed by law.

Recorded Duty Station Actual physical location where active duty military personnel perform duty on a permanent basis.

Recruit See Enlistee.

Regular Military Compensation Total value of basic pay, allowances, and tax savings, which represents the amount of pay a civilian worker would need to earn to receive the same take-home pay as a service member.

Reserve Components The Army National Guard of the United States, Army Reserve, Naval Reserve, Marine Corps Reserve, Air National Guard of the United States, Air Force Reserve, and Coast Guard Reserve.

Reserve Officers' Training Corps (ROTC) Training given to undergraduate college students who plan to become military officers. Often they receive scholarships for tuition, books, fees, uniforms, and a monthly allowance.

Reserves People in the military who are not presently on full-time, active duty. In a national emergency, reservists can be called up immediately to serve on active duty because they are highly trained by the services and drill regularly. During peacetime, they perform functions in support of the active duty forces in our country's defense, such as installation and repair of communications equipment. Reservists are also entitled to some of the employment benefits available to active military personnel.

Retired Reserves Those individuals whose names are placed on the Reserve Retired list by proper authority in accordance with law or regulations. Members of the Retired Reserve may, if qualified, be ordered to active duty involuntarily in time of war or national emergency declared by Congress, or when otherwise declared by the Congress, or when otherwise authorized by law.

Reveille The start of a new day.

S

Secure Lock, put away, or stop work.

Security Classification A category to which national security information and material is assigned to denote the degree of damage that unauthorized disclosure would cause to national defense or foreign relations of the United States and to denote the degree of protection required. There are three categories:

Top Secret: National security information or material that requires the highest degree of protection, the unauthorized disclosure of which could reasonably be expected to cause exceptionally grave damage to the national security. Examples of exceptionally grave damage include armed hostilities against the United States or its allies, disruption of foreign relations vitally affecting the national security, the compromise of vital national defense plans or complex cryptologic and communications intelligence systems, the revelation of sensitive intelligence operations, and the disclosure of scientific or technological developments vital to national security.

Secret: National security information or material that requires a substantial degree of protection, the unauthorized disclosure of which could reasonably be expected to cause serious damage to the national security. Examples of serious damage include disruption of foreign relations significantly affecting the national security, significant impairment of a program or policy directly related to the national security, revelation of significant military plans or intelligence operations, and compromise of significant scientific or technological developments relating to national security.

Confidential: National security information or material that requires protection, the unauthorized disclosure of which could reasonably be expected to cause damage to the national security.

Security Clearance An administrative determination by competent national authority that an individual is eligible, from a security standpoint, for access to classified information.

Service Academy Cadet or Midshipman A person in training at one of the service academies to become a commissioned officer.

Service Classifier A military information specialist who helps applicants select a military occupational field.

Service Obligation The amount of time an enlisted member agrees to serve in the military, as stated in the enlistment agreement.

Station A place of assigned duty.

Subsistence Food.

Swab Mop.

T

Taps Time to sleep; end of the day.

Topside Upstairs.

Tour of Duty A period of obligated service; also used to describe a type of duty tour, such as a Mediterranean tour.

Transients All military members who are available for duty while executing permanent change of station orders. Transients comprise all military personnel in a travel, proceed, leave enroute, or temporary duty enroute status on orders to execute an accession, separation, training, operational, or rotational move.

W

Warrant Officer A person who holds a commission or warrant in a warrant officer grade.

X

XO Executive Officer.

THE AUTHOR

Donald B. Hutton served in the United States Coast Guard as a reservist from 1976 until 1992 in the following capacities: Boatswain's Mate, Pollution Investigator, Special Agent in Intelligence, and Mobilization/Augmentation Administration. During his tours of duty he received several awards and letters of praise for his outstanding performance. In 1992 Hutton received an Honorable Discharge *Semper Paratus*.

In his civilian life, he worked progressively for several law enforcement agencies: with the New York State Office of Inspector General as Executive Deputy Inspector General; as a Delaware & Hudson Railroad Police Department Special Agent; U.S. Department of Veterans Affairs Police Officer; and as a U.S. Customs Service Inspector.

Hutton has a master's degree from the State University of New York College at Buffalo. In 1994 he served on the National Assessment of Educational Progress Panel (NAEP), also known as the Nation's Report Card. NAEP advances its findings and recommendations to the U.S. Department of Education as part of the Goal 2000 program for improving education throughout the country.

The author also wrote Barron's *Guide to Law Enforcement Careers* (1997).

MILITARY CAREERS
ACTION (TEAR-OUT) SHEET

How to Use

Listed below are the main recruiting phone numbers and Web sites. Call the phone numbers for information and free publications in the areas of military careers and opportunities (most are toll free). The Web sites can be main sources of information about military careers and opportunities. If you do not have a computer or Internet access, go to your public library; they will most likely have access or know where you can access the Internet, free of charge. Remember, Web pages and phone numbers do change.

Check the boxes that you have contacted.

U.S. Department of Defense
☐ Main Web   www.defenselink.mil
☐ Careers Online   militarycareers.com

U.S. Army
☐ Recruiting Phone   800-USA-ARMY
☐ Main Web   www.goarmy.com

Military Academy, *West Point*
☐ Phone   800-USA-ARMY
☐   www.usma.edu

AROTC
☐ Phone   800-USA-ROTC

Army Reserve
☐ Phone   800-USA-ARMY

Army National Guard
☐ Phone   800-638-7600

U.S. Air Force
☐ Phone   800-423-USAF
☐ Web   www.usaf.mil

Military Academy, *Colorado Springs*
☐ Phone   800-443-9266
☐ Web   www.usafa.mil

AFROTC
☐ Phone   800-522-0033

Air Force Reserve
☐ Phone   800-257-1212

Air National Guard
☐ Phone   800-423-USAF

U.S. Coast Guard
☐ Phone   800-GET-USCG
☐ Main Web   www.uscg.mil

Military Academy, *New London*
☐ Phone   800-GET-USCG
☐ Web   www.dotgov.usgca

Coast Guard Reserve
☐ Phone   800-GET-USCG

U.S. Marine Corps
☐ Recruiting Phone   800-MARINES
☐ Main Web   www.usmc.mil.

Marine Corps Reserve
☐ Phone   800-MARINES

Military Academy/NROTC
(See U.S. Navy)

U.S. Navy
☐ Phone   800-327-NAVY
☐ Web   www.navyjobs.com

Military Academy/Annapolis
☐ Phone   800-638-9156
☐ Web   www.nadn.navy.mil

NROTC
☐ Phone   800-NAV-ROTC

Navy Reserve
☐ Phone   800-USA-USNR

ENLISTMENT PROGRAMS CHECKLIST

Enlisted Programs
☐ Guaranteed Training Enlistment Program
☐ Delayed (how long)
☐ Buddy Deal
☐ Advanced Rank Enlistment Program
☐ Enlistment Bonus
☐ GI Bill/Tuition Assistance Programs
☐ Commissioning Programs
☐ Reserve Enlistment
☐ National Guard
☐ Reenlistment Bonus

Officer Programs
☐ Military Academy Preparatory Schools
☐ Military Academy
☐ Officer Candidate School
☐ Direct Commission
☐ ROTC
☐ ROTC Scholarships
☐ Graduate Degree Programs
☐ Aviation Programs
☐ Medical Programs
☐ Legal Programs

Enlisting in the Military

Meet with Recruiters
☐ At least more than one branch
Qualify for Enlistment (MEPS)
☐ ASVAB or Officer Testing
☐ Physical Examination
☐ Paperwork Process
Before you sign
☐ Select a Military Occupational Specialty or Program
☐ Agree on the number of years of service obligation

Dealing with Recruiters
☐ Bring a friend or relative (preferably someone who is a veteran)
☐ Have a prepared list of items to discuss
☐ Be careful to sign nothing on your first meeting. Recruiters are geared for high-pressure dealings and will try to have you sign up on the first meeting.
☐ Meet with each branch you are interested in for the best deal (shop around!)
☐ Obtain all the official publications that clearly explain the programs you are interested in.

Military Entrance Processing Stations
(MEPS) 65 key U.S. locations; call the listed number that will automatically route you to the MEPS nearest you

☐ Phone   800-323-0513

What happens at MEPS
☐ ASVAB or Officer Testing
☐ Medical/Physical Examination
☐ Administrative Processing
☐ Career Counseling

What to Bring
☐ Identification
☐ Parent/Friend/Veteran
☐ Necessary Paperwork

List of Military Careers
☐
☐
☐

List of Military Opportunities
☐
☐
☐